JK524 .P36
The Past and future of Presidential
Kennedy Sch of Govt   AEA9821

P9-AQC-663

The Past
and
Future
of
Presidential
Debates

The Past
and
Future
of
Presidential
Debates

Edited by
Austin Ranney

WITHDRAWN

American Enterprise Institute for Public Policy Research
Washington, D.C.

2122

M- 422

RECEIVED

FEB 25 1981

KENNEDY SCHOOL OF
GOVERNMENT LIBRARY

Library of Congress Cataloging in Publication Data
Main entry under title:

The Past and future of Presidential debates.

(AEI studies ; 228)
"Bibliography, Evron M. Kirkpatrick": p. 215
1. Presidents—United States—Election—1960.
2. Presidents—United States—Election—1976.
3. Television in politics—United States.   4. Campaign
debates—United States.   I. Ranney, Austin.   II. Series: American Enterprise Institute for Public Policy
Research.   AEI studies ; 228.
JK524.P36   329'.023'73092   78-26778
ISBN 0-8447-3330-X

AEI Studies 228

© 1979 by American Enterprise Institute for Public Policy Research,
Washington, D.C. All rights reserved. No part of this publication may
be used or reproduced in any manner whatsoever without permission
in writing from the American Enterprise Institute except in the case of
brief quotations embodied in news articles, critical articles, or reviews.

The views expressed in the publications of the American Enterprise Institute
are those of the authors and do not necessarily reflect the views of the staff,
advisory panels, officers, or trustees of AEI.

"American Enterprise Institute" is the registered service
mark of the American Enterprise Institute for Public Policy Research.

Printed in the United States of America

CONTENTS

PREFACE

Austin Ranney

The televised joint appearances (like most people, we shall call them "debates" in this book[1]) of John F. Kennedy and Richard M. Nixon in 1960 and of Jimmy Carter and Gerald R. Ford in 1976 played critical roles in the two campaigns. They were watched and heard by far more Americans than any other campaign event in history: some 107 million adults watched or listened to at least one debate in 1960,[2] and in 1976 the number rose to 122 million.[3] Both debate series had major impacts on the election's outcomes, and some analysts say they were decisive. Both series were widely hailed, here and abroad, as American democracy operating at its best. And both were widely criticized as travesties of reasoned discussion, disservices to the American people, and electoral disasters for some of the participants.

The 1960 and 1976 debates shared other traits as well. As Chapters 1 and 2 detail, setting them up involved a number of legal and constitutional complications stemming from Section 315(a) of the Federal Communications Act of 1934—the so-called equal time rule.

---

[1] Not everyone agrees—see, for example, Evron Kirkpatrick's comments in Chapter 1. The argument is made that in true debates, such as those between Abraham Lincoln and Stephen Douglas in Illinois in 1858 and between Thomas Dewey and Harold Stassen before the Oregon Republican presidential primary in 1948, only the candidates participate and each is given time to present his views, to question his opponent directly, and to refute the opposition's statements. Most people, however, appear to take the more latitudinarian view of Webster that a debate is any "regulated discussion of a proposition between two matched sides as a test of forensic ability" (*Webster's Third New International Dictionary of the English Language Unabridged*, 1966 edition, p. 582). So in this book as, sadly, in most employment of the language, usage triumphs over logic.

[2] Elihu Katz and Jacob J. Feldman, "The Debates in the Light of Research: A Survey of Surveys," in Sidney Kraus, ed., *The Great Debates* (Bloomington: Indiana University Press, 1962), pp. 187–192.

[3] See Chapter 3, p. 82.

Chapters 1, 3, and 4 make clear that the candidates' decisions to participate were made tardily and in response to their perceptions of their strategic needs, not as a result of disinterested reflection upon how best to bring the issues to the people. Chapters 1, 5, and 6 show that the formats of the debates resulted from ad hoc compromises among the sponsors and the candidates' representatives, with each participant seeking to maximize his special advantages and minimize his handicaps. And neither series offered a guarantee that the debates would be resumed in any future presidential campaign.

Shortly after the election, James Karayn, who had organized and directed the 1976 debates for their sponsor, the Education Fund of the League of Women Voters, proposed that the American Enterprise Institute sponsor a conference on the impact of past debates and the status and format of future debates. The conference met at the International Club of Washington, D.C., on October 19–20, 1977. First drafts of the chapters of this book were presented to and discussed by an audience of political scientists, print and television journalists, members of congressional staffs, and persons associated with AEI, the American Political Science Association, the Brookings Institution, Common Cause, the Federal Communications Commission, the Federal Elections Commission, the League of Women Voters, and the Russell Sage Foundation. The recorded and transcribed exchanges between authors and audience were frequently provocative and illuminating, and selected passages have been included after each chapter.

The book generally follows the order of the conference. Evron Kirkpatrick describes the origins, conduct, and impact of the 1960 debates. Nicholas Zapple analyzes the changing constitutional and legal status of the debates in both 1960 and 1976. Steven Chaffee and Jack Dennis summarize the results of several empirical studies of the impact of the 1976 debates on the voters' interest, knowledge, and presidential choices. Richard Cheney presents an insider's account of why President Ford decided to challenge Jimmy Carter to debate and why he conducted himself as he did during the debates. Stephen Lesher, in association with Patrick Caddell and Gerald Rafshoon, sets forth a comparable account of Carter's participation. James Karayn argues that the debates should be made permanent and compulsory, and offers a number of suggestions for improving their format. Nelson Polsby challenges the debates' utility as devices for helping voters make intelligent choices between the candidates. Jack Germond and Jules Witcover conclude by arguing that, while debates can be useful adjuncts to presidential campaigns, they should never be allowed to dominate them as they did in 1976. And Evron Kirkpatrick appends a bibliography of the leading published studies of both the 1960 and the 1976 debates.

Sometime before mid-1980 the decision will be made whether or not there will be any debates between—or among—the presidential candidates in 1980. If the decision is negative, that will conclude the matter until 1984 and perhaps beyond. If it is positive, then many other decisions will have to be made about the format, sponsorship, location, and funding of the 1980 debates.

This book considers most of the issues involved in making all of these decisions, but let us be clear that the first decision is the most critical of all. In the past it has been made nominally by both major party candidates, but in fact it has been made by the incumbent president running for reelection or by the incumbent vice-president running for the presidency. Whatever conclusions they reached, Nixon, Johnson, Humphrey, and Ford all made their decisions because they and their advisers believed that debating would (Nixon in 1960, Humphrey in 1968, Ford in 1976) or would not (Nixon in 1968 and 1972, Johnson in 1964) help them enough to warrant the risk involved. If they saw an advantage, ways were found to slip past Section 315(a). If they saw no advantage, the equal time rule became an insurmountable barrier.

This is probably—though not certainly—how the decision will be made about holding debates in 1980. We should not be shocked or repelled by this. After all, the candidates' stakes in the decision are very high, and it would be foolish to expect them to make those decisions without regard to their consequences for their chances of winning the election.

But the candidates' prospects are not the only stake. There is also the stake of the American people in having presidential campaigns organized and conducted in a manner most likely to provide them with correct information about the candidates' personal qualities and positions on issues.

The critical role played by the debates in 1960 and 1976—to say nothing of the role they might play in the future—make it highly desirable that we reflect on their future status and format well before the next campaign. If the debates deserve a continuing place in the American political system—the vexed central question on which this book focuses—that place should be determined on its merits, preferably far enough in advance of the next election that it will be free from the tremendous pressures exerted by the special interests of particular candidates and parties in any election year.

I hope that this book will make a contribution to the making of that decision. Several people have been especially helpful in putting it together. James Karayn was an invaluable source of suggestions for topics and people. People attending the conference generously gave permission to reproduce selections from their remarks. Andrea Kozak cheerfully performed the tedious chores of checking footnotes and bibliography. Randa Murphy and Paula Simmons kept close watch on the manuscript's successive stages. And above all, the authors not only produced authoritative, informative, and stimulating analyses of their topics but also kept the editor's labors at a minimum. On all these matters, at least, there is no debate.

1
Presidential Candidate "Debates": What Can We Learn from 1960?

Evron M. Kirkpatrick

The "great debates" (actually, neither great, nor debates) held in the 1960 presidential election campaign between candidates Richard Nixon and John Kennedy had more viewers and listeners than any broadcast of a political event up to that point. Not only was the audience larger but also interest in and advance knowledge of the "debates" was enormous. The "debates" themselves may very well have determined the outcome of the election, and the amount of research on and writing about these television encounters has been extraordinary.[1]

In the spring of 1963, the American Political Science Association appointed a Commission on Presidential Campaign Debates, which was asked to "review past experience, consider the implications of future television and radio debates between Presidential candidates, and make recommendations regarding format and procedure for such debates" if held (from the preface to the *Report of the Commission on Presidential Campaign Debates*, 1964). The commission included Carl J. Friedrich, chairman, Evron M. Kirkpartrick, Harold D. Lasswell, Richard E. Neustadt, Peter H. Odegard, Elmo Roper, Telford Taylor, Charles A. H. Thomson, and Gerhard D. Wiebe and was financed by a grant from the National Broadcasting Company. A report (now out of print) was published in 1964. It was a report of the commission, not of the association or NBC. The association's executive director, writing on behalf of the commission, invited all members of Congress, all governors, and all state and national party chairmen of the two major parties to submit their views on the format and procedures for presidential debates. Replies were received from about one-third of the members of the House, one-third of the state chairmen, more than a third of the senators, and over half of the governors. In this paper I have drawn freely on the letters and on the report.

[1] Strictly speaking, the Nixon-Kennedy "debates" should, in my judgment, be referred to in quotation marks to distinguish them from true debates, such as the Lincoln-Douglas debates of 1858. For ease of reading, however, the 1960 debates will henceforth appear without special punctuation. The best single source on the 1960 debates is Sidney Kraus, ed., *The Great Debates* (Bloomington: Indiana University Press, 1962). For other works on both the 1960 and the 1976 debates, see the bibliography at the end of this volume.

An unexpected consequence of the 1960 debates was that several other countries including Germany, Sweden, Finland, Italy, and Japan, instituted campaign

Advance knowledge of and interest in the Kennedy-Nixon debates was very high. Gallup found 55 percent of adults had "a lot" of interest in the upcoming debates, and Sindlinger reported that 90 percent of the population over age twelve had advance knowledge of the debates.[2] It is generally agreed that "some 70 million to 107 million—and perhaps another 10 to 15 million younger people—watched or listened to the first 'debate.'" While the number declined for subsequent debates, it has been conservatively estimated that at least 55 percent of the adult population listened to each debate and that over 80 percent saw or heard at least one.[3] Elihu Katz and Jacob J. Feldman surveyed thirty-one independent studies of opinions and attitudes about the debates and concluded that "this is the largest number of studies of a single public event in the history of opinion and attitude research."[4]

While there is still some difference of opinion about the overall "winner," it seems quite clear that Kennedy made a better impression ("won"?) in the first debate and that Nixon did so in the third. The second and fourth were quite close.[5] Reviewing the voluminous writing and the numerous polls suggests that Kennedy probably gained a slight edge. Given the closeness of the 1960 election, this edge may have made the difference between victory and defeat.[6]

---

debates, briefly described in Sig Mickelson, *The Electric Mirror* (New York: Dodd, Mead, 1972), pp. 208–210. These debates were longer and more complicated because more parties were represented, for example, four in Sweden, seven in Finland, eight in Italy.

[2] See Elihu Katz and Jacob J. Feldman, "The Debates in the Light of Research: A Survey of Surveys," in Kraus, *The Great Debates*, pp. 193–195.

[3] Ibid., pp. 187–192.

[4] Katz and Feldman summarize the findings of the thirty-one studies in chapter 11 of Kraus, *The Great Debates*. Six of the studies are reported in some detail in the Kraus volume.

[5] Katz and Feldman in Kraus, *The Great Debates*, p. 195.

[6] Ibid., pp. 195–200. A table at pages 196–197 presents data on who won from thirteen of the surveys. See also the results of the Deutschmann study, pp. 242–252; the Carter study (dealing mainly with images), pp. 260–269; Tannenbaum, Greenberg, and Silverman, pp. 271–288, who conclude "Kennedy did not necessarily win the debates, but Nixon lost them"; and Lang and Lang, pp. 315–329; Ben-Zeev and White, pp. 332–337. Many observers thought Kennedy had a slight edge as a result of the debates. For example, Mickelson, *The Electric Mirror*, p. 194, says that "Many experts credit John F. Kennedy's election to the presidency to his success in the first of these encounters." Also, see the data set forth by Theodore H. White, *The Making of the President 1960* (New York: Atheneum, 1961), pp. 293–294. Kennedy is reported as saying on November 12, the Monday following the election: "It was TV more than anything else that turned the tide." Nelson W. Polsby and Aaron Wildavsky, *Presidential Elections: Strategies of American Electoral Politics* (New York: Charles Scribner's Sons, 1976) comment, "With the benefit of hindsight, many observers now suggest that Nixon was obviously foolish to engage in the debates" (p. 178).

In this chapter, I am concerned with certain aspects of the debates between Richard Nixon and John Kennedy in the course of the 1960 campaign. I have not attempted a history of these appearances, nor presented all the evidence concerning their impact on the campaign; neither have I attempted an explanation of why no debates occurred in 1964, 1968, or 1972. I have been concerned mainly with those aspects of the debates in 1960 from which we can learn something about the following matters:

- How is a decision made to debate or not to debate and what factors and considerations determine such decisions?
- How is a format determined, and how does it influence TV encounters?
- What was and is likely to be the impact on voters of joint appearances and how does this differ from or relate to the impact of other campaign activities?
- What is the impact of debates and of the electronic media on the parties and on the political system?
- Is there good reason to encourage or discourage further debates?

I have, where appropriate, used data from years other than 1960 and from debates other than Kennedy-Nixon but have used little data from or about 1976; the 1976 experience is treated in other chapters of this book.

To Debate or Not to Debate

The decision whether or not to engage in debates is one that will be made, in the future as in the past, by the presidential candidates. Almost no one has suggested that debates be required by law. James Karayn's proposal, in this volume, for a National Debate Commission chartered by Congress and supported by public funds is an exception, as are some parts of the proposal of Minow, Martin, and Mitchell reported later in my paper. There are some, to be sure, who hoped that Kennedy's announcement of his willingness to debate whoever might be the Republican candidate in 1964 would lead to such debates and establish a tradition that would be difficult to break. But, after Kennedy's death, Lyndon Johnson, an incumbent president with great personal popularity, estimating that he had nothing to gain, refused to get involved, though Barry Goldwater and his staff tried very hard to get Johnson to debate.[7]

---

[7] Polsby and Wildavsky, *Presidential Elections*, p. 179. I have checked this with persons associated with the Goldwater campaign; they verify that such efforts were made.

The Johnson decision was not surprising. There is little, if any, incentive for an incumbent president to engage in debate. A president running for re-election certainly is better known than his opponent and has facilities and resources for campaigning that his opponent does not. Every act of a president is news; he is continually involved in matters that bring him to the attention of the voting public through the press and the news programs on TV and radio. Further, a number of people feel there are sound reasons for a president not to debate and will try to discourage such debates.

In 1968, the campaign staff of Hubert H. Humphrey tried hard to involve Nixon in debate, but Nixon, having been burned once, had no intention of risking debates that might, in a close election, result in his defeat, as he believed had happened in 1960.[8]

Obviously, there could be no question of television debates until television itself was developed and its use widespread. Thus, TV debates were not a possibility before 1952. There had been radio debates between Thomas Dewey and Harold Stassen in the 1948 Republican presidential primary campaign in Oregon, though such joint appearances on radio were rare. In July 1952, Senator Blair Moody of Michigan, participating in the CBS program "People's Platform," suggested that TV debates be held between the presidential candidates. Robert W. Sarnoff reports that NBC responded rather quickly and wired candidates Dwight Eisenhower and Adlai Stevenson that its TV and radio facilities would be available for such debates.[9] Sarnoff's invitation to both candidates was flatly rejected.

Sig Mickelson reports that only ten days after Moody's comment, Dr. Frank Stanton, president of CBS, wrote Moody expressing "interest, if not enthusiasm, for the idea." Both Stanton and Moody pointed out that the debates in 1952 would have required suspension of Section 315 of the Federal Communications Act, which states that if a station provides time to a legally qualified candidate for public office it must provide equal time to other legally qualified candidates. The section was suspended in 1960 to make the Kennedy-Nixon de-

---

[8] Richard Nixon, *Six Crises* (New York: Doubleday, 1962), p. 257, expresses the view: "Looking back now on all four of them, there can be no question but that Kennedy had gained more from the debates than I. While many observers give me the edge in the last three, he definitely had the advantage in the first—and especially with the television audience. And as I have pointed out, 20 million people saw the first debate who did not bother to tune in the others."

[9] Sarnoff in Kraus, *The Great Debates*, pp. 57–58. The text of the Moody statement is in Robert E. Danders, *The Great Debates*, Freedom of Information Center Publication no. 67 (Columbia, Mo.: University of Missouri School of Journalism, 1961).

4

bates possible. The act, as amended, exempts bona fide newscasts, bona fide news interviews, bona fide news documentaries, and on-the-spot coverage of bona fide news events from the equal time requirement. The ambiguity about what falls within these categories has led to varied interpretations. A debate between Edmund Brown and Richard Nixon in the 1962 campaign for governor of California—before a convention of United Press International—was held not to be exempt, but a debate between George McGovern and Hubert Humphrey in the California Democratic primary in 1972 was held to be exempt.

In 1975, the commission made a new ruling that coverage of a debate *did* come within the exemption of on-the-spot coverage of a bona fide news event. On the basis of this ruling, which was upheld by the courts, the League of Women Voters set up debates between the two major presidential candidates. Nicholas Zapple's paper in this volume deals in detail with Section 315.

Stanton, following his letter to Moody, did get in touch with the Eisenhower campaign suggesting an Eisenhower-Stevenson debate. General Eisenhower referred the matter to Bernard C. Duffy, president of the Batten, Barton, Durstine, Osborn Advertising Agency, who advised a "flat and abrupt turndown."[10]

In 1956 there seems to have been little or no discussion of debates, and it certainly would have been unlikely that Eisenhower, then president, would have accepted. Even Stevenson, famed for his articulateness, was reluctant because of his belief that he had fared badly in his TV debate with Kefauver in the presidential primary in Florida that year. Stevenson had entered that debate with Kefauver because he and some of his advisers believed that Kefauver's victory in the Minnesota primary made it nearly obligatory for Stevenson to debate him. All who participated in the decision thought that all the spring primaries might turn on the outcome. The debate was, in fact, quite dull. Stevenson and Kefauver spent the first part of the debate on a fuzzy, blunted discussion of foreign affairs. Moving to domestic affairs, both took firm stands on civil rights. Immediately after the debate Stevenson phoned Willard Wirtz, Newton Minow, and John Bartlow Martin, who were watching in Minow's home in a Chicago suburb; Stevenson felt he had been totally unprepared and had done badly. Later, he angrily told George Ball, "What I should have done was destroy him in some blinding oratory. But I didn't have any

---

[10] Sig Mickelson, *The Electric Mirror*, p. 196.

notes." In fact, Stevenson had spent the two days before the debate going over questions that were likely to be asked.[11]

It is clear that, except in rare cases, American major parties and major party candidates make decisions about campaign strategy and tactics on the basis of what is likely to gain votes. They want to win, to gain office, and to hold onto it. Campaigns are designed to accomplish these ends. Campaign tactics are adopted or rejected because of their assumed contribution to these objectives.[12] In making decisions about strategy and tactics, parties and candidates have little firm scientific knowledge to guide them. Very little is known or can be learned about the influence of different elements of a campaign. The campaign is made up of thousands of separate activities and carried on in a context of rapidly changing and developing events over many of which the parties and candidates have little or no control. To determine in such circumstances what works or what would be a serious blunder is extraordinarily difficult, if not impossible.[13]

In addition to the difficulties inherent in all campaigns, in 1960 there was very little historical experience or evidence to guide candidates and their advisers in assessing what impact the debates might have on their prospects and most of that was of dubious relevance to the Kennedy-Nixon contest.

The Lincoln-Douglas debates of 1858 were the most famous previous forensic contests. The two candidates for the U.S. Senate from Illinois were both considered excellent platform speakers; each clearly thought he would benefit from the debates. It also is noteworthy that they did not debate again when they were presidential candidates two years later, in 1860. It is widely believed that the debate between Stassen and Dewey in the 1948 Oregon primary over national radio networks eliminated Stassen from the race for the presidency. Kefauver had debated Stevenson in the Florida presidential

[11] John Bartlow Martin, *Adlai Stevenson of Illinois: The Life of Adlai Stevenson* (New York: Doubleday, 1976), pp. 328–329.

[12] Polsby and Wildavsky, *Presidential Elections*, pp. 19–41; also chapter 6 discusses the role of the "amateur" or "purist" in the reform activities based on the desire to create a more programmatic party. For an early discussion of the nature of party and the argument that it is office-oriented, not policy-oriented, see Pendleton Herring, *The Politics of Democracy* (New York: W. W. Norton, 1940). Also, see James Q. Wilson, *The Amateur Democrat* (Chicago: University of Chicago Press, 1962); Joseph A. Schlesinger, "The Primary Goals of Political Parties: A Clarification of Positive Theory," *American Political Science Review*, vol. 69 (September 1975), pp. 840–849; Austin Ranney and Willmoore Kendall, *Democracy and the American Party System* (New York: Harcourt, Brace, 1956), pp. 84–87, 198–199; and Joseph Schlesinger's discussion in the *Encyclopedia of the Social Sciences* (New York: Macmillan, 1968), pp. 428–430.

[13] Polsby and Wildavsky, *Presidential Elections*, pp. 184–191.

primary of 1956, and John Kennedy and Hubert Humphrey debated in the West Virginia primary in 1960. Lyndon Johnson debated John Kennedy at the Democratic convention in Los Angeles in 1960, but neither Johnson nor anyone else believed the debate had a significant effect on Kennedy's nomination.

Descriptions of the 1960 decisions by Kennedy and Nixon to engage in debates may illuminate the calculations made by candidates and their advisers as they approach a decision about debating. Doubtless such descriptions are incomplete, but from them there emerges a rough notion of the cognitive maps of the two candidates. These maps reflect the candidates' understanding of themselves, the political context, and their places in it. The offer of TV and radio time for debates was quickly accepted by Kennedy, probably out of the feeling that TV debates would win him greater visibility and would aid him in overcoming the charge of youth and inexperience. Kennedy was quite aware that he was unknown to many voters and far less known than Nixon, who had been vice-president for eight years. Kennedy's great self-confidence permitted him to believe that the debates would give him an opportunity to display his broad knowledge and good looks. Also, Kennedy, prior to his nomination, had asserted that he wanted to debate the Republican candidate during the campaign.

Nixon's decision was more difficult. Mickelson reports that, in a meeting early in May at the Statler Hotel in Washington, Nixon had made clear to his campaign staff that he would not participate in debates at any time: "There can be no conversations about debates. I won't tolerate it." President Eisenhower, in unmistakable terms, had advised him against debates. When he accepted, it was a shock to his campaign staff, with whom he evidently did not discuss the matter. There were reports that Leonard Hall threatened to resign because of dissatisfaction with the decision.[14] What, then, led Nixon to his decision? He fully recognized that he was better known and that TV debates would provide Kennedy with an opportunity to be seen and heard by many who would not otherwise see and hear him. But his success with his Checkers speech in 1952, his debating success in high school and college, his greater experience with television, his belief that he was more experienced and more knowledgeable, his underestimation of Kennedy, and his concern that refusal would subject him to the charge that he was unwilling to face Kennedy— all these combined to produce his wire of acceptance (July 31) two days after Kennedy's letter of acceptance (July 29).

It is clear that each candidate agreed to debate because of his

[14] Mickelson, *The Electric Mirror*, p. 198.

7

expectation that he would derive political advantage from the decision. In considering the Kennedy-Nixon decisions, it should be noted that neither was an incumbent, neither had a clear lead in the election contest, both had good reasons for expecting to do well in television appearances. Foresight in such decisions is not easy. It is much easier in retrospect to see that Kennedy and Leonard Hall were right, Nixon wrong. Nixon himself, subsequent to 1960, was quite clear about the matter and, as noted above, expressed the view that Kennedy gained more from the debates than he did.

Although the presidency is a unique office and campaigning for it involves some special considerations, the factors involved in Kennedy's and Nixon's decisions to debate also occur in the decisions of others. Incumbency, the closeness of the race, and the television personality of the candidate figure importantly in the answer to the question: Under what circumstances and on the basis of what considerations do candidates decide to debate?

Murray Levin has provided a valuable account of the background of the debates between Edward J. McCormack, Jr., and Edward M. Kennedy in the 1962 Massachusetts senatorial primary. In this case too each candidate carefully calculated the potential benefits to his campaign. McCormack wanted to confront Kennedy; he thought he "could 'expose' him as a 'name's the same' candidate, a non-voter, a brash young man who was cashing in on his family's influence. Television, McCormack thought, admirably suited his needs."[15] He and his advisers assessed the situation and the personality of his opponent. They calculated

> that in a debate with Ted Kennedy, Ed McCormack can light Mr. Kennedy's extremely short fuse. I think this is a guy who could blow it on television. Ted Kennedy could be angered to the point where he could make a public display of his very famous temper. . . . This would be highly injurious and accrue to our benefit.[16]

At the same time Kennedy aides and advisers thought their man would profit by the debates on television. One aide commented:

---

[15] Murray Levin, *Kennedy Campaigning: The System and Style as Practiced by Senator Edward Kennedy* (Boston: Beacon Press, 1966), p. 182. R. W. Apple, Jr., reports that there were hundreds of debates in state and local elections in 1962; it is likely that the same has been true in each election year since then. The number, in fact, may have increased. To the best of my knowledge, no one has done a comprehensive account, critique, or evaluation. For Apple's report on 1962, see "The Little Debates," *Reporter*, December 6, 1962, pp. 36–38.

[16] Levin, *Kennedy Campaigning*, pp. 183–184.

I think Kennedy looks extremely well on television. If I was Kennedy, I would welcome these debates, and I would debate in every town and city in Massachusetts. . . . What has Kennedy got going for him? That he looks like his brother. That he looks like a Kennedy. That he talks like a Kennedy. That he's got vigor, that he's an excellent and articulate person, and he makes a very strong presentation. And Eddie McCormack, although very capable, has got kind of a bad smile, unfortunately, and a little bit of lisp . . . and doesn't come through quite as well on television as he does in person.[17]

Kennedy's campaign manager summarized the views of those who thought Kennedy ought to debate because he projected so well on TV and McCormack did not:

We felt that it would probably be in the best interest of Ted Kennedy to have the debate. . . . His brother was going throughout the country saying that people running for office should debate. And we felt in the very beginning that Ted has a peculiar amount of stage presence. He does very well when he's in situations which the average individual wouldn't do too well in. And we felt that he's big, strong, he's vigorous. McCormack himself doesn't project too well on television. We thought it would be a pretty good idea to get them both together. The only problem that we had, we just didn't want to spring into this because it seems Mr. McCormack doesn't have too much going for him in terms of organization, or any type of planned effort. . . . Their feeling was we were out in front, . . . and McCormack had a great amount of difficulty gathering any kind of a crowd. And we felt that this would be building him, and I think, in a sense, we did build him. We brought him up to a certain point. There was a lot of coverage, a lot of notoriety to it. . . . And their feelings were that this is not such a good idea, to give him all of this opportunity for exposure. And I think underlying the whole thing was that Teddy does well on television, McCormack doesn't. We felt we had nothing to fear. Some people thought that every ball team, even the Yankees, have one bad day, and it's courting a little bit of danger, but we weighed all the pros and the cons, and the advocates of the debate seemed to win out. And then we just didn't want to get into the position of running away.[18]

---

[17] Ibid., p. 223.
[18] Ibid., p. 186.

Murray Levin summarizes the problem of decision:

Pragmatic politicians who are underfinanced, who sense that they are likely to lose, or who know that they are less well known than their opponents, should press for television debates—they have much to gain and little to lose in such confrontations. It is always possible that a witty remark, a pointed barb, a flurry of statistics, or a startling revelation can turn the tide or that the front runner may "blow the election," as one McCormack aide noted, by "being stupid, impolite, or who the hell knows what." Televised debates not only present the underdog with a unique opportunity to get in a crippling blow but also provide him with badly needed free time and equal exposure. Professional politicians agree, therefore, that it is wise for the candidate who is behind to debate unless he is hopelessly inept, stupid, or physically repulsive. They also agree that it is unwise for the favorite to accept the challenge.[19]

In addition to considerations of visibility, good looks, popular standing, stage experience, and articulateness, these comments on the Kennedy-McCormack debates introduce another factor that influences the decision to debate: the possibility that, in an unrehearsed confrontation, a candidate may lose control of himself. He may show to millions of viewers an unattractive trait: a bad temper, arrogance, ignorance, a mean streak normally hidden from public view. Certainly, Gerald Ford's error about Eastern Europe in his second debate with Jimmy Carter in 1976 was damaging to him. For the underdog, the possibility of provoking a more famous opponent into unintended self-revelation is enormously attractive. The notion that candidates will reveal on television their "true" selves and that TV debates will permit voters to assess the "true" merits of the man is an argument frequently made by proponents of TV debates. It seems clear, however, that the candidates themselves are concerned with communicating the true self and the dark side only of their opponents. The candidates are concerned above all with political advantage. Murray Levin succinctly sums up the candidates' priorities: "Neither Kennedy nor McCormack was seriously concerned with the problem of how best to make the debate a vehicle for educating and informing the public. The rational candidate makes strategic decisions in terms of political expediency, not civic duty."[20]

If candidates are left to decide the question whether to debate

---

[19] Ibid., p. 182.
[20] Ibid., p. 185.

or not to debate, the decision will normally reflect careful calculation of the potential political advantages or disadvantages. Some disadvantage, of course, may derive from refusal to debate. Media spokesmen typically support debates, and their voices, added to that of a challenger, can create a great deal of pressure on a candidate to meet his opponent in a verbal duel.

Robert MacNeil has noted that the skillful campaign manager needs a technique for keeping his candidate out of debates that might be harmful and at the same time not lose face. He notes that Joe Napolitan has revealed how he would approach the problem:

> If I had a candidate who was a clear favorite, I'd try to keep him off TV debates. But I would never openly refuse to debate. If challenged to a debate, you say, "Yes, sure. How about my campaign manager meeting yours at 4 P.M. on Thursday?" Then at five to four on Thursday, you call and say, "We've had a real crisis here, can we make it on Saturday?" And on Saturday you put it off till next Wednesday. . . . and so on.[21]

Since it is clear that the candidates make self-serving, or what they think to be self-serving, decisions to debate or not to debate, it is reasonable to ask whether the decision should be left to them and their advisers. Does the public have an overriding interest and, if so, how might that interest best be served?

Some of the respondents to inquiries from the Commission on Presidential Debates of the American Political Science Association (APSA), established in 1963, thought there were very good reasons for an incumbent president not to participate in televised debates, regardless of his preferences or campaign needs. One distinguished Georgia Democrat said:

> While I believe that the Nixon-Kennedy debates of 1960 played a vital role in the 1960 election campaign, nevertheless, I am firmly of the opinion that no President of the United States, while serving as the President, should ever engage in a television or radio debate with an opposing candidate. When both candidates are first seeking the office, then the debates are helpful, and, I am sure, of great value to

---

[21] Robert MacNeil, *The People Machine: The Influence of Television on American Politics* (New York: Harper and Row, 1968), pp. 174–175. That negotiations are likely to be prolonged in any case is evidenced by the *Worcester Telegram* comment about the Kennedy-McCormack negotiations: "The attempt to arrange a meeting between Edward J. McCormack and Edward Kennedy . . . is only slightly less involved than the disarmament talks in Geneva." Levin, *Kennedy Campaigning*, p. 185.

the electorate in making a decision. However, I do not believe that the President of the United States, even though he is a candidate for re-election, should participate in these debates because of the office he holds. It is one thing for a Presidential aspirant to participate in a debate, it is something else for the occupant of the most important office in the world to participate in a debate which may be televised to all parts of the world.[22]

Another legislator wrote in the same vein:

In the first place there is some doubt in my mind as to whether an incumbent President should engage in such debates. In order to defend his position, it may be necessary to say things which might rise to haunt him later or which might cause embarrassment internationally. Certainly, a President can find ways of acquainting our citizens with his views which do not possess such inherent danger of being misunderstood.[23]

The *New Republic* took the same view in an editorial on November 7, 1960, saying:

Are a Chief Magistrate and the policies, the secrets, and the prestige of his regime to be made targets of direct, unrehearsed partisan interpellation—perhaps at a dangerous moment of world affairs? Can a President in office afford to gamble on losing ascendancy in a sharp debate within sight of tens of millions? Can the questioners be expected to press a President as relentlessly as they do his opponent? Is a President to be held to a rigid time limit in answering questions involving the heart of national policies? Can the dignity of the office be upheld without conditions unacceptably disadvantageous to the challenger?[24]

None of the letters received by the APSA commission favored requiring debates—though a number felt debates, under the proper circumstances, would be a good thing. An Ohio Republican expressed a view held by many: "Certainly no candidate should be compelled to either enter into a debate with a particular format or to enter into any debate at all. . . . I believe also that where there is an incumbent president involved, there are serious questions of national security that have to be considered."[25]

---

[22] APSA Commission, *Report*, p. 24.

[23] Ibid., p. 3.

[24] *New Republic*, vol. 143, no. 20 (November 7, 1960). Also see Bernard Rubin, *Political Television* (Belmont, Calif.: Wadsworth, 1967), p. 65.

[25] APSA Commission, *Report*, p. 23.

The commission also took the view that the debates should be voluntary, that they were not the only form appearances might take, and that, while they "might play a critical role in some campaigns," they "are not likely to become the sole—or even the most important—method of campaigning for the Presidency." The commission also cautioned that a presidential candidate who is also president should carefully consider his full duties and responsibilities of office before agreeing to and participating in debates.[26]

Format: The Ground Rules for Debate

In 1960, there were three major participants in establishing ground rules: the two candidates and the networks. They had to decide how many joint appearances there would be and under what conditions and rules. Each candidate had a set of requirements he thought would serve him well; so did the network representatives.

The format for the 1960 debates was the product of the original suggestions of the networks, the needs and views of the media, Nixon's requirements as set forth in his telegram of acceptance, and the concerns, desires, and demands of Kennedy and his negotiators. The networks had offered eight hours, four for the debates and four for optional appearances on scheduled programs. CBS, for example, offered four hours on its "Face the Nation" panel interview show and additional exposure on "Person to Person." Both NBC and CBS insisted on controlling the nondebate hours. Sarnoff's NBC invitation specifically suggested a series of confrontations called by the formal title "The Great Debates."[27]

Nixon, in his acceptance telegram of July 28, said: "In general, it is my position that joint television appearances of the presidential candidates should be conducted as a full and free exchange of views without prepared text or notes, and without interruptions."[28]

The first negotiating session was held in the Waldorf Astoria Hotel in New York City on August 9. The meeting included representatives of all the networks and representatives of the candidates. Mickelson reports that the meeting produced little that was conclusive. There was a general agreement that there would be joint appear-

---

[26] Ibid., pp. 6–7.

[27] Kraus, *The Great Debates*, pp. 61, 63, 64. The chapter by Seltz and Yoakem provides a brief discussion of the negotiations about format. Sig Mickelson's *The Electric Mirror*, chapter 8, has a longer discussion of negotiations. Mickelson's account is particularly valuable since he represented CBS in the negotiations; Mickelson reports that the term "Great Debates" was Sarnoff's, p. 203.

[28] Mickelson, *The Electric Mirror*, pp. 197–198.

ances or confrontations, each an hour in length. The details were to be worked out later.

One set of differences concerned the number of appearances. Theodore White describes the candidates' differences on this matter:

> The Nixon negotiators fought to restrict the number of debates—their man, they felt, was the master of the form and one "sudden-death" debate could eliminate Kennedy with a roundhouse swing. They viewed the insistence of the Kennedy negotiators on the maximum possible number of debates as weakness. ("If they weren't scared," said one Nixon staffman, "why shouldn't they be willing to pin everything on one show?") The Kennedy negotiators insisted on at least five debates, then let themselves be whittled to four. ("Every time we get those two fellows on the screen side by side," said J. Leonard Reinsch, Kennedy's TV maestro, "we're going to gain and he's going to lose.")[29]

Both candidates having agreed to debates, the Congress proceeded to set aside Section 315, the equal time provision, as it applied to candidates for president, making it possible for the networks to present the debates without giving time to all minor candidates. This led immediately to another negotiating session on August 31, in Washington, D.C., where representatives of the candidates agreed on four appearances. They wanted only very broad topics to be discussed, rather than specific propositions that would limit the areas of debate. The network representatives wanted debates and not press conferences. CBS, particularly, pushed the Oregon plan used by Dewey and Stassen in 1948, in which the two candidates after opening statements would question each other and then end with concluding summaries. The candidate representatives from both sides, Leonard Reinsch for Kennedy and Fred Scribner, Jr., for Nixon, would not budge. They insisted on a panel of interviewers or questioners, preferably four, on all four programs. The networks agreed but insisted that the networks select the panel. This led to further argument, since the candidates wanted to be sure that representatives of the wire services, newspapers, and news magazines would be included. Agreement seemed near, but Scribner again raised the question of the other four hours of the eight originally offered; Scribner, speaking for Nixon, wanted the hours to be provided for any program the respective candidates might want. The networks refused, however, and Scribner and Reinsch abandoned the claim to the extra four hours.

The discussion then moved rapidly, as Scribner spelled out what

---

[29] White, *The Making of the President 1960*, p. 283.

both sides apparently had agreed to: on two programs there would be eight-minute opening statements by each candidate, a thirty-four minute question-and-answer period, and three-minute summaries; and on the other two programs, the two candidates in tandem would answer questions from a panel of the working press, including wire services, newspapers, news magazines, radio, and television.

There still remained the questions about the dates of the programs and the selection of the moderator and panelists. As moderator, the networks wanted a public figure—an outstanding jurist or college president. The candidates wanted a broadcasting professional. The networks, with reluctance, accepted this proposal. It was agreed to issue a press release designating the four dates September 26, October 7, October 13, and October 21. It was left to the networks to offer a specific hour for each date, to decide on the division of production responsibilities, and to agree on a title for the series. The meeting ended without deciding on the panelists, an item that became a subject of considerable controversy later on.

Sarnoff had called the series "The Great Debates," but within the network group there was considerable dissatisfaction with that title. It was decided that the title on the screen introducing each debate would carry the words: "Face to Face" and that in the body of the program it would be called "joint appearance."[30]

In the first and fourth debates, each candidate would make an opening statement of approximately eight minutes and a closing statement of approximately three minutes. In between there would be a question-and-answer period. In the second and third appearances there were to be no opening statements and no closing summation. Each candidate was to be questioned in turn by members of the panel; each was to have an opportunity to comment on the answer of the other; each panelist was to ask only one question in turn and was to be free to ask any question he wished.[31]

It is clear, as already indicated, that "The Great Debates" were not debates as that term is generally understood. Afterward there was a good deal of criticism of the networks for encouraging or permitting the press conference format. This was unjust since the networks,

---

[30] The above account follows the report of Mickelson, *The Electric Mirror*, pp. 197–203.

[31] See the introductory statement in the first debate by Howard K. Smith and the opening statements of the other moderators, Frank McGee in the second debate, Bill Shadel in the third, and Quincy Howe in the fourth. The texts of all four debates are printed in Kraus, *The Great Debates*, pp. 348–430. The four debates cover only 92 printed pages. Each man had fewer than 46 pages in which to state his views on important issues of foreign and domestic policy.

from the start, had wanted a formal debate format but the candidates insisted on the format adopted.[32]

It is unfortunate that the term "debate" was used to refer to the joint appearances in 1960 and in much of the writing and discussion since. Many have noted that acceptance of the word led to excessive discussion and argument about who won. Data were collected and analyzed in large part to try to find the winner. The fact is that winning is an artificial concept as applied to these appearances, except insofar as the term signifies a positive public response.[33]

In 1960, Douglass Cater expressed the view that:

> The format of the Great Debate was neither fish nor fowl, not permitting the relentless interrogation of the "Meet the Press" type of quiz show or the clash of ideas that can occur in a genuine debate. The candidates had quickly mastered its special form of gamesmanship. No matter how narrow or broad the question, we could watch by the timing the way each of them extracted his last second of allotted image projection in making his response. The panel's role was hardly more than to designate categories—animal, vegetable, or mineral—on which the two might or might not discourse.[34]

It may be that there is some format that would produce a genuine discussion, enlightening to all who watched and listened, but there is little to support such a view. As Cater points out:

> As they approached this brave new frontier of television, the two candidates were far more concerned about their images than their arguments. . . . Nobody around the candidates seemed to think that clarity of argument was the objective. . . . One kept wondering about those silent millions who sat before their television sets. Did they come any closer to a knowledge of their candidates? Not even a trained political observer could keep up with the crossfire of fact and counterfact, of the rapid references to Rockefeller Reports, Lehman amendments, prestige analyses, GNP, and a potpourri of other so-called facts. Or was the knack of merely seeming well informed what counted with the viewer? . . . Last but not least, was the viewer really edified by the frantic clash on foreign policy? Neither of the men showed any regard

---

[32] See Mickelson, *The Electric Mirror*, pp. 203–204.

[33] See the comments of White, "Presidential Debate of 1976," and Mitofsky in his paper, "The 1976 Presidential Debate Effects." Also, see J. Jeffery Auer, "The Counterfeit Debates," in Kraus, *The Great Debates*, chapter 8.

[34] Cater in Kraus, *The Great Debates*, p. 128 (also printed in the *Reporter*, November 10, 1960, pp. 19–20).

for the fact that some things are better left unsaid if one of them expects to conduct that foreign policy next January. It was like a bastardized version of Art Linkletter's "People Are Funny" in which the contestant had to tell how he would deal with Castro in 150 seconds flat.[35]

Cater's view is borne out both by reading the debates and by an examination of the survey studies that were done. Reading the debates makes clear how little can be said about any important issue of domestic or foreign policy either in a short opening statement, in an even shorter answer to a question, or in still shorter comments on answers. Kennedy, having memorized a lot of facts, managed to get them in no matter what the question and created the impression of great knowledge. Nixon's comments often seemed so general as to be meaningless. One hour for a discussion of foreign or domestic policy is very little indeed, and it is important to keep in mind that each man had only half an hour, minus the time taken by the moderator and the panelists.

The surveys confirm that, in this format, it was the image of the man and not the issues that most impressed the viewers. Nixon's appearance in the first debate is generally believed to have been greatly disadvantageous, and those who heard the debate on radio tended to have a more favorable attitude to Nixon than those who viewed the debate on TV.

What kind of format might have produced different and better results? No one has seriously suggested that the format of the Lincoln-Douglas debates be adopted. In 1858, the rivals for the Senate seat from Illinois engaged in seven debates, one in each congressional district. Each debate lasted three hours. The first speaker, Douglas in four debates and Lincoln in three, spoke for an hour. His opponent then spoke for an hour and a half. The first speaker ended the debate with a final half hour. The debates drew large crowds, as many as 15,000 in some places; as low as 1,500 in others. The slavery issue was the primary one in all the debates.[36]

While the Dewey-Stassen debate dispensed with the panel of questioners, it was no more successful than the 1960 debates in dealing with the issues. The *Oregonian*, in an editorial said, "if any votes were won by either debater, we fancy they were won by his debate

---

[35] Ibid., pp. 129–130.

[36] Robert N. Sarnoff in Kraus, *The Great Debates*, pp. 56–59. See also Lloyd B. Dennis, "Lincoln Debates Easily Arranged," *New York Times*, September 26, 1960, p. 25. The complete texts of the Lincoln-Douglas debates are printed in Paul M. Angle, ed., *Created Equal? The Complete Lincoln-Douglas Debates of 1858* (Chicago: University of Chicago Press, 1958).

conduct, rather than by what he said," and the *Oregon Journal* called the event a "Debate of Tweedledum and Tweedledee."[37]

Not many distinctive formats are available for joint appearances of presidential candidates, though there are many minor variations. They can be either like the 1960 joint appearances (or 1976), with a panel asking questions; or like the Dewey-Stassen radio debates in Oregon, where each speaker had twenty minutes for opening argument and each had eight and a half minutes for rebuttal; or like the Lincoln-Douglas debates, with each speaker given a long period for developing his position and attacking his opponent and a shorter, but still long, period for rebuttal; or part of the time could be used for the candidates to question one another.

The replies received from the letters sent out by the APSA commission in 1963 included a wide range of comments about format. A number of replies expressed doubt that there is one good format. An Ohio Republican House member said, "My opinion is that circumstances, personalities, and abilities of the candidates will vary so widely that I doubt the value of drawing up any rules."[38] He and others were strongly of the opinion that these matters should be left to the candidates. Other respondents suggested specific changes. Several were adamantly against the use of a panel of interviewers. A Michigan Democratic member of the House wrote, "My frank feeling is that witnessing a bunch of reporters acting as prosecutors is not always the most appealing form of television programming, and this at all costs should be avoided."[39] A number favored the traditional debate including direct questioning of each candidate by the other. For moderator, some suggested a U.S. Supreme Court judge; another suggested that one candidate present the other with names of three members of Congress from which one would be chosen; another suggested that an important educator preside; and others that a Nobel Prize winner or a former president do the job.

Some replies suggested that the format vary from program to program, sometimes using the debate format and sometimes the "statement technique." A Republican House member from the Southwest recommended that the candidates not meet face-to-face but have the same question put to them by the same people separately. Such a program, he proposed, should be taped in advance and would allow each presidential candidate "to give true and complete answers about

---

[37] Quoted in Kraus, *The Great Debates*, p. 40. See also *Oregonian*, May 19, 1948, p. 10, and *Oregon Journal*, May 19, 1948, p. 13.

[38] APSA Commission, *Report*, p. 13.

[39] Ibid., p. 13.

his philosophy, without the temptation to vary his presentation a bit to 'sock the other guy.' "[40]

A number of congressmen suggested the debates be longer and that issues be explored in depth; on the other hand, one House member warned that allowing too much time was conducive to long speeches. The most commonly suggested lengths ranged from one to two hours, the number of debates from three to six.

A considerable number of congressmen recommended measures they believed would result in a more meaningful discussion of issues. A Maryland Republican said, "I think that debates should be limited to topics which establish the maturity, humanity, judgment, and wisdom of candidates rather than their encyclopedic memory, their histrionic ability, or their sex appeal."[41] Only a few replies raised the question whether there should be a studio audience; all were in favor. An Iowa Republican suggested an audience "evenly divided with half the seats going to the backers of one candidate and half to the backers of the other."[42]

The state chairmen who responded, with two exceptions, favored debates but were dissatisfied with the 1960 format. All but one were against having a panel of interviewers; only one, a Republican from the Midwest, approved the panel approach but recommended, instead of reporters, a six-member panel representing both political parties. A number of state chairmen favored longer debates. A midwestern Democratic state chairman said:

> Each participant should be allowed adequate time for a definitive opening statement on the subject, and each participant should be given an opportunity to comment on the opening statement of his opponent; a panel of experts, preferably those with news or political backgrounds, should direct questions at the participants, each of whom would be allowed to comment on the question regardless of to whom it was addressed; the participants should have the opportunity to question each other; the panelists ought to be permitted a series of follow-up questions on particular points so that neither candidate can gloss over a point with a generality or catch phrase; if an area of intense disagreement arises, there ought to be sufficient flexibility in the debate to permit remaining on the subject and thoroughly exploring the area of disagreement.[43]

[40] Ibid., p. 14.
[41] Ibid., p. 14.
[42] Ibid., p. 15.
[43] Ibid., p. 18.

A midwestern Republican suggested that participants be separated and give their respective presentations in adjoining but separate facilities.

Because of its serious approach to the problems, the response of the spokesman for one of the national committees deserves to be quoted at length:

A great deal has been written about the 1960 debates. In preparing our answer to your request for the views of the National Committee, we have consulted these writings and have discussed the matter with journalists, political scientists, and politicians who were in a position to give us expert advice. A number of suggestions have been made which we believe should be transmitted to your Study Committee for their consideration.

One of the most striking things we discovered was the extent of agreement about changes from the 1960 procedures which were thought to be desirable. This also turned out to be one of the cases in which the feelings of the "average viewers" were very much the same as those of the experts. Of the many studies of the 1960 debates, apparently the only one which specifically asked respondents for suggestions for improvement was conducted by Richard F. Carter of the Institute for Communications Research at Stanford University. Three comments were made much more frequently than any others. The debates should be longer. The interviewing newsmen should be eliminated. And there should be only one topic per debate. Each of these suggestions can be documented with arguments we have heard from experts.

Somewhat longer debates would be desirable. It might not be possible to hold an audience for two hours but a debate ought to hold their attention for an hour-and-a-half. And this additional time could be usefully employed. The candidates could begin with a statement of their own positions. They could follow this with cross-questioning and still have time for summary statements.

The role of the press ought to be restricted because they frequently ask a particular type question, one which will produce a newsworthy answer. As is said on Meet the Press: "The questions which the reporters ask do not necessarily reflect their own opinions, but are their way of developing a story for you." Good stories often result when a reporter asks a provocative question, but the campaign ought to be run for the benefit of the candidates and the electorate, not the reporters.

Reporters are also concerned with the partisan implications

of the questions they ask. They do not want to appear as pro-Republican or pro-Democratic, and therefore avoid asking questions which might give that impression to their viewers. Often it is the frankly partisan questions which stimulate good debate. I believe that it would be better to have frankly political questions asked by acknowledged political opponents.

Of course, there is no reason why two formats cannot be used in the same series. One or two appearances could be presented as joint press conferences. The others could be debates in which the candidates cross-examine each other. Both of these formats can be used to develop information for the viewers, and perhaps both should be used.

If it is decided to use a panel of interviewers, the interrogators should be allowed at least one follow-up question. An experienced politician can evade any question in his first answer. If a reporter is allowed a follow-up question, he at least has a chance to probe.

The selection of the topics to be debated is clearly going to have to be a matter of agreement between the candidates. The topics which are being discussed are just as much a part of the debate as the words which the candidates speak. Some topics give an advantage to one candidate; other topics give an advantage to his opponent. Defining the issues is the business of the candidates. That's what they are supposed to be doing during a campaign.

In 1960, the debates seemed to lack a focus. There was too much randomness, too much generality, and too much back-and-forth between the candidates. There was not enough serious discussion of the issues. The candidates ought to be encouraged to reach agreement on the topics they will discuss on each debate. The goal here ought to be narrow enough to provide a focus for discussion, but broad enough that it does not constrict the discussion. Something narrower, say, than "foreign policy," but not as restricted as "The Alliance for Progress."

There is some danger that trying to achieve agreement on the exact topics to be discussed could bog down the whole negotiations. A committee of experts, such as your Study Committee, could facilitate agreement. Each candidate could submit a list of topics he would be willing to discuss. The committee could then prepare a proposed schedule for the debates which could be referred back to the candidates as an agenda for their final negotiations. Agreement between the candidates on the specific subjects to be discussed might be easier to reach if the first debate, or the final debate, were retained as a general debate when topics not covered in the other debates could be discussed.

The timing of the debates is another important question. In 1960 it was not possible to schedule any debates during the final two or three weeks of the campaign, the traditional period in which the real heat is put on. The impact of the debates would be greater if they were spread out during the campaign period so that there were one or two during the climax of the campaign.[44]

The principal criticisms of the 1960 format concerned (1) their duration—which many believed to be too brief; (2) their focus, or more accurately their lack of focus; and (3) their reliance on a panel of interviewers interposed between the candidates. The 1960 debates, the comments about them by viewers and critics, and the responses to the APSA commission letters sharply suggest a variety of possible changes that could be made to improve the format. The responses from politicians make clear that debates are not likely to be required by law and the format of debates almost certainly will be decided by the candidates and their advisers.

It also is worth remembering that disagreement on format may not be real disagreement but a way of postponing or avoiding debates. A candidate who wants to avoid debate can best do so by prolonging discussion of format.[45] He can, for example, list a number of seemingly reasonable conditions that will be unacceptable to his opponent but which, if his opponent does accept, will be favorable to himself. Stassen finally acceded to all Dewey's terms in the Oregon radio debate in 1948 and was damaged by the debate. There were protracted negotiations; Stassen wanted an audience with applause and heckling, Dewey did not. Stassen wanted a wide-ranging discussion of issues; Dewey wanted the debate limited to outlawing of communism. There was still no agreement three days before the scheduled debate. Stassen capitulated saying, "We will let Dewey write his own ticket and we will meet his terms—reluctantly."[46]

Finally, in evaluating format in the 1960 experience, it should be remembered that candidates appear on television in many formats other than joint appearances. These include campaign spots, filmed biographies, staged or spontaneous press conferences and interviews, and telethons. Further, if free of a requirement for equal time for all

---

[44] Ibid., pp. 19–21.

[45] MacNeil, *The People Machine*, pp. 174–175.

[46] Kraus, *The Great Debates*, p. 39. Also see the *Washington Evening Star*, May 28, 1948, p. 8.

candidates, TV is likely in the future, as it has in the past, to provide for a number of appearances by the candidates in formats established by the networks. In 1960, Vice-President Nixon appeared on the Jack Paar "Tonight" show (NBC), "Meet the Press" (NBC), "Presidential Countdown" (CBS), "The Campaign and the Candidates" (NBC), and "Person to Person" (CBS). The Republican vice-presidential candidate Henry Cabot Lodge appeared on "Meet the Press," "The Campaign and the Candidates," "Face the Nation," and "Presidential Countdown."

The Democratic candidate, Senator Kennedy, appeared on "Presidential Countdown," "Tonight," "Person to Person," "The Campaign and the Candidates," "Meet the Press," and "Face the Nation." Senator Johnson, the Democratic vice-presidential candidate appeared on "Presidential Countdown," "Face the Nation," "The Campaign and the Candidates," and "Meet the Press."[47]

Programs like the above provide the possibility for very considerable television exposure. Their formats, in fact, have one major advantage over the 1960 debate format: they provide an opportunity for follow-up questions by the panel that force greater exploration of the problem or policy being discussed.[48] Joint appearances should be considered in the total context as only one device for presenting the candidates to the voters. Networks, parties, and candidates need

---

[47] Robert E. Gilbert, *Television and Presidential Politics* (N. Quincy, Mass.: Christopher Publishing House, 1968), p. 165. Such programs make extensive use of politicians, but the political influence of television extends far beyond these programs.

Michael J. Robinson has several excellent articles on the impact of television in American politics. See "Public Affairs Television and the Growth of Political Malaise: The Case of the Selling of the Pentagon," *American Political Science Review*, vol. 70, no. 2 (June 1976), pp. 409–432; "Television and American Politics, 1956–1976," *Public Interest*, no. 48 (Summer 1977), pp. 3–39; "The TV Primaries," *Wilson Quarterly* (Spring 1977), pp. 80–83; "American Political Legitimacy in an Era of Electronic Journalism: Reflections on the Evening News," in Richard Adler, ed., *Television as a Social Force: New Approaches to TV Criticism* (New York: Praeger, 1976), pp. 79–83; with Clifford Zuken, "Television and the Wallace Vote," *Journal of Communication* (Spring 1976), pp. 79–83. Also see Morris J. Gelman, "TV and Politics: '62," *Television Magazine* (October 1962), pp. 64–67, 82–87; Thomas E. Patterson and Robert D. McClure, *The Unseeing Eye: The Myth of Television Power in National Politics* (New York: G. P. Putnam's Sons, 1976).

A number of interesting and useful articles on the mass media and American politics are published in L. John Martin, ed., "The Role of the Mass Media in American Politics," *Annals of the American Academy of Political and Social Science*, vol. 427 (September 1976).

[48] See Stanley Kelley, Jr., "Campaign Debates: Some Facts and Issues," *Public Opinion Quarterly*, vol. 26, no. 3 (Fall 1962), p. 364. Kelley's whole article is worth reading since it discusses most of the issues raised by the debates.

to canvass all alternatives and exercise their creativity in establishing more effective contributions to presidential and other campaigns.

The commission established by the American Political Science Association recommended that seven programs should take place between Labor Day and Election Day, on a suitable evening in prime television time. It recommended that the first program should provide the candidates—including the vice-presidential candidates—an opportunity to present an overall statement of issues. Four of the succeeding appearances should be devoted to exploring key issues in depth. The sixth should be given over to candidates of minor parties; the seventh might be a summing up by the presidential and vice-presidential candidates. The commission expressed the view that these programs should be held in a studio, not before an audience, that actual presence of the participants should be required, that one or more of the programs might include a senator and a representative. The commission, in other words, proposed a set of programs differing substantially from the 1960 debates but agreeing with the viewer comments in those studies that explored the matter: more time, more specific issues, and elimination of interviewer panels.[49]

Impact on Voters

There are, in principle, several influences televised debates might reasonably have on voters. These include (1) stimulating voters' interest and turnout; (2) affecting voters' knowledge and/or understanding of one or more issues; (3) altering voters' perception of one or both candidates; (4) influencing voting intention or voting behavior. It is also possible that debates have no influence whatsoever. How can one estimate the impact, if any, of given debates on the voting population or some segment of it? It is quite clear that we cannot do so in any definitive or precise way. Debates, and all other campaign events, take place in a complex personal, social, and political context. Not only is it impossible to isolate respondents from all other influences that impinge on their attention or feelings, but voters bring to debates identifications and expectations that shape and perhaps determine their reaction to specific political events. Each viewer before each television has not only a mind set but also a feeling set which predisposes his evaluation of candidates and their comments in one way rather than another. The viewer is in no sense a *tabula rasa*, a blank page, on which television writes. Furthermore, it is unlikely that

---

[49] APSA Commission, *Report*, pp. 6–10.

the viewer could describe (indeed could know) everything about his own predispositions. The prestige of "open mindedness" further complicates the problem. Not many respondents are prepared to affirm that their institutional loyalty to Democrats or Republicans is so strong that they could not be swayed by a rational discussion of the issues. Even if it were possible to know all the relevant expectations and predispositions of a voter—which it is not—there remains another virtually insoluble problem: simultaneity of campaign events. Many forces impinge on the voter at every moment: conversations with family, friends, and colleagues; events reported on radio and TV, in newspapers and magazines; interpretation of the meaning and consequences of events—or of the debates—by radio and television commentators, editorial writers, and news and magazine stories; events outside the political system—all these affect the perception and evaluation of political occurrences. It seems reasonably well established that Ford's statement concerning the extent of Soviet influence in Eastern Europe made less impact on viewers than did the comments and discussion of journalists—radio, newspapers, TV, magazines— in the days that followed.[50]

Beyond these virtually insoluble problems lie some more routine but nonetheless knotty technical difficulties: the cost of an adequate sample, so that inferences made from the responses can be applied to larger populations; the development of techniques for getting data on a comparable group of nonviewers; the difficulties and costs of panel studies carried on through sufficient time for comparisons to be made of an individual's responses at different times. There is also, of course, the problem of recall and the distortion it introduces.[51]

Paul Hagner and John Orman in their study of the 1976 debates call attention to one of the most critical difficulties:

> The methodology of critical event analysis faces inescapable problems which vary according to the degree of control present in the observation. At one extreme, asking respondents at t_3 to recall their attitudes at t_1 and their evaluation of an event which occurred at t_2 raises serious questions of voter recall and rationalization. At the other end of the spectrum,

---

[50] See Chapter 4 of this volume, by Richard B. Cheney; his conclusion (p. 129) is that "the data indicate that for much of the viewing public, the misstatement about the status of Eastern Europe was not a significant item until it received extensive comment and coverage in the press after the debate."

[51] Most, if not all, of those who did studies in 1960 were well aware of the shortcomings of their own studies. For example, see Katz and Feldman, pp. 213–218, and Lang, p. 314, in Kraus, *The Great Debates*.

laboratory-condition experimental designs may sacrifice external validity for observational control.[52]

Conceding then the impossibility of achieving perfectly accurate and reliable information on the impact of the debates, we must settle for findings based on imperfect studies and make allowances for the imperfections in evaluating the conclusions. In fact, a great many studies were done on the impact of the 1960 debates. In considering them, it is well to recall certain longstanding findings of voting behavior research. From studies of voting behavior it was long ago concluded that voting behavior is influenced by both short- and long-range factors. Among the long-range factors are party identification and fundamental beliefs. These determinants of voting behavior are difficult to change, in part because selective exposure and perception enables the voter to avoid those things that might call into question existing commitments.[53] Warren Miller pointed out in 1960:

> Much evidence can be assembled to illustrate the ponderous slowness with which political attitudes actually do change. And it can be suggested that the dominant source of change which does occur is not to be found in the deliberate act of a publicist or a campaign manager, but in the non-political events which impinge on the daily routine of the voter.[54]

Voting studies also have documented the existence of short-range factors that may be determining in any given election. These

---

[52] Paul R. Hagner and John Orman, "A Panel Study of the Impact of the First Debate: Media Events, 'Rootless Voters,' and Campaign Learning," paper delivered at the annual meeting of the American Political Science Association, Washington, D.C., September 1–4, 1977, appendix.

[53] It has been argued that selective exposure and perception enables the voter to avoid being confronted with information that might call into question existing commitments. But the usefulness of these concepts has been called into question by recent studies. See Sidney Kraus and Dennis Davis, *The Effects of Mass Communication on Political Behavior* (University Park, Pa.: Pennsylvania State University Press, 1976), chapter 4. This is a very useful volume and the abstracts and bibliography at the end of each chapter provide an excellent guide to the literature. For a further critical examination of selective exposure, see David O. Sears and Jonathan L. Freeman, "Selective Exposure to Information: A Critical Review," *Public Opinion Quarterly*, vol. 31 (Summer 1967), pp. 194–213; Stanley Kelley, Jr., has an excellent discussion of the use of the mass media in election campaigns in "Elections and the Mass Media," *Law and Contemporary Problems* (Spring 1962), pp. 307–326.

[54] Warren E. Miller, "The Political Behavior of the Electorate," in Earl Latham, ed., *American Government Annual, 1960–1961* (New York: Holt, Rinehart, and Winston, 1960), p. 55. Elihu Katz asserts that campaigns in the mass media, political and nonpolitical, convert very few; see "Platforms and Windows: Broadcasting's Role in Elections Campaigns," *Journalism Quarterly* (Summer 1971), pp. 304–314.

include the state of the economy, the personality of the two candidates, the character of the campaign (including such media events as debates), and the flow of information. Short-run factors have less influence on those who are well-informed and strong partisans and on those with virtually no information and no commitments than they have on those with some information and weak loyalties.[55] This means that any significant increase in the flow of information to the poorly informed increases the probability that they will receive new information and be affected by it. Those with much information and high involvement and those with no information and *very* little involvement have a high degree of stability of voting intention. The floating voter is more likely to have some but little information; new information is likely to influence his intentions.[56] However, Edward Dreyer, examining the elections between 1952 and 1964, concludes:

> With the growing availability of mass media (primarily television since 1952), and the increased utilization of the media by candidates and parties, the flow of short-term political stimuli—both during campaigns and in the lengthy lulls between them—has effectively penetrated all segments of the electorate. These data also suggest that the more or less immediate circumstances that surround any given election have eroded and probably will continue to erode the stabilizing influences normally associated with the electorate's partisan loyalties. This weakening of the party identification— party vote relationship will be manifested across the total electorate. . . . Converse's modification of the floating voter hypothesis, while probably applicable to an earlier era of rather weak political communication, no longer seems to apply to the current situation.[57]

With this background, we look now at the effects of the debates— insofar as this is possible—on questions raised at the beginning of this section: audience size and voting turnout; knowledge of issues; voters' images of candidates; and voting intentions and behavior.[58]

---

[55] Philip E. Converse, "Information Flow and the Stability of Partisan Attitudes," in Angus Campbell, Philip E. Converse, Warren E. Miller, and Donald E. Stokes, *Elections and the Political Order* (New York: John Wiley and Sons, 1966), chapter 8.

[56] Ibid.

[57] Edward C. Dreyer, "Media Use and Electoral Choices: Some Political Consequences of Information Exposure," *Public Opinion Quarterly*, vol. 35 (Winter 1971–1972), pp. 544–553.

[58] A very large amount of research has been done that might illuminate the impact of the 1960 debates as they relate to the above matters. This research includes studies by university groups designed specifically to study the debates;

Audience Size and Turnout. A dramatic feature of the debates was their enormous audiences. As noted earlier, in 1960 some 70 million of the total of 107 million adults viewed or heard the first debate, and it is estimated that at least 55 percent of the adult population watched or listened to each debate. The same phenomenon occurred in 1976. As Chaffee and Dennis note in their paper, the first debate in 1976 had an audience of at least 67 percent (Gallup) and with a figure of 89 percent reported by Market Opinion Research. For the second debate the median viewing estimates were 67 percent; for the vice-presidential debate 50 percent, and for the third debate 56 percent.[59]

Did the massive audience for the debates result in a massive increase in voter turnout at the polls? The answer is no; there was no massive increase in turnout at the polls. The turnout, using Census Bureau figures, was 61.6 percent in 1952, 59.3 percent in 1956, 62.8 percent in 1960, 61.9 percent in 1964, 60.9 percent in 1968, 55.5 percent in 1972, and 54.4 percent in 1976. Thus, in 1960, the turnout was only 1.2 percent above 1952 when no debates were held; 3.5 percent above 1956, and 0.9 percent above 1964.[60]

We also know that the massive viewing audience for the 1976 debates was not matched at the polls. Turnout, in fact, was down to 54.3 percent, the lowest since 1948. It is clear that debates did not

some questions on the debates included in the election study done by the Survey Research Center at Michigan; the work of the Gallup and Roper organizations; various state polls; work done for the candidates (Opinion Research Corporation for Nixon and Louis Harris and Associates for Kennedy); Albert I. Sindlinger and Co., which paid special attention to the debates in its elaborate study of the campaign; and the opinion research firms of John H. Kraft, R. H. Bruskin and Associates, and others. As noted in footnote 4, Elihu Katz and Jacob Feldman list all the studies, including information on locale, size of sample, timing, characteristics of the sample, data collection procedures, and principal concerns. With respect to impact on the audience, the studies reviewed by Katz and Feldman were concerned with images of the candidates, who won, change of voting intention, issues, role of debates in decision, and evaluation of performance. But the studies varied greatly in their subject matter, locale, size of sample, and the like. While it is difficult to arrive at definitive judgments of the impact of the debates on the viewing audience from these studies, it is possible to draw some conclusions.

[59] For 1960, see Katz and Feldman in Kraus, *The Great Debates*, p. 190; for 1976, see this volume, p. 82. Chaffee and Dennis take their data from a paper by David O. Sears prepared for the American Political Science Association annual meeting, September 1–4, 1977, Washington, D.C. Also, Arthur Miller, study director of the Center for Political Studies, reports that the debates were used more extensively than any other media source in 1976; see *ISR Newsletter*, vol. 6, no. 1 (1978), p. 5.

[60] U.S. Department of Commerce, Bureau of Census, *Statistical Abstract of the United States, 1977*, p. 508, table 813.

greatly stimulate interest in voting. This coincides with Angus Campbell's judgment in 1962 that there had been only a small, proportionate increase in the presidential vote since the advent of TV. Campbell further noted that the midterm elections did not even show that increase.[61]

The Impact on Issues. It is most difficult to assess whether the debates had any significant impact on voters' concern for or knowledge of issues, even though political scientists have had a great interest in how much election campaigns influence and are influenced by substantive knowledge of issues. We do know, of course, that voters have a very slight knowledge indeed of almost any given issue, and that a great many voters are committed to vote for the candidate of their party, no matter what discussion of issues takes place. At the same time a number of students of politics believe that issues and matters of public policy are having an increasing importance in election campaigns.[62]

After reviewing all of the survey data from 1960, Katz and Feldman conclude:

> As far as issues are concerned, then, the debates seem to have (a) made some issues salient rather than others (the issues made salient, of course, may or may not have been the most important ones); (b) caused some people to learn where the candidates stand (including the stand of the opposition candidate); (c) effected very few changes of opinion on issues; and (d) focused more on presentation and personality than on issues.[63]

In fact, the material they are able to bring together under the heading "Learning from the Debates: The Issues" is very slight, little more

---

[61] Angus Campbell, "Has Television Reshaped Politics?" *Columbia Journalism Review* (Fall 1962), pp. 10–13. Also, see MacNeil, *The People Machine*, p. 9.

[62] It may be that increased issue voting is attributed to debates when, in fact, issue voting is increasing even though there are no debates. For example, see Norman H. Nie, Sidney Verba, and John R. Petrocik, *The Changing American Voter* (Cambridge, Mass.: Harvard University Press, 1976), chapter 10. See also John Kessel, "Comment: The Issues in Issue Voting," *American Political Science Review*, vol. 66 (June 1972), pp. 459–465; David E. RePass, "Issue Salience and Party Choice," *American Political Science Review*, vol. 65 (June 1971), pp. 389–400; Benjamin I. Page and Richard Brody, "Policy Voting and the Electoral Process: The Vietnam Issue," *American Political Science Review*, vol. 66 (September 1972), pp. 979–995; Richard W. Boyd, "Popular Control of Public Policy: A Normal Vote Analysis of the 1968 Election," *American Political Science Review*, vol. 66 (June 1972), pp. 429–449; and Warren Miller and Teresa Levitan, *Leadership and Change* (Cambridge, Mass.: Winthrop, 1976).

[63] Kraus, *The Great Debates*, p. 203.

than two pages. They noted that the Carter study (approximately 100 respondents in four cities near Stanford, California) reported that a high proportion of respondents believed that—on most issues— neither candidate had the best of it; the same study, however, reported that 27 percent of the respondents believed the debates contributed to their learning about issues. (The respondents, it should be noted, were probably well above average in social and economic status.) They note that the Kraus-Smith study (142 respondents in Indianapolis), which attempted to assess the amount of actual change of opinion on issues as a result of the debates, reported no change at all.[64]

The national polls (Opinion Research Corporation and Sindlinger) indicated that foreign affairs was the paramount issue in the campaign and increased in importance as the campaign went on. In the debates, the Quemoy-Matsu matter appeared to benefit Nixon. The Roper poll asked a specific question on this issue: "How do you feel about this— that Nixon scored against Kennedy in these discussions about the off-shore islands of Quemoy and Matsu—or that Kennedy scored against Nixon or that neither of them handled the issue well?" Nixon support-ers were more certain that Nixon handled the issue well than Kennedy supporters were that Kennedy handled it well.[65] This, however, does not tell us much about what voters knew or learned about the issue, particularly since Republicans generally were surer that their man handled foreign policy issues well than Democrats were that Kennedy did. This may simply reflect a feeling that Nixon had more experience in foreign affairs and have little to do with specific issues. At the same time, the Roper poll indicates that confidence in Kennedy's ability in the foreign affairs field increased as a result of the debates.[66] In gen-eral, Nixon rated higher in handling foreign policy and Kennedy in handling domestic issues, but this is probably a reflection of views about party, or about the man, or about their respective experience, not a reflection of any detailed knowledge of issues.

These findings should not surprise us. Even though the Lincoln-Douglas debates lasted three hours and concentrated on the slavery issue, much of the reporting demonstrates that it was the voters' perception of the candidates and not the substance of the arguments that made the greatest impression on the crowd and on the reporters.

---

[64] Ibid., pp. 253–270, 289–312. Kraus and Smith conclude that "It is difficult, if not impossible, to determine which candidate was helped or hindered by par-ticipating in the debates. Certainly, this study cannot award victory to either candidate," p. 311.

[65] Ibid., p. 202.

[66] Ibid.

This was due, in part at least, to the very striking differences in appearance and style.[67] In regard to the 1960 candidates, Douglass Cater reports that they were "far more concerned about their images than their argument," and "not even a trained observer could keep up with the crossfire of fact and counter fact."[68] Reading the texts of the Nixon-Kennedy debates provides a lively reminder of how little time was spent on any topic and how inadequate was the time set for rejoinder. The topics were very complex and there is no way a voter could have learned very much. But time was not the only factor. The interposition of a panel of questioners added to the problem. Questions were not always well chosen to bring out adequate discussion, and no questioner could follow up a question with another question to illuminate the topic. The candidates often pushed aside the question in order to make a point on a different topic. Time consumed by the panel of newsmen not only shortened the time of the candidates but also failed to provide an effective means of getting at important issues.

It is important to note, however, that Steven H. Chaffee and Jack Dennis in their study of the 1976 presidential debates in this volume are more optimistic about the extent to which debates provide a means of educating voters about issues and, thereby, contribute to an issue effect on voting behavior. They say, after reviewing a number of relevant studies of the 1976 debates:

> In general, we conclude that the debates clearly performed one of their major social tasks, that of providing information about the candidates and their positions that was new to many voters. Further, the debates might well have been the only mechanism that would supply such information to a significant number of these people, despite their apparent need for it in connection with the impending vote. Prior to the debates people had fairly well established in their minds

---

[67] Michael Kraus, *The United States to 1865* (Ann Arbor: University of Michigan Press, 1959), p. 473. Douglas was five feet tall, solidly built, with fire and frenzy in his speech. "Lincoln, said a reporter, was 'built on the Kentucky type,' very tall, angular, awkward, with big feet, and clothes much too short for his long arms and legs. His deep-set eyes reflected quickly his mirth or sorrow. When he was stirred he became truly impressive—'his eye glows and sparkles, every lineament, now so ill-formed, grows brilliant and expressive, and you have before you a man of rare power and of strong magnetic influence. He *takes* the people every time, and there is no getting away from his sturdy good sense, his unaffected sincerity, and the unceasing play of his good humor, which accompanies his clear logic and smoothes the way to conviction.' His shrill, penetrating voice carried to the farthest edges of the patient crowds who stood for hours to listen to America's most famous debate."

[68] Kraus, *The Great Debates*, p. 129, 130; see also chapter 6.

which issues were of greatest concern to them, but the positions of the candidates were not clear. The debates thus enabled voters to apply their own priorities to the political decision that they, collectively, had to make.[69]

In spite of the studies reviewed, my pessimism remains. The debates, as we experienced them in 1960 and 1976, do not furnish a very effective mechanism for providing information about issues or the issue positions of the candidates. I find myself in agreement with Nelson Polsby who concludes:

> The debates are best understood not as an occasion for the ventilation of ideas or the exploration of genuine disagreements about the future course of events, but as a trial by ordeal, pure and simple. Whoever holds his hand over the fire for the prescribed period without flinching survives. There are no winners, however, just losers—those who say something that sends the press baying like a pack of beagles into the next week or ten days seeking after clarifications, revisions, apologies, or concessions. It is no wonder that the candidates themselves are so fixated on preparation, on control over the setting, on elaborate ground rules, and are so little inclined to emphasize the potential of the debates to encourage spontaneity.[70]

Impact on Voters' Perception of the Candidates. In 1960 as in 1858, in spite of the increased salience of issues such as foreign affairs, most viewers formed more of an impression of the men than of the issues. Samuel Lubell found this to be the case. From his 1960 interviews he reported comments like the following: "I heard so much about Kennedy being inexperienced that I was surprised at how well he did in 'debate.' " "He (Kennedy) seemed intelligent and educated"; he is "sharp" and "aggressive." Voters saw Nixon as "conservative," "mature," "knowledgeable," "experienced." "Nixon knows the value of a dollar."[71] On balance, the impressions voters formed supported Kennedy's candidacy. Both Kennedy and Nixon subsequently expressed the view that Kennedy benefited most. Kennedy asserted that "we wouldn't have had a prayer without that gadget (television)," and Nixon summed it up by saying "there can be no question but that

---

[69] See p. 89.

[70] See p. 178. See also Arthur H. Miller and Warren E. Miller, "Partisanship and Performance: 'Rational' Choices in the 1976 Presidential Elections," paper prepared for the Annual Meeting of the American Political Science Association, Washington, D.C., September 1–4, 1977.

[71] Kraus, *The Great Debates*, p. 158 and the whole of chapter 9.

Kennedy . . . gained more from the debates than I."[72] To a great extent, this effect was probably a result of Nixon's appearance in the first debate, which was due in part to makeup and lighting but even more to his health. He looked pallid and grey, because he had only recently been released from the hospital and was tired from the intensity of the effort to make up lost campaign time. In any event, the important things seem to have been appearance, style, personality. How could it have been otherwise? Although voters acquired some information about issues and candidates' stands on issues, they were not, and could not have been, knowledgeable enough to make a decision on the merits of Nixon's and Kennedy's positions on the complex matters that were discussed in the debates.

> Katz and Feldman, reviewing the survey studies, conclude:
> We have already seen that the viewers learned something about the issues though perhaps not very much. But there is considerably more reason to believe that they learned something about the candidates themselves. They discovered how well each candidate could perform in debate and they formed images of each candidate's character and abilities.[73]

The relevance of these vivid TV images to a valid assessment of a candidate's presidential potential is a difficult question that will be discussed later. A plausible argument can be made that judging the men is even more important than judging the issues, because the issues are so complex and the knowledge required to think about them so arcane that voters simply cannot make sound judgments about the individual issues. It also is quite possible that issues discussed in the campaign may differ from those confronted by the winner when he takes office. However this may be, it remains true that the TV debates of 1960 "educated" the voters more about the candidates than about the issues. Some viewers may have left their TV sets with a little more interest in Quemoy and Matsu than they brought with them to the debates, but many more left with a vivid impression of the candidates. There was nothing in the 1960 debates to encourage those who view the principal objective of the party to be educating voters, or who view the debates as the royal road to such a goal. Samuel Lubell concluded that "future TV debates will continue to put the prime emphasis on the personality of the candidates rather than on party or issues." He agrees with a Detroit auto worker who told him "It's all phony. This has become an actor's election."[74]

---

[72] Nixon, *Six Crises*, p. 357.
[73] Kraus, *The Great Debates*, p. 203.
[74] Ibid., p. 154, 155.

adian Broadcasting Corporation study in seven major
es conducted by telephone interviews with 4,800 re-
ectively summarizes their judgment in a way that seems
h the U.S. data; their study supports the view that personality and style were most important. The subject matter of the
debates—the issues—were rarely mentioned as affecting the viewers'
positive or negative opinion of the candidates. They say:

> The questions we asked here were carefully worded so as to
> allow respondents to talk either about what the candidates
> said or about the two men themselves and how they per-
> formed. . . . The fact that so little comment was directed at
> the subject matter of the debate or at any of the arguments
> involved, and so much more at the candidates themselves
> and the general quality of their respective performances as
> debaters, would seem to confirm what some commentators
> have already suggested. This is that a television debate of
> this kind, which focuses attention so sharply on the con-
> testants themselves, leaves a mass audience with (as we have
> seen) some very distinct impressions of the capabilities of
> the two men as debaters and as persons, but (as our results
> suggest) with very little idea of what the debate was all
> about.[75]

Influence on Voting Intention and on Voting. Most difficult of all, as
Katz and Feldman note, is to ascertain how much impact the debates
had on voting decisions.[76] Very few studies included interviews with a
panel of the same respondents before and after the debates and after
assessing voter intentions. In some studies that did use a panel, the
sample was not such that an inference could be made to a larger population. Further, there is little adequate comparison of viewers and
nonviewers. Studies of trends tell us about aggregate changes but
little about internal shifts of opinion and their causes.[77]

Even in the best of circumstances, it is difficult to be sure that
changes in voting intention or voting are due to a single aspect of a
campaign—the debates, for example—rather than to the other campaign activities and events that take place simultaneously. Still, most
of our information concerning motives suffers from the same limitations. While the voters' recollection and reconstruction of the process
by which they made up their minds is not wholly reliable, it should

---

[75] Ibid., p. 200.

[76] Ibid., pp. 205–208.

[77] Ibid., pp. 208–210.

never be wholly discounted. From the studies of the debate impact, some conclusions can be drawn.

In a study for CBS conducted by Elmo Roper—based on a national sample—Roper estimated that 57 percent of those who voted believed that the debates influenced their decision. Another 6 percent (over 4 million voters) ascribed their final decision on voting to debates alone. Of these, 26 percent voted for Nixon and 72 percent for Kennedy. As Theodore White points out, if these extrapolations are true, then 2,000,000 of the Kennedy margin came from television's impact on the American mind—and since Kennedy won by only 112,000 votes, he was entirely justified in saying on the Monday following the election, November 12: "It was TV more than anything else that turned the tide."[78] In the study conducted by R. H. Bruskin, 39 percent said that the debates were the most important thing that led to a Kennedy victory.[79]

The Gallup poll figures show a significant increase in favor of Kennedy between mid-August and November 7, from 44 percent to 49 percent. Nixon at the same time dropped from 50 percent to 48 percent. In the actual vote, Kennedy received 50.1 percent, Nixon 49.9. There is very little evidence in the Gallup survey, however, for attributing this change to the debates.[80] To be sure, the 1960 election was one of the closest in our history; in *Elections and the Political Order*, Campbell, Converse, Miller, and Stokes commented:

> The 1960 election is also a classic in the license it allows for explanation of the final outcome. Any event or campaign stratagem that might plausibly have changed the thinnest sprinkling of voters across the nation may, more persuasively than usual, be called "critical." Viewed in this manner, the 1960 election hung on so many factors that reasonable men might despair of cataloguing them.[81]

On the basis of the ORC and Lang studies, it seems possible to say that the debates, particularly the first, resulted in strengthening the

[78] White, *The Making of the President 1960*, p. 294. For another report on the Roper study see Katz and Feldman in Kraus, *The Great Debates*, pp. 211–212.

[79] Katz and Feldman in Kraus, *The Great Debates*, p. 213. See also their footnote 22 reporting that ORC got a different figure (8 percent, debates) from a slightly different question: What do you think were the most important issues or factors in deciding who won the election? For a discussion of the impact of the Kennedy-Nixon debates on voters in Tallahassee, Florida, see Russell Middleton, "National Television Debates and Presidential Voting Decisions," *Public Opinion Quarterly* (Fall 1962), pp. 426–429.

[80] Kraus, *The Great Debates*, p. 211.

[81] Campbell and others, *Elections and the Political Order*, p. 78.

commitment to the viewer's party; this was more the case for the Democrats than the Republicans. Further, the ORC study indicates that individual commitment was strengthened for the person who "won" and weakened for the loser. In general, it seems safe to say that the debates did have some effect—again, particularly the first—in accelerating Democratic support for Kennedy.

Converse concludes that viewers were more apt to revise their voting intentions than the relatively small proportion of the population that saw no debates, and he also concludes that the debates helped to bring some Democrats back to the party.[82]

The authors of *Elections and the Political Order*, in discussing in chapter 5 the short-term forces that influenced the 1960 election, do not mention the debates. They note that the two Eisenhower victories, in 1952 and 1956, were deviating elections in which short-term forces brought defeat to the majority party without prompting a realignment in party identifications. This made the 1960 election a reinstating election with victory going to the majority party. In their view, short-term forces—the most important of which was the religious issue—prevented the victory from being bigger than it was. It is significant, however, that the debates may, in fact, have muted the Catholic issue. Converse points out in his essay "Religion and Politics: The 1960 Election" that the debates served to demonstrate that Kennedy was "quick witted, energetic, and poised" and these traits are "valued across religious lines and act at the same time to question some of the more garish anti-Catholic stereotypes."[83]

A number of studies asked questions of the "Who won?" sort—Who made the better impression? Who benefited? Who gained the most? Who outscored? Who did the best job stating his case?[84] Almost the only conclusions that can be drawn are: (1) Kennedy rated best in debate 1; (2) things were more nearly even in debate 2; (3) Nixon had a slight edge in debate 3; and (4) the fourth debate showed a mixed response. In the Opinion Research Corporation poll on who did the best job stating his case, Nixon was ahead 39 percent to 35 percent; in the Roper poll on who did the best job, Kennedy was ahead 36 percent to 31 percent; in the Schwerin Research Corporation poll on who outscored the other, Kennedy led 52 percent to 27 percent; in the Sindlinger poll on "Who won?" Kennedy had a one point margin, 36 percent to 35 percent. The Opinion Research Corporation poll was a national sample of 2,672 conducted by personal interviews;

---

[82] Ibid., pp. 124, 146–147.

[83] Ibid.

[84] Kraus, *The Great Debates*, pp. 196–197.

the Roper poll was a national sample of approximately 3,000 conducted by personal interviews; the Schwerin poll was a New York City poll of about 250–300, conducted by self-administered questionnaire; the Sindlinger poll was a national poll of approximately 3,000 conducted by telephone. It is obvious that the national polls (Opinion Research, Roper, and Sindlinger) do not give a very definitive answer.

If one takes all debates in studies by Carter, Gallup, Iowa poll, Kraft, Minnesota poll, Roper, and Wallace, Kennedy seems to have won or benefited most. The margin in all cases is significant, and in the three national polls Kennedy had a clear margin—Gallup, 42 percent Kennedy and 30 percent Nixon; Kraft, 42 percent Kennedy and 30 percent Nixon; Roper, 37 percent Kennedy and 21 percent Nixon.[85]

These data coincide with the judgments of informed observers and with that of the candidates themselves; both Nixon and Kennedy thought Kennedy benefited most from the debates.

While it is difficult, if not impossible, to translate the "Who won?" scores into voting behavior, there seems to be widespread agreement among students of politics that the debates had some small influence on voting intentions and on actual voting. The debates tended to solidify or reinforce Kennedy's Democratic supporters while they loosened Nixon's hold on some independents and Republicans. They improved Kennedy's image somewhat, causing him to seem more knowledgeable, more mature, more competent. Meanwhile, Nixon's image deteriorated, most sharply after the first debate in which Nixon's five o'clock shadow, lack of makeup, and haggard appearance from his illness played an important role.

In conclusion, about all we can say is that in some contexts debates are a short-term force that may aid one candidate against another. The extent of the aid is not likely to be great, but given the difficulty in predicting who will be aided and given the fears of candidates and campaign managers and given the closeness of many elections, debates are not likely to be the usual practice in presidential campaigns.

Impact on Parties and the Political System

It is, I believe, impossible to separate entirely the impact of televised debates on the parties and the political system from the larger subject: the general impact of television on politics. The presidential debates are simply the most important single type of televised campaign event; they command the largest audience and the most attention from other media. Some of the effects of the debates are effects of the media. Some are shaped by the format in which the debates are cast; still others from the views of media commentators about these encounters. The debates become especially important because so many influential persons say they are especially important, and also because the notion of a "contest" or "confrontation" in public view between two men, one of whom is about to be chosen president, stimulates interest beyond that aroused by the appearance of a single candidate.

Thus, while debates between presidential candidates on TV have occurred only twice (1960 and 1976), with a gap of sixteen years in between and, therefore, could not have had a continuing impact on parties in recent years, it is clear that any attempt to explore the effects of debates leads one directly to the influence or impact of the electronic media generally. It is this general influence of the media on parties that I propose to explore.

Selection of Candidates. Along with TV generally, television debates contribute to the recruitment of candidates who do well on TV. The importance is well stated by Theodore White:

> For of all those matters in which organization is important, the direction of television in a political campaign in modern America is incomparably the most important. Here is where the audience is; here is where the greatest part of all money is spent; here is where creative artistry and practical commercialism must join to support the candidates' thrust.[86]

Size, shape, voice, dress, poise, articulateness, and wit attain tremendous importance when TV becomes a major campaign medium. Debates reinforce and enhance these qualities. In debate, in almost any form of joint appearance, in the give and take of oral argument or discussion, the quick reply is rewarded; the candidate with a tendency to think before he speaks is penalized. Image assumes ever increasing importance. Appearance becomes a reality of great potential importance. Does the candidate give the impression of maturity, sincerity, ability, experience, knowledge? Unfortunately, the impression of thoughtfulness is not always best conveyed by thoughtfulness any more than the appearance of sincerity guarantees sincerity.

Television influences the nominating process not merely because it can be used to win support; its greatest influence is on the criteria

---

[86] Theodore H. White, *The Making of the President 1964* (New York: Atheneum, 1966), pp. 321–322.

by which candidates are evaluated. It makes style a factor as important as, perhaps more important than, experience, expertise, or service to the party.

Television campaigning influences nominations in another way as well. It gives those who seek the nomination direct access to masses of potential primary voters and thereby reduces or eliminates entirely the influence of the party leaders or regulars whose opinions about candidates would be much more influential in a two-step communication process. Television magnifies the impact of primaries on the selection process by making it possible for candidates to communicate directly with voters. For this reason it becomes one more instrument for the realization of the populist goal. Its very existence lends—or seems to lend—substance to the dream of direct popular control of government. The fact that candidates seem to be "visiting" in the living rooms of potential voters is far less important than the impression of immediacy that is achieved and the elimination of party representatives as middlemen between the voters and party leaders.

Television and Party. Through most of our history political parties have been a principal, probably the principal, intermediary institution linking the individual to his government. Parties have performed such major political functions as structuring the electorate, recruiting leaders, selecting and presenting candidates, mobilizing voters, and eliciting the resources needed to perform these functions. In recent years, however, symptoms of the decline, or what some call the decomposition, of the parties have accumulated.[87] The 1976 election provided fresh evidence. The near success of Reagan in wresting the party nomination from an incumbent who enjoyed virtually the unanimous support of the party's leadership and the success of the complete outsider, Jimmy Carter, in winning his party's endorsement provide fresh proof of the inability of the two parties to control the nominating process. The continuing decline of party identification and the rise in split-ticket voting are evidence of a growing incapacity to structure the electorate. Meanwhile, as one observer noted, "there was accumulating evidence that the functions of the parties were being

---

[87] See Samuel P. Huntington in Michel J. Crozier, Samuel P. Huntington, and Joji Watanuki, *The Crisis of Democracy* (New York: New York University Press, 1975), pp. 85–91; Jeane J. Kirkpatrick, *The New Presidential Elite* (New York: Russell Sage Foundation and Twentieth Century Fund, 1976), pp. 369–373; Jeane J. Kirkpatrick, *Dismantling the Parties: Reflections on Party Reform and Party Decomposition* (Washington, D.C.: American Enterprise Institute, 1978); Frank J. Sorauf, *Party Politics in America*, 3d ed. (Boston: Little, Brown, 1976), pp. 414–426; Polsby and Wildavsky, *Presidential Elections*, chapter 6 and pp. 35–39.

progessively assumed by government, public relations firms, professional campaign consultants, and candidate organizations."[88]

Obviously, there are multiple causes for such far-reaching social and political events; changes in social structure, in culture, in the kinds of people attracted to politics have all played a role. But it seems likely that the two most important sources of party transformation are technological change and changes in the authoritative rules under which parties—especially the majority party—must operate. These changes "have hampered the capacity of the parties to carry out their historical tasks and have encouraged the development of alternative institutions which perform some activities of political parties but are less effective than parties as instruments of recruitment, representation, and accountability."[89]

Organizationally debilitating rules changes include the proliferation of primaries; the McGovern-Fraser decision to "open" caucuses (eliminating them as a forum for party leaders and regulars); the new campaign finance legislation that reduced the dependence of candidates on parties. Technological changes that have had a negative effect on parties in this country include the development of the electronic media, rapid transportation, computerized mailing lists, and scientific polling.

The development of polling provides information more accurate than that supplied by state and local party leaders and, at the same time, reduces dependence on them. The advent of television and of easier and speedier means of travel reduces the need for national, state, or local party organizations to carry the campaign to the voters. Alongside these changes there have emerged new powerful candidate organizations whose staffs duplicate those of the parties and frequently supplant them. Meetings in a given locality are most frequently arranged by advance men from the candidate's personal organization, who often, if not usually, bypass the local leaders, antagonizing them.

These developments have not gone unnoticed by the professionals. Stimson Bullitt in his interesting book *To Be a Politician* asserts:

> The mass media have done to the campaign system what the invention of accurate artillery did to the feudal kingdom: destroyed the barons and shifted their power to the masses and the prince. While the Reformation removed the intermediary between deity and communicant, the media substi-

---

[88] Kirkpatrick, *Dismantling the Parties*, p. 2.
[89] Ibid., p. 3.

tute themselves for the party in an intermediary role, enabling more nearly direct contact between politician and citizen because they transmit more and translate less. Without the media, candidates are as lost as once they would have been without the party apparatus through which to operate. Candidates now pay less attention to district leaders than to opinion polls, and citizens no longer need party workers to advise them how to vote. When a citizen can see and hear candidates on a screen at home, and read and hear news written by the best journalists from a variety of points of view, about candidates' public and private lives, he does not heed the precinct captain on his block.[90]

Robert Casey, beaten by Milton Shapp in the Democratic primary in Pennsylvania in 1966, makes a comparable point.

Politics is changing tremendously. The old ways no longer work. From that election, I learned that these days you need a combination of two things. First, the traditional grass-roots effort, the telephoning and the door-knocking. But more than that, you have to do what he did. You have to use the new sophisticated techniques, the polling, the television, the heavy staffing, and the direct mail. You can't rely any more on political organizations. They don't work any more. These days, who wants a job in the courthouse or with the highway department? Why, the sons of the courthouse janitors are probably doctors or professional men. You can't give those jobs away any more. We're at the tag end of an era in Pennsylvania.[91]

Cultural, technological, and political developments interact to produce a cumulative impact. Sophisticated techniques such as television, polling, and targeted mailing require specialists whose skills are technical rather than political. The rules give these technicians and the candidate organizations in which they operate even greater influence, partly by hamstringing their potential competitors, the parties. Television's impact, especially the impact of the presidential debates, occurs in this context. Because debates tend to be billed as more important than candidates' other activities and because they focus almost inevitably on persons and personality, they contribute to the growing

---

[90] Stimson Bullitt, *To Be a Politician* (New Haven: Yale University Press, 1977), p. 81; the whole of chapter 5 deals with "Communication Brokers."

[91] Sorauf, *Party Politics in America*, p. 234. See Sorauf's discussion, pp. 234–235, where he says: "It is clear that the new professional managers, media specialists, pollsters and advertising men have become a new and powerful force in American political campaigning. It is equally clear that they threaten to replace the party organization as the major planner and executor of campaigns."

personalism of American politics. Weak parties are more easily influenced by media events which, in turn, further weaken the parties. Frank Sorauf describes the dynamics of this process:

> Thus the two major American parties are dominated by a concern for contesting elections, but their party organizations have great difficulty in controlling those electoral activities. In many parts of the country the ability of the candidates and the party in government to control them has led to dominance of the party organization itself. If these are electoral parties and if groups other than the party organizations control the electoral processes—the picking of candidates and the staging of campaigns—then those groups control the parties.
>
> The failures of the party organizations inevitably frustrate them. Domination by candidates and incumbent officeholders mattered little when the partisans of the organization wanted only patronage and preference. They and the candidates could agree that electoral victory was their common goal on whatever terms were necessary to win it. The victory itself and its later fruits were all that mattered. But today the tension between these two sectors of the party is far greater as the organization recruits ideological and issue-oriented activists. The electoral goals of the new activists include more than mere electoral victory; they would like to control electoral choices so that they might expound issues and select candidates loyal to them. Thus the inability of the organization to control nominations and election campaigns means simply that it, of all the sectors of the party, has the most difficulty in achieving its goals and rewards at the election.
>
> Through their ability to control nominations and election campaigns, the candidates are freed of organizational domination, both in the affairs of the party and in the decisions of public office. And the failures of the party organizations also enhance the competitive position of the non-party political organizations that want to play electoral politics. It is easier than ever before to influence nominations and elections, for the skills and techniques of electoral politics are more widely available than ever. Whoever bids successfully for them can compete on even terms with the party organization.[92]

---

[92] Ibid., pp. 264–265; Sorauf's discussion in chapters 10, 16, 17, and 18 is among the best in the party literature. Also see Dan Nimmo, *The Political Persuaders: The Techniques of Modern Election Campaigns* (Englewood Cliffs, N.J.: Prentice-Hall, 1970); MacNeil, *The People Machine*; Patterson and McClure, *The Unseeing Eye*.

As usual, complex political events are susceptible to more than one interpretation. There are those who see the debates not as media events, which heighten the personalist trend in American politics, but as "national debates," which can heighten voters' awareness of issues and of candidates' positions on issues. They see debates as creating a more informed, issue-oriented electorate and as leading to a politician of the same type. American parties today contain substantial numbers of activist leaders with an intense overriding interest in the issues and a powerful drive to make political contests the purveyors of issue education, clarification, and choice. For those who see campaigns principally as a clash of ideas and programs, presidential debates can be conceived as one more "classroom of the air." What an extraordinary opportunity to have candidates focusing their own and voter attention on the important issues of the day, each candidate stating his own views and commenting on his opponent's—all in the full view of a hundred million voters. Dr. Frank Stanton, speaking in December 1960, affirmed his conviction that the presidential debates were the mechanism that would make politics more rational, dispassionate, judicious.

> Much of the old style campaigning of the torchlight parade era was based on a calculated effort to reinforce old emotional attitudes. . . . We can't afford the emotional landslide that defies reason and negates the judiciousness that ought to be inherent in the grave act of choosing our leaders. I would hope very much—with some of you who have already commented on the lessons of this past campaign—that whatever else it did, it spelled the end of the time when the voters listened only to one side. This was the singular achievement of the debates as an aid to the democratic process: by their very nature they exposed the audience that tuned in to hear one man, the one it favored, to the views of the other man, the one it thought it opposed. . . .
> The debates not only brought an added voter participation; I submit they brought a more thoughtful participation.[93]

For those who, like Stanton, believe voting can and should be "a judicious act, a dispassionate appraisal of contending approaches to the problems facing the nation," and who further believe (as media specialists are perhaps disposed to believe) that nationwide TV debates will lead voters to focus more on issues than on style and personality, the debates have obvious appeal. Among certain kinds of activists (and some others) there is a tendency to think that discussion

---

[93] Kraus, *The Great Debates*, p. 67.

has intrinsic, or nearly intrinsic, merit. Such attitudes are frequently part of the syndrome that has been termed "purist." Such purists might well approve debates even if such a decision made winning harder or unlikely, as long as it appeared to further their principles and programs. The purist or other amateur reformers, at some time, may well seek to require debates by law or by party regulation. One can also conceive that the responsible party advocates might support such a course. It should be remembered, however, that the impact of presidential debates and other TV appearances on parties is to some extent a function of the nature of the parties. If we had programmatic major parties, candidates selected by those parties, and campaigns in which those candidates stood squarely on their parties' platforms, *then* candidate debates would have less tendency to distract voter attention from parties to candidates, though the media's tendencies to personalization would, of course, still be operative. To say this is to re-emphasize that the impact of such media events depends on their total context. In the existing American context, the debates—and political television generally—tend to accelerate the decline of parties by focusing on such visual factors as good looks and such entertainment factors as style. Who doubts that TV was a necessary ingredient in the construction of Camelot?[94]

To Have or Not to Have: The Future of Debates

Dr. Frank Stanton, Richard Salant, and some others have been so enthusiastic about debates that they have argued that TV debates should be made a fixed part of national presidential campaigns.[95] It is suggestive that many persons of that opinion are from the media and have a sanguine view about the relations between television appearances and political reality.

The proponents of debates make several arguments: (1) that they involve more voters in listening to and viewing candidates than any other campaign effort; (2) that they provide a situation in which Democrats have to listen to the Republican candidate and vice versa; (3) that they provide a better mechanism for exposing issues and so provide voters an educational experience they might not otherwise

---

[94] Compare with MacNeil, *The People Machine*, chapter 6. MacNeil says, "TV has made the actor-politician inevitable," p. 147.

[95] Richard S. Salant, "The Television Debates: A Revolution That Deserves a Future," *Public Opinion Quarterly*, vol. 26, no. 3 (Fall 1962), pp. 335–350; and Frank Stanton, "Case for Political Debates on TV," *New York Times Magazine*, January 19, 1964, p. 16.

have; (4) that they provide a better basis for deciding how to vote than is otherwise available because voters have the chance to see the candidate and determine how he reacts under pressure.

Some critics of debates support their use in political campaigns but propose specific revisions. Gilbert Seldes, for example, suggests that debates be used in primaries but not become fixed or traditional factors in the choice of president. Seldes argued in his essay "The Future of National Debates" that "since we are going to have them," we should take all possible steps to see that the "informational, and not the entertainment, side of the medium . . . prevail." Seldes also has argued that it is better to have "too much rather than too little scepticism. It will do little harm to move cautiously into a new and at moments obscure terrain."[96]

Newton Minow, John Bartlow Martin, and Lee M. Mitchell support the debates but propose some reforms in presidential television which go well beyond simple changes in format. Their proposal looks to the institutionalization of televised encounters between the major parties.

THE OPPOSITION PARTY: (1) *Response Time:* Presidential television and opposition party television should be deregulated—taken out of the hands of the FCC. The national committee of the opposition party should be given by law an automatic right of response to any presidential radio or television address made during the ten months preceding a presidential election or within the ninety days preceding a congressional election in nonpresidential years. . . . The national committee should control format if the president has had control of his format. The national committee would not be limited to addressing only those issues raised by the president in his appearance. When a presidential appearance has been carried simultaneously by all three networks, the national committee response should also be carried simultaneously by the networks. The national committee should choose its spokesman or spokesmen. The opposition response should be exempt from the "equal time" law and the fairness and political party doctrines.

(2) *National Debates:* Between elections, the national committee of the opposition party, the national committee of the president's party, and the commercial and public television networks should together develop a plan to present live debates—"The National Debates"—between spokesmen

---

[96] Kraus, *The Great Debates,* pp. 168, 169.

the two major parties with agreed topics and formats quarterly each year (but only twice in federal election years). All debates should be scheduled during prime time and broadcast simultaneously by all networks. This proposal should be carried out voluntarily by the parties and networks rather than be required by legislation. Minor parties would participate in "The National Debates" according to the guidelines set forth in *Voters' Time* (the 1969 report of the nonpartisan Commission on Campaign Costs in the Electronic Era, sponsored by The Twentieth Century Fund, Inc.). "The National Debates" should be exempt from the "equal time" law and the fairness and political party doctrines.

(3) *Voters' Time:* The reforms proposed in *Voters' Time* should be adopted to ensure all significant presidential candidates a minimum amount of free, simultaneous television time. The two major party candidates would receive six thirty-minute prime-time program periods in the thirty-five days preceding a presidential election; candidates of minor parties of sufficient size (based on a formula contained in the *Voters' Time* report) would receive one or two half-hour periods depending on their party's relative strength.[97]

It should be noted that only a portion of the proposals of Minow, Martin, and Mitchell require legislative action, and they, happily, place emphasis on party, not on candidates, an emphasis that would at least tend to diminish the negative impact of TV on parties.

Opponents of debates argue that there is no evidence that debates so grip, stimulate, and interest the voter that many more citizens go to the polls. In fact, the vote in 1960 was up only slightly over 1952, 1956, and 1964, when there were no debates. Further, the debates in 1976 did not stem a downward slide of turnout that has continued since 1960; in 1976 turnout was 54.4 percent, down from 1972 by 1.1 percent and down from 1960 by 8.4 percent. Opponents of debates also argue that there is virtually no evidence that debates educate the voters in any unique way, nor that they improve the rationality of voting decisions. It has not been shown that the debates in 1960 resulted in a better understanding of issues or that the acquired knowledge enabled the voter to vote more intelligently. While there is some evidence in 1976 studies that debates had the effect of improving voters' understanding of issues, the evidence does not seem to me to be very conclusive.[98] As a matter of fact, many critics of the

---

[97] Newton N. Minow, John Bartlow Martin, and Lee M. Mitchell, *Presidential Television* (New York: Basic Books, 1973), pp. 161–163.
[98] See Chapter 3 in this volume.

debates—both in 1960 and 1976—criticize them because they adversely affected understanding of the issues.[99]

Numerous commentators express the view that debates place too great an emphasis on personality, glibness, and appearance, on the clever jibe or the quick reply rather than knowledge or understanding. Max Ascoli, for example, said:

> At the end of the fourth Great Debate, many questions were crowding my mind, and above all: Why has such punishment been inflicted on so many of us ... with an audience that can be counted in tens of millions, the competition of ideas cannot possibly be real. The protagonists are bound to behave like two talking univac machines, each conditioned to recite a pre-taped message in answer to a foreseeable challenge from the other.[100]

Norman Cousins expressed a similar view: "The trouble with the Nixon-Kennedy debates is that they run counter to the educational process. They require that a man keep his mouth moving whether he has something to say or not. It is made to appear that the worst thing that could happen to a man is to be caught without an instant answer to a complex question."[101]

Henry Steele Commager argued that some of our best presidents could not have been elected if they had been forced to appear on TV.[102] Samuel Lubell asserted that (1) "debates tend to lessen somewhat the importance of issues and party and to elevate the significance of personality, particularly on its theatrical side," and (2) "debates threaten to upset one of our most deeply rooted political habits—the habit of not listening to candidates." In his interviewing Lubell said he systematically asked each voter, "Did you listen to any of the TV debates?" and "What do you think of them?" The overwhelming majority "responded in terms of how the candidates looked and handled themselves rather than in terms of the issues that were argued about." Lubell does not believe this can be cured by changes in format. He asserted that "comprehension of complex issues is never achieved easily through any media, let alone through an exchange of verbal punches."[103] Douglass Cater, as we noted above, has

---

[99] See, for example, Nelson Polsby's argument in Chapter 7 of this volume, with which I find myself in general agreement.

[100] Max Ascoli, "Intermezzo," *Reporter*, November 10, 1960, p. 18.

[101] Norman Cousins, "Presidents Don't Have to Be Quiz Masters," *Saturday Review*, November 5, 1960, p. 34.

[102] Henry Steele Commager, "Washington Would Have Lost a TV Debate," *New York Times Magazine*, October 30, 1960, pp. 13, 79–80.

[103] Kraus, *The Great Debates*, pp. 152, 153.

the same view of the debates.[104] R. W. Apple, Jr., commenting on the many state and local debates in 1962, asserted that it would be reassuring to report that they helped educate the public, "but they did not. . . . They produced far more intensity than intelligence. They kept the focus of American politics . . . on personality rather than issues."[105]

If TV debates do not educate or elevate voters we should not be overly concerned. Neither does other campaigning. Furthermore, the American system of representative government does not require that voters be able to identify the most important issues facing the country, have a reasoned position on each of these issues, know where their party's candidates stand on them, and vote on the basis of a congruence or incongruence between their own views and the candidates' views about these issues. There are few well-educated voters who could make decisions on the above model.

As volumes of voting studies (in the United States and elsewhere) demonstrate, voters vote orientations, values, and especially parties. The Miller-Stokes study, "Constituency Influence in Congress," clarifies these relations. As Philip Converse points out, their study reports "a fairly satisfying degree of congruence between mass wishes and ultimate, official outputs achieved largely through popular elections." The Miller-Stokes study also made clear—as other studies have—that "most voters under the routine conditions that prevailed knew next to nothing in policy terms or otherwise about the specific figures they chose to represent them."[106] The "mechanism that intervenes to salvage meaning, of course, is the system of political parties, with the gross policy images that specific parties have come to evoke over time." Parties fulfill an important role that is seldom ascribed to them; they give shape and sense to government at the same time they bridge the gap between the individual and the government.[107] As Converse emphasizes, "What is important is that a variety of such mechanisms exist, including the simple one of aggregation, such that the discrepancy between a bleak portrait at the individual level and elections of shape and sense is no perplexing contradiction." Those disposed to worry about institutional arrangements to further democracy would do well to focus their attention here.

---

[104] Ibid., chapter 6.

[105] Apple, "The Little Debates," p. 38.

[106] Philip W. Converse, "Public Opinion and Voting Behavior," in Fred I. Greenstein and Nelson W. Polsby, Handbook of Political Science (Reading, Mass.: Addison-Wesley, 1975), vol. 4, chapter 2, pp. 157–158. Warren E. Miller and Donald E. Stokes, "Constituency Influence in Congress," was reprinted in Campbell and others, Elections and the Political Order, pp. 351–372.

[107] Greenstein and Polsby, Handbook of Political Science, vol. 4, pp. 157–158.

The medium shapes the message, and it also shapes those who send and receive it. The technology of communication determines who can see and hear and "know" whom. It has a profoundly important influence on the way we think about politics and especially on the criteria by which we judge public figures. The fact that political leaders can present themselves on television results in many, if not most, voters and opinion leaders expecting them to—and so they do. In the process they invite being judged by the standards previously reserved for anchormen, newscasters, and other television entertainers. Nowhere is the impact of medium (including format) on standards of evaluation greater than in TV debates between presidential candidates. Such appearances—and appearances they are—bring with them their own criteria: good looks, poise, a quick mind, and a quick tongue.

Theodore White reflects an overwhelming consensus when he says of the first Nixon-Kennedy debate, "it was the sight of the two men side by side that carried the punch." Nixon's five o'clock shadow, lack of makeup, poor lighting, and physical fatigue assumed a paramount political importance that utterly overshadowed discussion of the issues. For White and many other observers, the Kennedy-Nixon debates "did little to advance the reasonable discussion of issues." They were judged valuable because they gave voters "a living portrait of two men under stress and let the voters decide, by instinct and emotion, which style and pattern of behavior under stress they preferred in their leader."[108] This view has become commonplace. But it and the assumption on which it is based deserve closer scrutiny than they usually receive. There is, first of all, the assumption that the performance of a potential president, confronted by unrehearsed questions on nationwide TV, tests his capacity to respond to "stress" as president. This analogy implies that there is some general condition, stress, which elicits characteristic responses, and that the stress caused by trying to form a good answer quickly on nationwide television at the height of a presidential campaign is comparable to the stress a president might be under on learning, as Kennedy was to learn, that the Soviet Union had installed nuclear missiles in Cuba. The assumption is curious since both the problems and the appropriate responses are utterly different. In TV debates the problem is to articulate a credible answer; in presidential crises, the problem is to find a solution, a way out, a program of action. In the debate the candidate must rely on being able to recall relevant information on the spur of the moment. The president, knowing that he can never possess in his own head all the information needed to make good de-

---

[108] White, *The Making of the President 1960*, pp. 288, 292–293.

cisions on important matters, sets up task forces and calls on experts to brief him. In the debate success depends on being articulate and plausible. In the presidency success depends on being wise—on the selection of good advisers and on the effective evaluation of their advice. To win a debate it is necessary to look good, to be relaxed and good humored, to appear well informed, to respond quickly and without stammering. A debate might reasonably be considered relevant for judging how a candidate will, if elected, perform in presidential press conferences. The required skills are those of an actor, not of political leaders.

Ronald Reagan demonstrated, in his enormously successful half-hour TV show in 1976, that it takes a professional to look charmingly natural under conditions of high pressure media performance. The most dangerous aspect of TV debates is that they encourage us to judge presidential candidates by their stage presence rather than their political performance.

Televised presidential debates invite us to apply to presidential contests criteria of evaluation irrelevant to performance on the job. Daniel Boorstin says of the debates:

> The drama of the situation was mostly specious, or at least had an extremely ambiguous relevance to the main (but forgotten) issue: which participant was better qualified for the Presidency. Of course, a man's ability, while standing under klieg lights, without notes, to answer in two and a half minutes a question kept secret until that moment, had only the most dubious relevance—if at all—to his qualifications to make deliberate Presidential decisions of long-standing public questions after being instructed by a corps of advisors.[109]

Debates reinforce the power of entertainment values in politics; they encourage choices for the wrong reasons; they accelerate the trend to personalism; they contribute to dismantling the parties; they discourage appropriate attention to the institutional aspects of presidential contests and the presidency. My own conclusion is still best expressed by the American Political Science Association commission: "The choice of Presidential candidates must not be limited to those who are masters of appearance on television. If the trend seems to be toward such a limitation on our choices, then emphasis must be placed on strengthening methods of campaigning that enable citizens to make judgments on other bases."[110]

---

[109] Daniel Boorstin, *The Image: A Guide to Pseudo-Events in America* (New York: Harper Colophon Books, 1964), p. 42.
[110] APSA Commission, *Report*, p. 4.

Discussion

CHARLS E. WALKER, cochairman of the 1976 Debates Steering Committee: Dr. Kirkpatrick has written an excellent paper, and I learned a great deal from it. But I do want to challenge his judgment that it is highly unlikely that incumbents will debate in the future. I would like to advance the hypothesis—but I believe it is more than a hypothesis—that there will be debates much more frequently than not, though perhaps not in every election. The reason for the change is that when incumbents are involved, they will find it an exceedingly difficult task for a president to do a good job of running this country, at least as perceived by the people. Thus, during his first term, a president is likely to be down in the polls more often than he is up, not because he is not able, but because of the very nature of the job, the nature of the pocketbook issues and the economic problems.

Some past experience here, I think, is misleading. If LBJ had decided to run for re-election in 1968, I think he would have been hard pressed not to debate, especially if Nixon had taken the advice of Richard Whalen in the spring of 1968 and come out strongly against the Vietnam War.

In 1972 the Democratic candidate did not go over well at all. This was a very high and rising period in the Nixon presidency, reflecting to no small extent the Connally-Nixon (and I put them in that order intentionally) economic policies, which had the country moving sharply ahead economically at the time of the election. But suppose the situation had been like 1970, when we Republicans were decimated in the congressional elections, largely because unemployment and inflation were rising rapidly at the time we went to the polls. If Nixon had been running at that time, I submit that he would have been hard pressed not to debate if so challenged. So, if I were a betting man, and I am a betting man, I would bet that we will have more debates than not in the future.

KIRKPATRICK: Well, I'm a betting man too; maybe we can arrange something. The candidates decide whether or not it is advantageous, politically expedient, for them to debate. If they debate, it is because each of them decides that it is expedient to do so. Unless the circumstances are very unusual, I just don't see any situation in which an incumbent has anything to gain by engaging in debates. His opponent, the challenger, is likely to be a relatively unknown quantity, as Kennedy was in 1960.

The great advantage of the debates to Kennedy was that he stood before people as a mature man with a lot of knowledge. He did not look, in comparison with Nixon, young, inexperienced, or unknowledgeable, and this image did him a lot of good. I think Nixon made a mistake in agreeing to debate. Nixon himself thinks he made a mistake; he said so on numerous occasions. In *Six Crises* he says that it is very clear he was wrong about debating in 1960.

My own guess is that no matter what the situation might have been if Johnson had run for re-election, he would have had nothing to gain by debating. But only time will tell. Maybe we can arrange a small wager on this matter.

AUSTIN RANNEY, American Enterprise Institute: I would suggest another possibility. It relates to your statement that in 1960 almost nobody suggested that the debates might be, or should be, or could be required by law.

KIRKPATRICK: As a matter of fact, a great many people made very clear that, while they were not saying there should be no debates ever, they certainly thought it should be decided by the candidates.

RANNEY: I want to suggest that these days one does hear some people say that the debates can and should be made a permanent feature of the American presidential election system. I would furthermore suggest, without endorsing or opposing its desirability, that this might well be in keeping with the increasing intervention of the law in almost every aspect of American politics. Our presidential campaigns are now much more closely regulated by law than they ever have been in the past. We have federal financing of campaigns. We require the candidates to live up to a good many requirements that they never had before. And I want to suggest, without saying it is good or bad, that it is much less possible now to dismiss legally compulsory debates than it was in, say, 1962 or 1963.

KIRKPATRICK: I think that's true, but not very likely. I don't doubt that one of these days some zealot will get out a statement saying that we ought to have debates required by law. But I don't think many people are going to buy it.

MICHAEL ROBINSON, professor of political science, Catholic University of America: I interviewed six members of Congress—four House members and two senators from the state of Oregon—and I was interested in their attitudes toward the media. I specifically asked them if they liked debates, whether or not they thought that debates should be institutionalized in any way, whether they should be required by law. All six said firmly, no, they would oppose the idea of institutionalizing the debates. In fact one member said something to the effect that there has been consideration of doing this only by political scientists and weirdos. [Laughter.]

RANNEY: I hope you didn't criticize his statement for being tautologous. [Laughter.]

ROBINSON: I was a bit surprised by the vehemence. I thought if there was any place in Congress I would find those who might think that it was a good idea, it would be the Oregon delegation.

JAMES KARAYN, director of the 1976 debates: I am one of the goons who are in favor of debates. I don't think it should be left up to candidates to decide whether they should be held. I think that is the wrong premise. If you leave it up to candidates, they decide only according to whether it is good for them or not good for them. I think it should be whether or not it is good for the electorate.

Debates are said to reinforce the power of the entertainment media in politics. All right, they do that. But if you listened to the debates in 1976 and listened carefully, they told you an awful lot about issues. They told you whether or not the candidates were committed to combating inflation or unemployment as their first priority. They told you where Jimmy Carter stood on building the B-1 bomber; they told you about his conservative nature on the economy; they told you he didn't have a plan, really, for a national health policy. They told you where each candidate stood on granting amnesty to Vietnam deserters and draft resisters; they told about their stands on increased aid to beleaguered cities. There was a lot of information there.

I think some people have the attitude that in the days long before television people voted more intelligently—voted much more on issues, and studied issues much more closely. I think that's poppycock.

KIRKPATRICK: So do I.

KARAYN: I think the people always voted for personality. And in the days when we picked candidates who had booming voices and could stand in beer halls or on the back of the train or in a park and project themselves without any kind of amplification, we picked them for their personalities.

There isn't a candidate alive today who cannot, with the proper assistance, be made presentable for television, without making him a joke, or an actor, or distorting him totally out of his character.

I will end with Norman Cousins, who, in sixteen years, has changed his mind about debates. This year he says: "The presidential debates represent a profound service to the American people. It is difficult, in fact, to think of any other single development in recent years that has done more to revitalize the democratic process." Then he goes on to tell of the arguments against debates. "In any event, none of the arguments against TV debates is likely to be persuasive. The American people have made up their minds that TV debates are going to be an integral part of presidential campaigns. Everything will probably be subordinate to these debates. The kinks evident in this year's debates will be eliminated. The debates will be sharpened and speeded up; questions will be shorter; so will the answers. There will be more direct exchanges between the candidates."

KIRKPATRICK: I have often found Norman Cousins on both sides of an issue. The problem is in deciding which time he was right and which time he was wrong. I happen to think he was right the first time. If he has changed his mind, so much the worse for him.

One thing you say that interests me is whether people vote more for issues or for personalities. I tend to think that the question of issues is not the major one in voting behavior now or in the past. But there is something very important here, and that is the extent to which party is important. An identification with party and voting on party recommendations are not entirely removed from issues. There is a sense in which the parties give direction to views about policy questions, and voters know that.

In one respect I am much more sympathetic to the Minow-Martin-Mitchell proposals than to the debate proposals—that is, I find it unfortunate that we do things in a way in which party has no real role. We should revive, not further decrease, the utilization of parties as links between the individual and the government. We ought to take account of ways in which we can make party more effective.

KARAYN: But the weakening of the parties started long before debates.

KIRKPATRICK: Oh yes. I am not saying it is due to debates.

KARAYN: That started with political image makers, the personalization of candidates.

KIRKPATRICK: Well, it started not only with the electronic media, but with a lot of other things too. Scientific polling was part of it. The pollsters became an integral part of the situation. Then, too, rapid transportation made it possible for the individual candidate to see more people, or feel that he was seeing more people. And television gave him an opportunity to speak directly to people, rather than using the party as an intermediary. Before these things occurred, the campaign in a state had to be conducted pretty much by the state party. The presidential candidate seldom visited a state more than once, and many states did not see him at all. The party played a major role.

But television tends to push that aside, and so does the use of a personal organization—an organization of experts of various kinds—in the campaign. I suppose the worst example of that was Nixon's decision in 1972 to use the separate organization he set up rather than the party organization. I think that some of the things that happened—such as Watergate—would not have happened if the party, and not CREEP, had been in charge.

2

Historical Evolution of Section 315

Nicholas Zapple

The application of the First Amendment principles to broadcast communications is a complex problem that has challenged the Congress, the Federal Communications Commission (FCC), and constitutional scholars since the early days of broadcasting. Efforts to regulate radio communication confront unique problems not present in other forms of mass communication. Because of the finite nature of the radio spectrum, substantially more individuals want to broadcast than there are frequencies to allocate.

As a consequence, those who have the good fortune to receive a license are treated as trustees of a valuable public resource and have imposed upon them certain responsibilities to serve the public—the viewer and the listener. These responsibilities were described by the Court of Appeals for the District of Columbia Circuit when it stated:

> A broadcaster has much in common with a newspaper publisher, but he is not in the same category in terms of public obligation imposed by law. A broadcaster seeks and is granted the free and exclusive use of a limited and valuable part of the public domain; when he accepts that franchise, it is burdened with enforceable public obligations. A newspaper can be operated at the whim or caprice of its owners; a broadcasting station cannot . . . [A] broadcast license is a public trust subject to termination for breach of duty.[1]

Origins and Early Interpretations of Section 315

One of the conditions imposed on every licensee was first set forth in Section 315(a), the so-called equal time section, of the Communications Act of 1934:

[1] Office of Communications of the United Church of Christ v. FCC, 359 FCC 2nd 994, 1003 (1966).

> If any licensee shall permit any person who is a legally quali-
> fied candidate for any public office to use a broadcasting sta-
> tion, he shall afford equal opportunities to all other such
> candidates for that office in the use of such broadcasting sta-
> tion: *Provided*, That such licensee shall have no power of
> censorship over the material broadcast under the provisions
> of this section. No obligation is imposed upon any licensee to
> allow the use of its station by any such candidate.[2]

A careful examination of the legislative history of the Section 315(a)
and its predecessor, Section 18 of the Radio Act of 1927, reveals clearly
the fundamental objective: Once any licensee allowed any legally
qualified candidate to use his facilities, the broadcaster was required
to afford equal opportunity to all other candidates for that same office.
Equal treatment of all candidates for a particular public office was a
sound principle. The equal time provision of Section 315(a) was
designed to assure a legally qualified candidate that he would not be
subjected to unfair disadvantage from an opponent through favoritism
in selling or donating time or in scheduling political broadcasts.

On February 19, 1959, in the *Lar Daly case*,[3] the FCC issued its
interpretation relating to the applicability of Section 315 to certain
newscasts by Chicago television stations. Primary elections for the
office of mayor of Chicago were scheduled for February 24, 1959.
Richard J. Daley, then mayor of Chicago, was a candidate in the
Democratic primary. Timothy Sheehan was a candidate in the Republican primary, and Lar "America First" Daly was a candidate in
both primaries. Prior to February 24, Daly filed a complaint with the
FCC alleging that certain television stations had, in the course of their
newscasts, shown film clips of his opponents in connection with certain events, that he had requested equal time, and that his requests
had been refused. After careful consideration, the commission held
that under Section 315 the use of the film clips entitled Lar Daly to
equal opportunities.

This ruling had a crippling effect on broadcast journalism. It required a broadcaster who devoted one minute to a legally qualified
candidate participating in any program—whether it be a discussion of
atomic energy or the need for adequate defense, a ribbon-cutting for
a new road or bridge, or the opening of a charity drive—to make available a minute of time to every other legally qualified candidate for the
same office.

It was quite evident that such a ruling constituted a deterrent to

---

[2] Public Law 86–274, *United States Code Annotated*, Title 47, Section 315, p. 226.
[3] 26 FCC 715 (1959).

stations, preventing them from showing one political candidate in any type of news program unless they were prepared to assume the burden of presenting a parade of aspirants. The ruling created a national furor. The general belief was that it would dry up meaningful radio and television coverage of political campaigns. The losers would be the public—the viewers and listeners.

The 1959 Amendment

Congress acted quickly and directly by enacting an amendment that created exemptions from the equal opportunity requirements of Section 315. The 1959 amendment added the following to the language quoted above:

> Appearance by a legally qualified candidate on any—
> (1) bona fide newscast,
> (2) bona fide news interview,
> (3) bona fide news documentary (if the appearance of the candidate is incidental to the presentation of the subject or subjects covered by the news documentary), or
> (4) on-the-spot coverage of bona fide news events (including but not limited to political conventions and activities incidental thereto),
> shall not be deemed to be use of a broadcasting station within the meaning of this subsection. Nothing in the foregoing sentence shall be construed as relieving broadcasters, in connection with the presentation of newscasts, news interviews, news documentaries, and on-the-spot coverage of news events, from the obligation imposed upon them under this chapter to operate in the public interest and to afford reasonable opportunity for the discussion of conflicting views on issues of public importance.[4]

The programs exempted by this amendment have one thing in common. They are generally news programs and documentaries designed to disseminate information to the public, and in almost every instance the format and production of the program is under the control of the broadcast station or, in the case of a network program, the network. The amendment affords the broadcaster freedom to exercise his good faith and judgment in handling news programs, despite the fact that such programs might involve legally qualified candidates for office.

The Congress was not unmindful of the danger that exemption from the equal time requirement would offer a temptation as well as

---

[4] As cited in footnote 2. The appendix to this chapter outlines the general background of the fairness doctrine.

an opportunity for a broadcaster to push his favorite candidate and to exclude others. But the alternative of maintaining the status quo would lead to a virtual blackout in the presentation of candidates on news programs. This would not serve the public interest. In any event, the Congress felt that any attempt on the part of broadcasters to feature a favorite candidate under the protection of the exemption would quickly be brought to the attention of the proper authorities, and Congress would move forward immediately with legislation to remedy the situation.

The 1960 Suspension of Section 315

By 1960 broadcast journalism had become a way of life. The public had become dependent upon it and was entitled to it. The liberalization of Section 315 was expected to lead to fuller and more meaningful news coverage of the actions and appearances of legal candidates during a political campaign. In the light of these developments, Adlai Stevenson, who had been a presidential candidate in 1952 and 1956, published an article urging that television time be made available for a continuing debate between presidential candidates.[5] When Stevenson was a candidate in 1952, the idea of a television debate with General Dwight D. Eisenhower had been suggested but was turned down by Eisenhower.

Following the appearance of Stevenson's article outlining his recommendation, Senators Warren G. Magnuson (D-Washington) and Mike Monroney (D-Oklahoma) drafted legislation that required each television broadcast station and television network to make available without charge the use of its facilities to qualified candidates for the office of president of the United States.[6] To qualify under this legislation, the candidate had to be the nominee of a political party whose candidate for president in the preceding election was supported by not fewer than 4 percent of the total popular vote cast.

Shortly thereafter, on May 16, 1960, the Subcommittee on Communications headed by Senator John O. Pastore (D-Rhode Island) opened hearings on the proposal. The broadcasters asked for an opportunity to develop a voluntary plan. It was during those hearings that Dr. Frank Stanton, president of the Columbia Broadcasting System, suggested that if Congress did not "want to change Section 315 permanently" it might be "possible to pass a resolution which would

---

[5] Adlai E. Stevenson, "Plan for a 'Great Debate'," *This Week Magazine*, March 6, 1960.

[6] S. 3171, 86th Congress, 2nd session, 1960.

set aside Section 315 as it applies to the presidential and vice-presidential candidates for 1960."[7]

After extensive hearings and extended floor discussion, the Congress enacted Senate Joint Resolution 207 temporarily suspending Section 315 insofar as it applied to presidential and vice-presidential candidates.[8] Thus, time could be made available to the major party candidates. The enactment of this resolution opened the door for the Kennedy-Nixon debates.

The rest is history. It worked—so well, in fact, that Senator Pastore introduced legislation in 1961 that was designed to suspend Section 315 not only for candidates for president and vice-president but also to include the candidates for U.S. Senate, House of Representatives, and governor of any state. Senator Pastore's effort was unsuccessful, and unfortunately this failure was subsequently repeated for many similar efforts.

Section 315 from 1961 to 1971

In 1961 President John F. Kennedy, by executive order, created the President's Commission on Campaign Costs and directed it to recommend improved ways of financing campaigns for the offices of president and vice-president. In April 1962 the commission noted in its report:

> During the presidential campaign of 1960, exercising the freedom granted by the temporary suspension of section 315 of the Federal Communications Act, the networks and radio-television licensees contributed important public information about the campaign by providing for a variety of broadcasts in which the candidates participated without charge to them.
>
> The leaders of the radio-television industry have stated their desire to render higher levels of performance in bringing information about campaigns to the public. There is also need to permit broadcasters further opportunity to experiment in the use of television in campaigns to develop practices fully compatible with the requirements of the American political system.
>
> Accordingly, we recommend that section 315, as it applies to presidential and vice-presidential nominees, be suspended

[7] See *Hearings before the Communications Subcommittee on Interstate and Foreign Commerce*, 86th Congress, 2nd session on S. 3171.

[8] Public Law 86–677, 86th Congress, 2nd session, S.J. Res. 207, approved August 24, 1960.

in the same form as in 1960 for the 1964 general election campaign. This will permit the networks and stations, in consultation with the candidates, to develop more fully their role in campaigns in mutually agreeable ways.[9]

On the basis of this report, President Kennedy, in letters to the president of the Senate and speaker of the House of Representatives on May 29, 1962, stated: "I believe that temporary suspension rather than permanent repeal is desirable so that the Congress can periodically review broadcasting and campaign practices that occur under ever-changing conditions."[10] With this strong endorsement, the suspension legislation passed both houses in the fall of 1963 (H.J. Res. 247, 88th Congress). A conference was required to iron out differences between the Senate and House versions. This was done successfully. But before final action on the conference report could be taken, President Kennedy was assassinated and Lyndon Johnson became president.

The atmosphere surrounding the suspension legislation began to change. When the conference report was finally called up for a vote in the Senate, a motion to table was entered and adopted on August 18, 1964, by a vote of forty-four to forty-one, thereby eliminating any chance to suspend Section 315 for the 1964 presidential campaign.

When it became apparent in 1968 that there would not be an incumbent in the presidential race, hopes began to rise that a suspension of Section 315 could be enacted. Bills were introduced in the Senate and the House of Representatives. Unfortunately, the legislation became a partisan matter. As Senate Joint Resolution 175 was being considered in the House, various delaying tactics were employed to prevent its adoption. There were thirty quorum calls over a period of twenty hours. In order to keep the members of the House on the floor, the doors to the Chamber were closed and congressmen were not allowed to leave. The bill was finally passed by the House on October 19, 1968.

When the legislation was scheduled for action in the Senate, Senator Everett Dirksen (R-Ill.), the minority leader, served notice that he was prepared to "use every weapon at the command of the minority leader in order to stop this resolution." He was successful, and the legislation was set aside. Once again a presidential campaign passed without a change in Section 315.

---

[9] *Report of President's Commission on Campaign Costs*, April 1962.

[10] Letter dated May 29, 1962, from President John F. Kennedy to the speaker of the U.S. House of Representatives and the president of the U.S. Senate submitting legislation that would implement the recommendation of the President's Commission on Campaign Costs.

In the meantime, various studies were being conducted of the costs of presidential campaigns. The total charges for broadcasters' time for all general election campaigns was $9.8 million in 1956, $24.1 million in 1960, $24.6 million in 1964, and $40.4 million in 1968.[11] The amount of and cost for broadcast time was also rising sharply.

The Campaign Reform Act of 1971

In spite of the frustrations experienced in 1964 and 1968, new suspension legislation was introduced and hearings scheduled in 1969. S. 3637 (91st Congress) took a comprehensive approach in an attempt to cap the spiraling costs of campaigning for public office via the electronic media. This bill repealed the equal opportunity provisions of Section 315 as it applied to the offices of president and vice-president in the general election. The other major features of the bill were:

1. Broadcast licensees were required to charge any legally qualified candidates for any public office the station's lowest unit rate charged any commercial time buyer for the same amount of time in the same period.
2. A limitation was set on the amount of money candidates for the office of president, senator, congressman, governor, or lieutenant governor—or anyone on their behalf—might spend in purchasing time in the broadcast media in the general election campaign. The formula was seven cents times the total vote cast in the last preceding election for that office, or $20,000, whichever was greater.
3. Before time was sold to or on behalf of a candidate, the candidate or his authorized representative was required to certify in writing to the broadcast licensee that the payment of such charge would not exceed the limitations set out in the legislation.

When the House of Representatives and the Senate were in conference on this legislation, the Republican members walked out because of disagreement with the Section 315 provision. The remaining conferees, all Democrats, resolved their differences and the legislation was enacted, including the repeal of Section 315 as it applied to the presidential and vice-presidential offices. President Nixon vetoed the bill, however, on October 31, 1970. His veto message suggested that a more comprehensive bill was necessary, one covering all aspects of political campaigning.

---

[11] *Voters' Time*, Report of the Twentieth Century Fund Commission on Campaign Costs in the Electronic Era (New York: Twentieth Century Fund, 1969).

When the 92nd Congress convened in 1971, a more comprehensive approach to the problem of political campaign reform and the high cost of campaigning was introduced (S. 382). The proposed legislation dealt with the communications media, campaign contributions, disclosure and reporting requirements, and tax incentives to encourage small donors to contribute to the candidates or parties of their choice. It also dealt with Section 315.

The original bill limited the repeal of Section 315 to presidential and vice-presidential candidates, but an amendment was adopted expanding the legislation to include senators and representatives. The Senate was warned that the House of Representatives would not accept the congressional exemption from Section 315. Over the years the House had steadfastly rejected any attempt to exempt congressmen from the equal time provision. It was felt that any such exemption would give too much power to broadcasters to develop programs that could favor one candidate or discriminate against a candidate, particularly in areas where there were only a few broadcast outlets. Sure enough, this comprehensive legislation, designed to control the spiraling cost of political campaigning, was passed by the House of Representatives, but the provisions relating to Section 315 were eliminated. To make matters worse, the House conferees refused to compromise on this issue in the conference.

When Senator Pastore, the manager of the legislation, was presenting the conference report to the Senate in December 1971, he stated:

> Many of us would also like to have seen the equal time requirements of Section 315 of the Communications Act repealed for the President and Vice President in the General Election. Here again, the House was absolutely adamant. We were again given the ultimatum that if we insisted on the equal time proviso we could forget the bill. . . .
>
> I repeat, the House was most adamant on this and there was no place to go except a compromise.[12]

Consequently, the first significant overhaul of the political campaign laws went into effect on February 7, 1972, without the repeal of Section 315.

Once again, when Congress convened in 1973, new legislation (S. 3044) was introduced updating the Campaign Reform Act of 1971. It was designed primarily to close the loopholes and refine the cost factors as well as the disclosure provisions of the 1971 act. The

---

[12] 117 *Congressional Record* 46943 (1971).

new legislation once more urged repeal of Section 315 as it applied to presidential and vice-presidential candidates. Unfortunately, the exemption was expanded to include all federally elected offices, and the House again deleted it.

The broadcasters and particularly the networks have always contended that Section 315 discouraged them from supplying free time to major party candidates because they would then be required to provide equal time to all the other candidates, significant third-party candidates as well as fringe candidates. In this respect, it is significant that the Federal Election Commission received disclosure reports for 230 candidates for president in 1976. This is not to say that all 230 became active candidates, but the number indicates the magnitude of the problem when equal time applies. Experience, therefore, seems to support the broadcasters' position.

What was the impact of the failure to suspend Section 315 in the presidential elections of 1964, 1968, and 1972? In 1964 the broadcasters made available only four and a half hours of free time, three hours in 1968, and one hour of free time in 1972, as compared with thirty-nine hours of free time provided candidates during the 1960 election. The figures speak for themselves. It was obvious that the public was the loser.

The Aspen Ruling and the 1976 Debates

In anticipation of the 1976 campaign, the FCC ruled on September 2, 1975, in the so-called *Aspen* case, that a presidential press conference, as well as any press conferences of any candidate for political office, broadcast live and in its entirety could qualify for on-the-spot coverage as a bona fide news event. The commission also ruled that candidates engaging in a debate sponsored by a nonbroadcast entity, such as the League of Women Voters, also qualified for this exemption.

The League of Women Voters proceeded to develop a series of debates between the presidential candidates that were televised by commercial and public broadcasters. To sustain the legality of these broadcasts under Section 315, a legal fiction had to be maintained to the effect that the broadcasters were merely covering an on-the-spot news event—a debate staged for the public and members of the League of Women Voters in an auditorium. The league and their associates are to be commended for taking the initiative and planning the debates, for the public was the beneficiary. But we must now look to the future and remove any obstacles that may affect the smooth functioning of such an event.

Section 315 and the commission's ruling are the law and policy, whether one agrees or disagrees. It is my firm belief that conditions have changed substantially and that Section 315 should be repealed at least for the presidential and vice-presidential races. All sham would be removed, and the broadcaster would be given flexibility and responsibility to inform the American public on important political races and issues effectively and fully. It would eliminate the legal jousting that appears to be endless in this area. It is my belief that the public would benefit from such an action.

In repealing Section 315, care should be taken to avoid endorsing any particular format. Rather, complete freedom should be given to the candidates and the broadcasters to develop program formats. As a condition for repeal, commitments must be made to ensure that time will be available on a fair basis to the candidates of any significant third party that might emerge, such as the States Rights party in 1948, the Progressive party in 1924 and 1948, and the American Independent party in 1968. Because third parties must be afforded an opportunity to be heard, some fair formula should be spelled out clearly in the legislation.

The Federal Election Commission currently has underway a proceeding involving the possible application of its statute to the sponsorship and financing of public debates between or among federal candidates. If the commission finds that corporate or labor financing of debates constitutes "contributions and expenditures" made in connection with an election and is therefore prohibited, gifts of free broadcast time by licensees to political candidates might also be considered illegal contributions. A decision by the Federal Election Commission that would limit the ability of a licensee to devote free broadcast time to political candidates would, in my opinion, be in direct conflict with the Communications Act.

Another problem would arise with certain educational and public broadcasting stations, which are prohibited from accepting compensation for broadcast time and fulfill their political broadcasting obligations through the offer of free broadcast time. Should the Federal Election Commission rule that such offers are illegal "contributions or expenditures," a direct conflict would exist between the FEC statute and the Communications Act. This is still another reason why action should be taken on Section 315 soon and legislative language employed to make clear the responsibilities of the respective agencies.

Television has become an integral part of political campaigning, and it is one of the most universal sources of information for voters about candidates. The public should not be deprived of the benefits that flow from this dynamic form of communication through the critical times of a political campaign.

The administration and Congress should move *now* to modify Section 315.

Appendix: General Background on the Fairness Doctrine

The fairness doctrine of the FCC provides that if a broadcaster presents one side of a controversial issue of public importance, he must afford reasonable opportunity for the presentation of contrasting views. Contrary to popular belief, the fairness doctrine does not require equal time as does Section 315 for political candidates. Instead, the broadcast licensee has an affirmative duty to encourage and implement the broadcast of contrasting views in its overall programming, which includes statements or actions reported on news programs.

The licensee has considerable discretion as to how to meet the obligations of the fairness doctrine. All sides of a given issue need not be presented in a single broadcast or even a series of programs, and no particular person or group is entitled to appear on the station. The fairness doctrine is intended to protect the right of the public to be informed rather than the right of any individual to broadcast his or her particular views. In summary, it is the responsibility of the broadcast licensee to determine whether views on a controversial issue of public importance have been presented, and, if so, how best to present contrasting views on the issue, considering format, scheduling, and selection of spokesmen. The FCC's review of fairness doctrine complaints is limited to determining whether the licensee has acted reasonably and in good faith in meeting its obligations, and in this review the commission will not overrule the licensee's judgment unless it is shown that the licensee has acted unreasonably or in bad faith.

The fairness doctrine was originally created by the FCC as a broadcast regulatory policy pursuant to the regard for the public interest expressed in the Communications Act of 1934. The 1959 amendment to Section 315 of this act exempted candidate appearances in certain specified news programs from the equal opportunities requirement. In considering this legislation, however, the Senate emphasized that "broadcast frequencies are limited, and, therefore, they have been necessarily considered a public trust. Every licensee who is fortunate in obtaining a license is mandated to operate in the public interest and has assumed the obligation of presenting important public questions fairly and without bias."[13] The bill was enacted with an amendment that affirmed the continued applicability of the basic fairness obligation.[14] As we noted above, the legislation also stipulated that the fairness obligation did not relieve broadcasters of their duty "to afford reasonable opportunity for the discussion of conflicting views on issues of public importance."[15]

In its landmark decision in *Red Lion Broadcasting Co.* v. *FCC*, 395 U.S. 367 (1969), the Supreme Court held that this amendment "vindicated the FCC view that the fairness doctrine inhered in the public interest standard of the Act." Thus, it can be argued persuasively that Congress, by the 1959 amendment to Section 315, "ratified" or "codified" the basic fairness doctrine obligation. The unanimous (8 to 0) *Red Lion* decision also upheld the fairness doctrine against claims that it was an unconstitutional infringement of broadcaster First Amendment rights. The court sustained the fairness doctrine on the so-called scarcity rationale. The following are considered the most significant excerpts from the Court's reasoning:

> The First Amendment confers no right on licensees to prevent others from broadcasting on "their" frequencies and no right to an unconditional monopoly of a scarce resource which the Government has denied others the right to use (395 U.S. at 391).
>
> As far as the First Amendment is concerned, those who are licensed stand no better than those to whom licenses are refused. A license permits broadcasting, but the licensee has no constitutional right to be the one who holds the license or to monopolize a radio frequency to the exclusion of his fellow citizens. There is nothing in the First Amendment which prevents the Government from requiring a licensee to share his frequency with others and to conduct himself as a proxy or fiduciary with obligations to present those views and voices which are representative of his community and which would otherwise, by necessity, be barred from the airwaves (395 U.S. at 389).
>
> It does not violate the First Amendment to treat licensees given the privilege of using scarce radio frequencies as proxies for the entire community, obligated to give time and attention to matters of great public concern. To condition the granting or renewal of licenses on a willingness to represent

---

[13] Senate, Committee on Commerce, Report 562, 86th Congress, 1st session (1959).

[14] 105 *Congressional Record,* 14439 (1959), amendment offered by Senator William Proxmire.

[15] Public Law 86–274, 86th Congress, 1st session, approved September 14, 1959.

> community views on controversial issues is consistent with the ends and purposes of those constitutional provisions forbidding the abridgment of freedom of speech and freedom of the press (395 U.S. at 394).

In short, in the context of the scarcity of frequencies and the resulting necessity for government licensing, the First Amendment supports, rather than prohibits, government action to ensure that the public will be informed of the important issues that confront it and of the views on those issues that may differ from the views held by a particular licensee. Because the government has in essence granted to a chosen few licensees the precious right to broadcast speech, it must recognize a concomitant obligation to the rest of the public to ensure that these licensees operate their stations so as to preserve "an uninhibited marketplace of ideas in which truth will ultimately prevail," rather than to permit the licensees' private interests to monopolize that market.

In 1973 the Supreme Court reaffirmed the constitutionality of the fairness doctrine as per *Red Lion* in the case of *Columbia Broadcasting System, Inc.* v. *Democratic National Committee*, 412 U.S. 94 (1973), commonly known as the *BEM* case (Business Executives Move for Vietnam Peace, one of the parties). In that case, the Court held that neither the First Amendment nor the public interest standard of the Communications Act *required* the creation of a direct "right of access" to the broadcast media for individuals wishing to express their political views. (BEM had argued that if broadcasters sold time to advertisers for product commercials, they could not constitutionally refuse to sell time for political messages.) In rejecting right-of-access arguments, the *BEM* Court relied heavily on FCC and broadcaster representations that the fairness doctrine protects the legitimate First Amendment interests of the public in having access to a diversity of views on important issues.

In 1974 the U.S. Supreme Court in *Miami Herald Publishing Co.* v. *Tornillo*, 418 U.S. 241 (1974), struck down a Florida right-to-reply statute as an abridgment of the newspaper's First Amendment rights of free speech and press. Some have argued that the reasoning of this case should apply to abrogate the fairness doctrine as well. The critical distinction between the print media and broadcasting still remains, however. There is no scarcity of printing presses in this country, and the government has not been called upon to license the print media in the public interest. What barriers exist to entry into the newspaper business are economic not governmental licensing barriers. By contrast, there are fewer frequencies available for broadcasting than there are individuals who want to broadcast.

Perhaps with the development and implementation of modern telecommunication technology, such as cable television, fiber optics, and small dish satellite receivers, we may move from scarcity to abundance and thereby eliminate both the basis and the necessity for the fairness doctrine.

Discussion

JOAN BERNOTT, Federal Election Commission: Mr. Zapple, I want to ask you whether any of the bills that were presented in the 1960s for repeal of Section 315 as regards vice-presidential and presidential and/or any Senate and House debates included a fair formula for determining which significant third-party candidates should be included, and what your own ideas are on that question.

ZAPPLE: I have always found that developing a formula creates more problems than it cures. As a consequence, we tried to write into the legislative history in our reports what the committee meant by a significant third-party candidate, regardless of the amount of votes he got. We expected the networks and the broadcasters to make time available to significant third-party candidates, and we used as an illustration the candidates for the States Rights party and the Progressive party of 1948. Three or four parties that we mentioned got less than 4 percent of the vote. During our hearings we brought up that subject, and we received affirmative responses from the networks and the broadcasters that they would accede to that kind of suggestion.

BERNOTT: By "that kind of suggestion," are you referring to a 4 percent vote share?

ZAPPLE: No. We tried the 4 percent vote standard originally, and we found that only one party up to 1972 had received 4 percent of the vote, and that was the Bull Moose party in 1912. A member of our committee, Senator Strom Thurmond, was a candidate for the States Rights party back in 1948. Rather than set a 1 or 2 percent level, which might increase the base or the number of people who would qualify, we suggested that recognition be given to a candidate who represented a party comparable to the States Rights party in 1948 and Progressive parties in 1924 and 1948, as well as the American Independent party that George Wallace ran on in 1968.

BERNOTT: What is your opinion on whether the 1976 debates conformed with the spirit and intent of the equal time provision of the

Communications Act by excluding a candidate of the stature of Senator Eugene McCarthy?

ZAPPLE: That is the reason I made the observation about the legal sham. The broadcasters were carrying out their news responsibility when they were covering an on-the-spot event, and the League of Women Voters didn't have any obligation to put Senator McCarthy on the program. The broadcasters very legitimately said, "We can't suggest that to the League of Women Voters. We only broadcast what was actually happening in the auditoriums where the debates took place."

BERNOTT: Do you think the Communications Act's spirit and intent would have been better served by inclusion of Senator McCarthy in some way?

ZAPPLE: No. I think it was a judgment made by a nonbroadcast group, the League of Women Voters. They selected their participants and the format. There is nothing in law or policy that would prevent the league or any other group from putting on Gene McCarthy or the candidate of the Socialist Labor party or any other candidate. The sponsors have to choose the participants and formats themselves.

I think it would be more significant for 315 to be suspended because the only time the broadcasters and the networks were given this freedom, in 1960, they did perform reasonably well. I'm not talking about the content of the debates, but the fact is that in making time available they lived up to their bargain.

On the third-party point, when we held our hearings in 1962, a representative of the Conservative party in New York was extremely concerned that if equal time were suspended for statewide offices, they would be penalized, and he testified to that effect. Nine months later, after the the 1962 election, he wrote the committee a letter in which he said: "I am happy to advise you that our experience in the election campaign has altered our estimate of the situation. We have found that broadcasters were quite fair in their treatment of all minor parties, including the Conservative party, which, in polling 141,000 votes, outpolled the Liberal party in fifty-seven of New York's sixty-two counties. We discovered, moreover, that the existence of the equal opportunity requirements actually disadvantaged the major parties."

AUSTIN RANNEY, American Enterprise Institute: In your judgment, what are the legal and constitutional problems and what are the

policy considerations involved in making the debates legally mandatory by, say, making the participation in presidential debates a condition of receiving federal matching funds for the candidates' campaigns,
at least for the major-party candidates?

ZAPPLE: I think that once you specify the format you run into significant legal problems. I would urge staying away from any mandatory
specific format. Give the discretion to the broadcaster to set the format.
I think there definitely are constitutional questions here, and I don't
think Congress would legislate it. In fact, this always was a problem,
even from the very beginning in 1960, when we first suspended 315.
Having had a hand in writing the reports, I was careful to stay away
from that particular point, because I knew the differences of opinion
that prevailed on our committee. Throughout the deliberations of the
next twenty years, we ran into that same question. We cannot dictate
the format. That is something that has to be worked out between
the candidates and the broadcasters. Unless the candidates agree, you
cannot have a debate, even with all the laws in the world; you cannot
force them to debate. There will always be skirmishing as to whether
there should be a stool, or whether there should be a platform, or
how many persons are going to ask questions, and the number of
questions.

RANNEY: But why not add on the condition that, while they don't
have to participate in debates, if they don't they will receive no federal matching funds for their campaigns?

ZAPPLE: I think there is a constitutional question there. In spite of
what we may think serves the public interest, I don't think the courts
would sustain such a condition. It just isn't broad enough. Why debates? Why not a back-to-back type of presentation? I think the
courts would construe such a condition to be a violation of the
Constitution.

RANNEY: I would like to solicit a comment from our British visitor,
Geoffrey Smith. In Britain, as I understand it, the basic idea is to make
a certain amount of free TV time available to each of the parties to
use as it sees fit. In their use of their free time the parties place their
emphasis on the *parties*, not on the all-powerful, all-glamorous party
leaders. Could you tell us more about that, because it just might be a
precedent we would want to consider here.

GEOFFREY SMITH, London *Times*: In British election campaigns there
are, as you say, party election broadcasts, which means a certain

amount of time is made available to each of the parties. The proportion of the total time available for each party depends on the proportion of votes it obtained in the last election. The way in which each party makes use of its time is entirely up to the party. It can decide to have its leader broadcasting directly to camera for each one of those broadcasts if it wishes to do so. No party has yet taken such a position, though quite frequently it is the practice to have the party leader figure prominently in the final broadcast of the campaign.

But British politicians increasingly attach importance not just to the formal party election broadcasts, which they themselves determine how to use, but to the regular discussion programs which take place during the election campaign under broadcaster control. These programs are much more popular with the viewers, attract much more interest, and probably exercise much more influence than do the party election broadcasts. Very often the smaller parties find themselves arguing with the broadcasting authorities and with the other parties over how much time should be afforded to them in the formal party election programs. What they really want is to say to the broadcasting authorities—though they don't put it quite like this—"Make sure that you give us a fair amount of time in the discussion programs and in the news bulletins." While they argue formally over the time to be allocated to them in the party election programs, they are really concerned about getting a decent showing for themselves in these discussion programs.

The discussion programs are of different kinds. Some have taken a format close to that of your presidential debates. Actual debates take place between prominent leaders, though not *the* party leader from each party. There are discussions, for example, on foreign affairs or economics, and each party nominates a spokesman to take part in that discussion. The discussion is led by a particular individual, not a panel. We have panel discussions as well, but that is something different.

Another experiment, tried in the election of October 1974, might conceivably be of some relevance for your discussions. For a program called "Granada 500" put on by one of the regional commercial program companies, Granada, 500 voters were chosen to represent a cross-section of opinion throughout the country. These voters were selected from two constituencies within the program company's area, and the program was on quite a long time, during which each of three main party leaders—Conservative, Labour, and Liberal—appeared in turn before this audience and answered questions from them. I think this relates to American presidential debates in the sense that the party leaders each appeared on the program and answered questions from a panel—in this case, obviously, a much larger panel than would ever be considered here—but they did not engage directly in debate with each other. This might conceivably be relevant here, though obviously I do not presume to say what would be the best arrangement for the United States.

But what does strike me in these discussions is that the spokesmen from both parties consider, rightly or wrongly, that one of the functions of the presidential debates is to focus attention upon issues rather than simply personalities. If that is correct, it seems to me that it is a function that should be served in a number of different ways and does not necessarily require the debate format. But the interest in the debate format, as I understand it, is that it brings within the compass of the one program the candidates from both parties and, therefore, is likely to attract both Democratic and Republican viewers, whereas separate programs would not. Republicans would not switch on the Democratic candidate and vice versa. Both those considerations would be met by a program in which the candidates appeared successively, answered questions, but did not engage directly in debate. I don't know if that would be appropriate for the United States, but I do know that a program of that kind has been tried in Britain and has attracted a good deal of favorable response.

3

Presidential Debates: An Empirical Assessment

Steven H. Chaffee and Jack Dennis

From the standpoint of society, the future of debates between presidential candidates rests upon two questions: Do debates make a sufficient contribution to the democratic process to merit their continuation? If so, in what form should the debates be institutionalized? Social research on the 1960 and 1976 debates has given more answers to the first question than to the second. But, as we shall see here, those answers are on balance encouraging enough that the second question also deserves serious attention.

In evaluating the debates we make some important assumptions. First, it should be clear that our assessment is specific to presidential elections and the news media as they exist in the United States. We examine the debates' contribution to the quality of democratic choice under conditions of universal adult suffrage, a national election that is ordinarily contested between two major parties, commercial national broadcast networks, and an aggressive political reporting tradition in a press system that is largely free of governmental constraints. The research we draw upon has been conducted under these conditions, and we would not recommend that any of our conclusions be exported without qualification to other kinds of situations.

For the debates themselves, we do not assume so much closure. Although we treat American democracy as a given and do not argue its merits against alternative government and press systems, we see the debates of 1960 and 1976 as pilot projects that are potentially open to a good deal of modification. Still, it must be recognized that those debates, which were organized along similar lines, give clues as to what general format is likely to be acceptable in the future. When discussing the debates we necessarily refer to those that have occurred; but it will also be possible to discuss debates as a general institution that would not necessarily have the precise features of the Kennedy-Nixon and Ford-Carter encounters.

Our third assumption is that some major trends in recent American history will not be reversed in the foreseeable future. Two deserve special mention because they are central to our analysis. One is the decline of identification with a political party as a determinant of voter behavior. Previous research on political mass communication has stressed the dominance of party affiliation not only in determining one's vote but also in conditioning a person's exposure and responses to the news media. For some decades there has been a decrease in the power of researchers to predict voter behavior on the basis of party identification alone. Correspondingly, there has been an increase in the predictive importance of the positions of candidates and voters on specific issues.[1] The two concepts overlap empirically, since each party represents a rough configuration of alternative positions on major and enduring political issues. But the voters' need to know where a presidential candidate stands on key questions seems to be on the rise.

The second trend of obvious relevance is the emergence of television as the medium from which most Americans get most of their news. Of every ten adults in this country, only about seven read a daily newspaper and two a weekly news magazine, but all ten (for practical purposes) watch television.[2] This does not mean that TV generates most of the news, nor that most of the political information held by U.S. citizens was received via television. To judge from the disappointing level of knowledge of those who rely solely on TV for their news, the print media are still responsible for disseminating most of the details that are known.[3] But with the rise of television such a significant proportion of the electorate is exposed to news by this mass medium that it must be considered the primary delivery system for most political enlightenment.

One nontrend should also be noted. There is no good evidence,

---

[1] Norman H. Nie, Sidney Verba, and John R. Petrocik, *The Changing American Voter* (Cambridge, Mass.: Harvard University Press, 1976), chapters 7–10.

[2] These estimates are based on unpublished data provided by F. Gerald Kline from national surveys conducted by the Center for Political Studies at the University of Michigan.

[3] Thomas E. Patterson and Robert D. McClure, *The Unseeing Eye: The Myth of Television Power in National Politics* (New York: G. P. Putnam's Sons, 1976); and Steven H. Chaffee with Marilyn Jackson-Beeck, Jean Durall, and Donna Wilson, "Mass Communication in Political Socialization," in Stanley Renshon, ed., *Handbook of Political Socialization* (New York: Free Press, 1977), chapter 8.

despite the many detractors of television, of any aggregate increase in voting on the basis of the personality or "image" of the candidates. The best empirical estimates of the predictive power of image characteristics indicate that it has remained approximately constant from one election to the next.[4] Unfortunately, since data for such studies began being collected only around 1950, we have no way of estimating the importance of candidate image before the mass diffusion of television. But the decline in partisan attachments seems in the past quarter century to have involved a trade-off with issue-based voting rather than any ascendance of the image factor. This is not to say that personal images of the candidates are not important. In 1960, for example, images were clearly significant, and the Kennedy-Nixon debates were interpreted by the research community as mainly image-building events.[5] But just as clearly, 1976 was not an image-based election; studies of the Ford-Carter debates have produced very little evidence of image enhancement.[6] The same contrast could be made in non-debate years; the 1952 election, for example, seems to have turned mainly on images, while those of 1964 and 1972 were dominated more by issues or ideologies.[7] A voter's perception of a candidate as a "good guy" or a "bad guy" seems to be determined heavily by which side of the issue the candidate is on; telegenic qualities may be important, but their importance has not risen with that of television itself.

Against this general background, we examine the debates—especially the more recent Ford-Carter (and Dole-Mondale) experience—for evidence that they have made a contribution to the electoral process that is worth maintaining. A number of discrete questions can be asked. For example, do the debates generate political information that would not otherwise become available? Do the debates deliver political information to people who would otherwise not receive it? Do people make use of information from the debates in making their voting decisions? Aside from the electoral process itself, do debates serve other valuable functions for the political system? Do the debates have dysfunctional as well as eufunctional consequences?

---

[4] Nie and others, *Changing American Voter*, chapter 10, n. 1.

[5] Sidney Kraus, ed., *The Great Debates* (Bloomington: Indiana University Press, 1962).

[6] This conclusion is based on approximately thirty separate studies of the 1976 debates. A review of some of the main findings in these studies is presented in David O. Sears and Steven H. Chaffee, "Uses and Effects of the Debates: An Overview of Empirical Studies," in Sidney Kraus, ed., *The Great Debates, 1976: Carter vs. Ford* (Bloomington: Indiana University Press, forthcoming).

[7] Nie and others, *Changing American Voter*, chapter 10, n. 1.

The Scope and Content of the Debates

At first blush, an experienced observer of the political scene might think it implausible that much "new" information emerges from presidential debates. The candidates have, after all, been making speeches through the primary season, the conventions, and on into the fall campaign for months before the debates take place. Few new questions are likely to arise in the last month or two before election day, and even fewer policy initiatives are likely to emerge unless one candidate finds himself far behind in the polls. A skilled politician would scarcely risk trying out a wholly novel political position, statement, or even slogan on live television before a huge audience. What happens instead is that the candidates respond to questions in ways that have already worked well. Their accumulated experience in speech making, press conferences, market testing via private polls, and debate rehearsals is brought into play.

Researchers have implicitly recognized this. Although there have been some content analyses of the debates themselves, none has given any indication that strikingly new information is provided by the candidates. The studies focus instead on the relative emphasis each candidate gives to certain broad categories of public policy—taxation, economic growth, defense, and the like—or on the rhetorical style employed by each candidate. For example, John F. Kennedy's Harvardian style featured a number of historical references, but other debaters have not been given to using them. And there is unsurprising evidence that Democratic debaters bring up certain favorite topics repeatedly, while their Republican opponents like to stress others; they of course emphasize their individual areas of strength, which are to a considerable extent their party's most appealing policies.[8]

But that is a narrow concept of the political content of the debates. The debate setting itself generates a great deal more. First, this is one of the few formats that allows comparison of political information, and the meaning of a statement clearly varies depending on the alternative statement with which it is juxtaposed. A sly or evasive response may serve a candidate well on the stump, but it is risky in the context of the debate. There is little in research to date to indicate

---

[8] Marilyn Jackson-Beeck and Robert G. Meadow, "Content Analysis of Televised Communication Events: The Presidential Debates," *Communication Research*, forthcoming; Robert G. Meadow and Marilyn Jackson-Beeck, "A Comparative Perspective on Presidential Debates: Issue Evolution in 1960 and 1976," in George F. Bishop, Robert G. Meadow, and Marilyn Jackson-Beeck, *The Presidential Debates: Media, Electoral, and Policy Perspectives* (New York: Praeger, 1978), pp. 33-58.

directly the value of this comparative (and competitive) feature of the debates in contrast with one-sided presentations, but it would seem to be a clear gain for the voter. As indicated below, there is indirect evidence that this two-sided presentation is helpful in overcoming voters' selective biases, which normally limit the impact of campaign communication.

A second source of added information is the questions asked by the reporters. This element too has been given little systematic scrutiny by social scientists. The central point has to do with the locus of control. Because of the comparative setting and the fact that the agenda for discussion is determined by the question askers, the candidates lose a great deal of the control over political communication that they normally enjoy. They cannot insure that a no-win issue (such as abortion in 1976) will not arise simply because neither of them wishes to take a position on it; they cannot prevent it from being injected into the debate. This loss of control cannot be counted as an unbounded gain for the information-seeking citizen, since it doubtless serves to make the candidates more wary of debating at all and of what they say when they do debate. But it should nevertheless tend to bring out the more difficult kinds of political issues.

A realistic concept of the political content of a presidential debate would include far more than this, however. Although the televised debate may last ninety minutes, the event as a whole is weeks, even months, in duration. Debate-related communication begins with the first announcement of the debate and with press speculation about what will occur in it. The first Ford-Carter debate was a front-page and magazine-cover story before it occurred and after. It was the news peg on which almost every political column for several days was hung, and it even led to sidebar features on the entertainment pages. Professional pundits from both political and media circles struggled to say something original about the debate, and politicians of every stripe (including the debaters themselves) were given the opportunity to react to it afterward. Ordinary citizens discussed it extensively with one another, producing their own interpretations of what had occurred and of what they had learned about the debate from the media—even if they had not watched it themselves.

In our Wisconsin Panel Survey of 1976, for example, we found that the debates and postdebate reporting claimed substantial attention and generated personal discussion. Table 3.1 summarizes the levels of attention to each of the four debates. The overwhelming majority of people in Wisconsin were tuned in to the three debates between the candidates for president, and one-third of the electorate

TABLE 3.1

DEBATE WATCHING AND LISTENING, ATTENTION TO POSTDEBATE PRESS REPORTS, AND DISCUSSION OF THE DEBATES, WISCONSIN, 1976

(percent)

	First Debate (N = 223)	Second Debate (N = 207)	Vice-Presidential Debate (N = 207)	Final Debate (N = 207)
"Did you happen to watch the debate between Ford and Carter (Dole and Mondale) on television, did you hear it on the radio, or did you miss the debate?"				
Saw it all on TV	35	44	24	39
Heard it all on radio	—	1	1	—
Saw part on TV	28	13	10	22
Heard part on radio	1	1	1	1
Part on TV, part on radio	1	1	1	1
Missed it	32	40	64	38
Not ascertained	1	1	—	—
Total	98	101	101	101

"Did you happen to read in the press or hear on the radio or TV about who won the debate after the debate was over?"

Yes	65	73	39	40
No	35	21	56	58
Can't remember	—	6	5	2
Total	100	100	100	100

"Let me ask you how much—if any—you have been discussing the debate with other people."

A great deal	15	10	2	6
Some	27	26	18	15
Very little	34	36	22	31
Not at all	23	28	58	48
Total	99	100	100	100

NOTE: Percentages do not always sum to 100 because of rounding.

Dash (—): Zero or negligible.

SOURCE: Steven H. Chaffee and Jack Dennis, Wisconsin Panel Survey (Madison, Wis., 1976).

saw or heard the Dole-Mondale debate. National samples yield even higher estimates. For the first debate, for example, our Wisconsin estimate of 66 percent attention can be compared with Gallup (67 percent), Associated Press (71 percent), Harris (71 percent), Roper (72 percent), Nielsen (72 percent), and Market Opinion Research (89 percent), according to a summary by Sears.[9] Local samples produced similarly high figures, ranging from 63 to 88 percent, and the median estimate across the fifteen studies reviewed by Sears was 75 percent. For the later debates the corresponding median viewing estimates were 67 percent (second debate), 50 percent (vice-presidential debate), and 56 percent (final debate). Not all the samples were weighted to take account of nonrespondents, who were probably less likely to watch. But the finding in the major postelection national survey that 83 percent of the adult U.S. population reported they had viewed or heard at least one debate is probably a fairly accurate assessment of overall penetration.[10] Finally, Table 3.1 shows—in concert with other studies —that television is much more important than radio as the medium for live reception of the debates.

We also found, as did other studies, considerable evidence of public attention to media reports after the debates, and evidence of personal discussion of the debates. The relevant data are also shown in Table 3.1. As with viewing, both attention to press reports and discussion were greatest for the first debate, remained fairly high for the second debate, but then dropped off following the vice-presidential and the final debate. This latter phenomenon—the drop of interest in the later debates—had also occurred in 1960, when there was no vice-presidential debate.

Although we have no comparable norms of attention to news stories against which to assess these figures in any precise way, they are impressive. The debates became the major political news story of the day, even of the campaign. This can be linked to an intriguing hypothetical cause and consequence: not much else seemed to be happening. Because of the debates, the press tended not to pay close attention to other elements of the campaign, and the candidates tended not to generate much other publicity for a time. When evaluating the political information generated by the debates, we should take into account that which was forgone—which either did not occur or was overshadowed—because of the overwhelming concentration on the debates. Unfortunately, the study of press content is to date not well

---

[9] Sears and Chaffee, "Uses and Effects."

[10] Arthur H. Miller and Michael MacKuen, "Informing the Electorate: A National Study," in Kraus, ed., *The Great Debates 1976*.

enough developed to assess the political information that was available but failed to get reported or was relegated to minor coverage because it was overshadowed by news surrounding the debates.

A central factor in identifying the total content of a debate is the construction given to the event by the press. Despite the journalistic credo that issues and information are all-important in political reporting, these are not emphasized in describing a presidential debate. Instead, the focus is on public reaction that determines which candidate "won" the debate.[11] This emphasis is manifested not only in the news accounts that follow the debate, but even more clearly in the massive research apparatus that the news industry assembles to get an instant decision. The situation is very much like a horse race with a photo finish or a boxing match in that the crowd must wait a few minutes—but only that long—to learn the decision of the judges. The event then becomes not what was said, but rather how the audience reacted to what was said.

There are several possible reasons, not mutually exclusive, why the press tends to treat a debate as analogous to sporting competition. First, journalists may assume that the broadcasting of the debate itself has served to report what was said, so that the real news is the public's reaction. Second, they seem to believe that the mass audience has little interest in the substantive issues of the campaign; accordingly, the media must focus on the combat in order to hold people's attention. Earlier research on mass political communication supports this belief more strongly than the first assumption and shows disappointing levels of mass interest in current public issues. But that would be all the more reason for presuming that people need more than the initial exposure to the debate itself in order to digest all the material presented.

The image of a politically apathetic mass audience is at best an oversimplified one, however, and was not an accurate characterization of the electorate in 1976. At the time the debates began, a great many people were undecided about their voting intentions and were seeking information about the substantive policy differences between the two major candidates. A significant number of voters appear to have used the debates as a means of cutting the costs of gathering such information and resolving their own decisional uncertainties.

Reporters may also have assumed that because *they* detected little that was new in the way of policy differences during the debates, some other "newsworthy" aspect of the event needed to be emphasized. Reporters and columnists had, after all, been following these speakers

---

[11] Ibid.

for months and had heard their positions expressed many times. Understandably, they felt a sense of *déjà vu* and projected it onto their audience. But television news in particular fails to report issue-related content, at least in its regular evening broadcasts.[12] Our data suggest that a significant portion of the electorate approached the debates with interest and an open mind, but not with much prior information—even about the candidate they might tentatively have chosen. For them, much of the content of the debates would have been novel, and it seems unfortunate that the postdebate coverage of the media dealt so much with the reactions of the more informed and committed voters rather than with a recapitulation of the major issue differences expressed by the candidates.

The character of the evidence on this point should be made clear, lest we overdraw the picture. One content analysis that used the same categories to analyze both the debates and subsequent newspaper and television coverage of them can be instructive.[13] Only 17 percent of the newspaper space and 10 percent of the television time dealt explicitly with the winner-loser aspect of the three presidential debates. But an additional 41 percent (newspaper) and 42 percent (television) was given over to statements about the performances of the candidates, the personalities and competence they projected, and the impact the debate would have on their campaigns. Thus more than half the press coverage was *about* the debates, but not *of* the debates themselves. The relative emphases the candidates placed on issues was preserved in the subsequent press reports, but the absolute level was not. For example, in the first debate 37 percent of the time was spent on economic issues. Press reports also mentioned economic issues more frequently than any other issue, but this amounted to only 14 percent of the coverage in newspapers and 5 percent on TV. Although the candidates had spent more than a third of their debating time on these issues, they were overshadowed by such topics as debate performance (20 percent newspaper, 19 percent TV), winner-loser (21 percent, 14 percent), and campaign implications (14 percent, 12 percent), themes which in toto came up in the debate itself only about 1 percent of the time. Across all the debates, foreign affairs and economics ranked first and second among the issues in all three presentations—debates, newspaper accounts, and TV reporting—but they occupied more than twice as much of the content of the debates as they did of the subsequent press coverage.

From a survey of the many studies of the debates, it appears as

---

[12] Patterson and McClure, *The Unseeing Eye*, n. 3.

[13] Miller and MacKuen, "Informing the Electorate," n. 11.

though the press and the audience engage in a series of interactions in the process of determining the outcome of the debate-as-horserace. First is an immediate reaction by the press in the time slot that follows the debate itself, as commentators begin discussing how the candidates fared. This "instant analysis," to use media-baiter Spiro Agnew's term, tends to consist mainly of summaries of what was said and speculation on the coming story, that is, who will turn out to be the victor. Meanwhile telephone calls are being made all over the country to randomly sampled households. In at least some cases, poll results are available by the end of the postdebate news special. These findings, which are ordinarily limited to the win-lose question, then provide the framework for subsequent speculation and interpretation. If a poll following the first debate shows that more people think Ford won than Carter, the press must look again at the debate to determine why. The resulting stories focus on what Ford (as a performer) did right and Carter did wrong. Separate studies, using quite different samples and methods, show that the popular perceptions of Ford's victory in the first debate, and of Carter's in the second, were much stronger the day following each debate than on the previous evening immediately after the debate ended.[14] It may well be that the press's interpretation of the debate, based on its initial information as to the apparent victor, is more important in determining the impact on the electorate than is the debate itself.

But to say that the debates generate communication is not to say that they produce new information that is useful in the electoral decision process. The perception that one candidate or another won a debate might change some votes,[15] but whether that kind of information should substitute in vote decisions for, say, comprehension of the candidates' positions on economic issues, is a dubious proposition. The debates activate both the media and the audience: the media response is to encourage people to concentrate on who won the debates and not on the substance of the campaign; the audience response is to discuss

---

[14] Gladys Engel Lang and Kurt Lang, "Immediate and Mediated Responses: The First Debate," in Kraus, *Great Debates 1976*, and Frederick Steeper, "Public Response to Gerald Ford's Statement on Eastern Europe in the Second Debate," in Bishop et al., *The Presidential Debates*, pp. 81–101.

[15] Miller and MacKuen, "Informing the Electorate," n. 11, present data showing only a temporary effect of debate victory on voter favorability, while other studies show a slight tendency for a candidate to gain intended votes following a debate he had "won." The net effect of the 1976 debates on the final vote seems to have been approximately zero because Ford's success in the first debate was nullified by Carter's later victories. See Jack Dennis, Steven H. Chaffee, and Sun Yuel Choe, "Impact upon Partisan, Image, and Issue Voting," in Kraus, *Great Debates 1976*.

the debates and to pay somewhat more attention to the campaign. In particular, the first two debates in 1976 appear to have instigated more widespread coverage of the campaign in the news media.[16] Overall there is little indication that the debates made important additions to the character of the political information available within the body politic. Their major societal benefit lies rather in stimulating the circulation of information throughout the system.

Learning from the Debates

The most obvious achievement of the debates of 1960 and 1976 is that huge numbers of voters watched them. Even by the ambitious standards of commercial television the audiences were large. Not all those viewers were greatly interested in politics. The debates seem to have attracted not only the politically interested but also the larger group of people who are accustomed to watching television. The debates were heavily promoted in advance, and all network prime-time programming was suspended to make room for them. For most habitual television viewers, then, there was nothing better to watch, and the debates promised novelty as well as the sense of doing one's often-neglected civic duty.

Several studies probed people's stated reasons for watching the debates and generally revealed an encouraging sense of civic responsibility. For example, McLeod and his associates applied a large number of mass media "uses and gratifications" items to the debates, in their study of a panel of Madison, Wisconsin, respondents. In the authors' words, their interviewees most often "said they were seeking things that we consider important to informed participation: learning candidates' stands on issues, deciding how to vote, and judging the personal qualities of the candidates."[17] In another panel study, O'Keefe and Mendelsohn found in Akron, Ohio, that two-thirds of their

---

[16] See Appendix Table 3.A of this chapter for data relevant to this point. A more thorough statistical analysis has been prepared by Sun Y. Choe in an unpublished paper at the Mass Communications Research Center, University of Wisconsin-Madison. In a regression analysis of the Wisconsin panel, Choe found that increases in attention to the campaign from before to after the first debate were significantly associated with viewing of the debate ($\beta = 0.25$ for television, $\beta = 0.19$ for newspaper/magazine). Discussion of the debate was an even stronger predictor of an increase in following the campaign in the media ($\beta = 0.26$ for television, $\beta = 0.30$ for newspaper/magazine).

[17] Jack M. McLeod, Carl R. Bybee, Jean A. Durall, and Dean A. Ziemke, "The 1976 Presidential Debates as Forms of Political Communication," paper presented to the 1977 meeting of the Association for Education in Journalism, Madison, Wisconsin, p. 26.

sample said they expected to be influenced by the debates in their choice of a candidate.[18] Other studies came to similar conclusions that people attempted to use the debates as a mechanism for arriving at a meaningful decision.[19] Such self-reported motivations are always suspect, of course; it is probably more common to describe oneself as behaving like a model citizen than actually to behave that way. But the McLeod data in particular suggest at least a modicum of validity in these findings, because the respondents were asked the extent to which the uses and gratifications they had sought from the debates had been achieved. The debates were rated most helpful in judging the personal qualities of the candidates—especially their weak points—and in judging their stands on issues and what they would do if elected. Regardless of the respondent's education or age, the debates were highly rated as sources of information about issue stands as well as personal qualities, ranking behind the regular news from TV and newspapers, and ahead of magazines, television advertisements, and campaign literature, in that order.[20] This is a remarkable evaluation when one considers that the debates occurred just four times while the other sources were constantly operating to provide information to the electorate.

Aside from people's self-perceptions of what they learned, did they actually gain significant political information from the debates? The available data suggest that they did, although the present methodological state of social science does not invite definite conclusions on such a question without controlled experimentation. A variety of studies statistically traced a substantial increase in election-relevant knowledge to the debates, even when other likely sources of information have been controlled. Miller, for example, using successive cross-sections of a national sample, found evidence that virtually all groups and demographic categories had widely used the debates to acquire information.[21] More important as a contribution to theory, this rather uniform pattern of dissemination of information via the

---

[18] Garrett J. O'Keefe and Harold Mendelsohn, "Media Influences and Their Anticipation," in Kraus, *Great Debates 1976.*

[19] W. Russell Newman, "The Visual Impact of Presidential Television: A Study of the First Ford-Carter Debate," Department of Sociology, Yale University, 1977; Everett M. Rogers, David Dozier, and Dorothy Barton, "Changes in Candidate Images as a Result of the Debates," Institute for Communications Research, Stanford University, 1977; Samuel L. Becker, Robert Pepper, Lawrence A. Wenner, and Jin Keon Kim, "Presidential Debates, Information Flow, and the Shaping of Meanings," University of Iowa, 1977.

[20] McLeod and others, "The Debates as Forms of Communication," n. 18, tables 12–13.

[21] Miller and MacKuen, "Informing the Electorate," n. 11.

debates applied at all levels of political interest and involvement. Ordinarily, studies of political information flow conclude that the people reached are primarily those who are already highly interested and involved in the campaign. Viewing the debates also appears to have produced perceptions of sharper differences between both the candidates and their respective parties, one of the key conditions for rational democratic participation.[22]

Other studies lead to similar conclusions. For example, after the first 1976 debate Morrison and others found in their national sample significant changes in public knowledge of where the candidates stood on certain leading issues. As they report: "We conclude from this evidence that media events of this type can perform a significant campaign function in terms of informing voters and enabling voters to clarify their perceptions of the images of the candidates."[23] Similarly, Wald and Lupfer concluded that the first debate conveyed a considerable amount of useful information about the candidates and about campaign issues.[24] All these conclusions are consonant with the voters' own perceptions that they had sought issue-relevant information from the debates and had found it.

It is also clear from several studies that people thought well of their experiences as viewers of the debates. This is most obvious in the findings of McLeod and others, but it is also underscored by Mendelsohn and O'Keefe who found a strong emphasis on anticipation and reception of issue-oriented information.[25] Nine of every ten of their respondents preferred issue-oriented to image-oriented information; put another way, the most important element of a candidate's debating "image" appears to have been his position on major issues.

At the same time, people saw ways of improving the debates. The McLeod sample, admittedly representing a highly liberal and politically aware community, expressed preferences for such format changes as inclusion of third-party candidates, separate interviews of each candidate, and more pressure by the interviewing reporters to get answers to the questions they posed.[26]

---

[22] Ibid., and tables presented by Arthur H. Miller at a conference on the 1976 debates at the University of Pennsylvania, May 12–13, 1977.

[23] Andrew J. Morrison, Frederick Steeper, and Susan C. Greendale, "The First 1976 Presidential Debate: The Voters Win," paper presented to the 1977 meeting of the American Association for Public Opinion Research, Buck Hill Falls, Pennsylvania.

[24] Kenneth D. Wald and Michael B. Lupfer, "The Presidential Debate as a Civics Lesson," Public Opinion Quarterly, vol. 42 (1978), pp. 342–353.

[25] O'Keefe and Mendelsohn, "Media Influences," n. 19.

[26] McLeod and others, "The Debates as Forms of Communication," n. 18, table 14.

Although issue-centered information was apparently sought, the debates do not seem to have established any new issues in the public consciousness, contrary to the theory that items would be added to the agenda in response to media influence. Several studies by leading students of the agenda-setting hypothesis concluded that the debates had no such effect.[27] This is not terribly surprising, since we have already noted the lack of evidence that the debate introduced novel content into the campaign. Atkin and others did note a slight increase in public interest in inflation, following some emphasis on that topic in the final debate.[28] And Jackson-Beeck and Meadow saw a mild relation between the content of the 1960 debates and subsequent perceptions of problems as reported in opinion polls.[29] In 1976 the candidates did in fact address many of the issues people were most concerned about, but Becker and others in a month-by-month analysis found no change in the strength of the correlation between debate content and public issue perceptions during the last half of 1976.[30] Whether significant new issues injected by the debaters would have raised the salience of these topics in the electorate is debatable; the mixed empirical literature on the agenda-setting hypothesis would not support a strong prediction that this would be the case.[31]

In general, we conclude that the debates clearly performed one of their major social tasks, that of providing information about the candidates and their positions that was new to many voters. Further, the debates might well have been the only mechanism that would supply such information to a significant number of these people, despite their apparent need for it in connection with the impending vote. Prior to the debates people had fairly well established in their minds which issues were of greatest concern to them, but the positions of the candidates were not clear. The debates thus enabled voters to apply their own priorities to the political decision that they, collectively, had to make.

While these conclusions seem to us inescapable on the basis of

---

[27] Lee B. Becker, David H. Weaver, Doris A. Graber, and Maxwell E. McCombs, "Influence of the Debates on Public Agendas," Newhouse School of Communication, Syracuse University, 1977; McLeod and others, "The Debates as Forms of Communication," n. 18.

[28] Charles K. Atkin, John Hocking, and Steven McDermott, "Homestate Voter Response and Secondary Media Coverage," in Kraus, *Great Debates 1976*.

[29] Jackson-Beeck and Meadow, "Content Analysis," n. 8.

[30] Becker and others, "Presidential Debates," n. 28.

[31] See Lee B. Becker, Maxwell E. McCombs, and Jack M. McLeod, "The Development of Political Cognitions," in Steven H. Chaffee, ed., *Political Communication: Issues and Strategies for Research* (Beverly Hills, Calif.: Sage Publications, 1975).

the 1976 research, any student of political mass communication would recognize them as standing at variance with the conventional wisdom. Voters are ordinarily conceived as partisans of predetermined intent who resist any information save that which supports the conclusions they have already reached. Whether 1976 was an exception to this rule or the first flowering of a new era in American democracy is a question that only future research can address. An encouraging note, at least for the informational gain, is that the one study of the 1960 debates that looked for selective patterns of effect found at most weak evidence. Carter examined panels of voters who had, prior to the debates, already decided how they would vote.[32] The pro-Nixon voters did indeed learn more from Nixon than from Kennedy, and the pro-Kennedy voters knew more of what Kennedy had said. When only those who had watched the entire debate were examined, however—that is, those who had not left the room or tuned out a portion of the debate—the Kennedy voters were as likely to know the information Nixon had presented as that which Kennedy had delivered, and the same was true of the Nixon voters. Thus, there was selective exposure but not selective perception when exposure was controlled.

Selective exposure to mass political communication is an undoubted fact; an election-eve telethon by a Republican candidate for governor is decidedly unlikely to attract Democrats, or even undecided voters.[33] But it may well be that a bipartisan device such as the debates can break through any selectivity of information reception. It may also be that selectivity is less an empirical reality and more an artifact of researchers who have organized studies around their own expectations. Meanwhile, there is a growing body of voters who shun overt partisan commitments and thus are less subject to that kind of selectivity. Instead they appear to concentrate on the issues and the personal qualities of the candidates as they are manifested in political positions.

The Debates and the Voting Decision

One reason for holding presidential debates is to help people make voting decisions. One of the biggest differences between the 1960 and 1976 studies is that most of the former concluded that the debates had not had much informational impact on the vote, whereas the latter

---

[32] Richard F. Carter, "Some Effects of the Debates," in Kraus, *The Great Debates*, n. 5, pp. 253–257.
[33] Wilbur Schramm and Richard F. Carter, "Effectiveness of a Political Telethon," *Public Opinion Quarterly*, vol. 23 (1959), pp. 121–126.

reached the opposite conclusion. Whether this resulted from a change in the voters, a change in pairs of candidates, or an improvement in the conduct of research is difficult to determine. We will rely here principally on the 1976 work, recognizing some danger of overstating the case by generalizing from the single election.

First, consider the evidence we gathered in Wisconsin.[34] The panel of Wisconsin voters we interviewed four times during the fall of 1976 can be broken down into three groups in terms of their attention to the debates. About one-fifth of the sample watched little or nothing of the debates. Two-fifths of the sample watched all or nearly all of each debate. And about two-fifths of the sample watched some of each debate or all of a few debates. For each of these three groups we performed detailed multivariate analyses of the major determinants of voting decisions, including socioeconomic status, party identification, liberal-conservative ideology, and the perceived images and positions of the candidates after the debates.

The three groups exhibited strikingly different patterns of decision making (Table 3.2). Those who did not watch the debates ("low exposure") changed the least from before to after the debates, as indicated by the strong relationship between their predebates intention and final decision. Before the debates began, they were most certain how they would vote, but they became no more decisive by the end of the debates, just before election day. The votes of these nonviewers were most strongly determined ($\beta = 0.35$) by the images they held of the candidates; party identification was only a weak factor in their eventual voting, and issues were not a factor at all when other predictor variables were controlled statistically.

Members of the medium exposure group, who watched the debates casually and sporadically, tended to make up their minds after the first debate and voted mainly on the basis of party identification ($\beta = 0.27$) and postdebates image perceptions ($\beta = 0.28$). Issues other than party affiliation were a negligible factor. It is as if these voters used the debates to assure themselves that the man nominated by their party was indeed worthy of their vote. One need not attend to every minute of every debate to make such a global judgment.

The third group ("high exposure") watched all or nearly all of every debate and consisted of issue-oriented voters. In this subsample, a substantial 40 percent of our total statewide sample, differences perceived between one's own position on an issue and the positions attributed to each candidate predicted the vote more strongly

---

[34] These results are reported more fully in Dennis, Chaffee, and Choe, "Impact of the Debates."

TABLE 3.2

SUMMARY OF EFFECTS OF MAJOR VARIABLES ON FINAL VOTING DECISION, BY AMOUNT OF EXPOSURE TO DEBATES

Independent Variable	Block		Low Exposure (N = 35)	Medium Exposure (N = 65)	High Exposure (N = 64)	Total Sample (N = 164)
Party identification	I	r	0.51	0.69	0.59	0.61
		β	0.12	0.27	0.06	0.15
Socioeconomic status	I	r	0.19	0.24	0.02	0.14
		β	−0.08	0.09	0.01	0.06
Predebates ideological difference	II	r	0.29	0.25	0.54	0.39
		β	0.16	−0.10	0.11	0.04
Predebates voting intention	III	r	0.82	0.79	0.71	0.76
		β	0.63	0.41	0.30	0.41
Postdebates issue differences	IV	r	0.46	0.53	0.72	0.59
		β	−0.12	0.04	0.31	0.10
Postdebates candidate images	IV	r	0.67	0.71	0.70	0.69
		β	0.35	0.28	0.22	0.28

NOTE: Beta weights (β) indicate direct effects of each independent variable on the final voting decision, calculated in a hierarchical regression analysis in which independent variables were entered in blocks as indicated, and the indirect effects of earlier variables through later ones in this model were calculated separately (not shown). r is the product-moment correlation coefficient.

SOURCE: Jack Dennis, Steven H. Chaffee, and Sun Yuel Choe, "Impact upon Partisan, Image, and Issue Voting," in Sidney Kraus, ed., *The Great Debates: Carter vs. Ford, 1976* (Bloomington: Indiana University Press, forthcoming), table.

($\beta = 0.31$) than did either party identification or image perceptions. Significantly too, these voters tended to delay their decisions until all the debates had been completed. Following the first debate they were the least certain how they would vote, but by the end of the fourth debate they had become the most certain of any group.

The time at which a voter makes the final decision is an important consideration here. Pretelevision, predebates research literature on presidential elections emphasized a paradox that has been discouraging to champions of democracy and of the mass media as instruments of it. Voters were seen as falling into two categories: (1) highly partisan, politically interested citizens, who follow the campaign news closely but who perceive it very selectively in favor of their own candidate and are consequently impervious to persuasion; and (2) uninterested, apathetic voters who pay little attention to the campaign and decide how they will vote only at the last minute and often for frivolous reasons. An analysis by Sun Yuel Choe shows that in 1976 a third group, larger than either of these, consisted of people who were quite interested, followed the campaign and the debates as closely as the highly partisan voters, but did not make up their minds until they had seen one or all of the debates.[35] It is to this type of voter that the debates are mainly addressed, and their message was received—at least in 1976. This middle group, which made up its mind during the debates rather than in advance of them, was the best informed of any of the three groups. Again, we see evidence of a more rational voter behavior than prior studies had suggested.

Let us consider now the special circumstances of 1976 that can be generalized to future presidential elections. On the eve of the first debate, only about 55 pecent of our sample reported that they had made up their minds how to vote, and some of these people were to experience doubts later. About 63 percent had decided after the first debate, and 70 percent by the time the debates were completed; finally, 83 percent of our respondents actually cast a ballot on election day. Although the phrasing of our question was not identical to those of previous election studies,[36] prior studies had led us to expect a larger

---

[35] Appendix Table 3.B summarizes some main findings from Choe's analysis (see also note 16 above). Those voters who decided how they would vote during the period of the debates are similar to predecided voters in their high levels of attention to the campaign and political knowledge, but more like late deciders in their lack of partisanship and active participation in the campaign. See also Steven H. Chaffee and Sun Yuel Choe, "Time of Decision and Media Use in the Ford-Carter Campaign," paper presented at the annual meeting of the Association for Education in Journalism, Seattle, Washington, 1978.

[36] The following questions were asked: (1) "So far as you know now, do you expect to vote on November 2, or not?" (2) (If yes to Q. 1) "Who do you think

percentage of the electorate who had decided before the debates, and fewer people who made up their minds during the debates period.

Considering the long-range decline in party identification, we should expect this lateness of decision to recur in future elections. To be sure, Carter was for many voters an unknown quantity before the 1976 debates, as Kennedy had been in 1960. The debates helped these candidates to become better known, on a par with their opponents. Would a significant number of voters wait to see the candidates debate before commiting their votes if both nominees were already well known? We cannot be certain, but the evidence that the debates contribute to informed voting decisions strongly supports continuing them on a regular basis.

System-Level Functions and Possible Dysfunctions

Beyond the services they provide for the individual voter, the debates have a function in the wider context of the political system. This function may be either positive or negative. In our research we gave special attention to people's feelings of support for, or alienation from, the institutions of American national government. Following the Vietnam and Watergate eras, public confidence in these institutions fell to a level that many political observers considered dangerously low.[37]

The process of holding elections is not merely a mechanism for choosing leaders; political theorists consider it a valuable source of support for all democratic institutions. Free elections are not simply a manifestation of a functioning democratic order, but one of its essential determinants as well. The more people are able to participate in competitive, free, and frequent choices of leadership, the more they are reinforced in the belief that democratic institutions are right and proper—or at least so the theory goes. We put the theory to an empirical test.

The debates are an especially vivid dramatization of democracy in

you will vote for in the election for president?" (3) (If no to Q. 1) "If you were going to vote, who do you think you would vote for in the election for president?" (4) (If undecided in Q. 2 or 3) "Would you say you are leaning more toward Ford or more toward Carter?" (5) (If Ford or Carter to Q. 2) "Are you sure you will be voting for him, or do you think there is a good chance you will change your mind?"

[37] Arthur H. Miller, "Political Issues and Trust in Government: 1964–1970," *American Political Science Review*, vol. 68 (1974), pp. 951–972, and "Changes in Political Trust: Discontent with Authorities and Economic Policies, 1972–1973," paper presented at the annual meeting of the American Political Science Association, Chicago, 1974.

action—they exemplify free political competition in a most compelling manner. The selected champions of the two major partisan armies appear in a format of direct and open confrontation, with the nation as judge. In addition to focusing public attention on specific issues, the 1976 debates emphasized the need to restore public confidence in the government. Ford, in his two years as president, had not fully repaired the damage to that confidence that had been done in the previous decade.[38] In the debates, as in other campaign appearances, both candidates emphasized the rightness of American institutions and put forth ways of using them to achieve national and social goals.

In Table 3.3 we summarize our main findings, abstracted from an elaborate statistical analysis. The coefficients in this table indicate the strength of relationship between the debates (the stimulating events) and increases in confidence in various institutions. Overall we found in the fall of 1976 statistically significant gains in all these indicators of confidence. Table 3.3 shows that much of this can be traced to the debates. Perhaps the "bottom line" in this table is the statistically significant coefficient ($\beta = 0.14$) representing the relationship of total viewing of the debates to total confidence in the four institutions. This figure is impressive when one considers that global feelings such as confidence in governmental institutions are ordinarily rather constant and not easily modified by passing events.

The effects shown in Table 3.3 are, somewhat puzzlingly, strongest in relation to the Supreme Court and the Congress, rather than the presidency, with no apparent effects for the federal government as a general entity. The legitimating impact of the debates is thus specific to certain governmental institutions. In this respect, it contrasts with analogous relationships between our measures of confidence and the respondents' general attention to the campaign via the media. Both newspaper and television attention are associated with modest gains in confidence in all four institutions—less than the debates in the cases of Congress and the Supreme Court, and more in the cases of the presidency and the federal government.

---

[38] In Ford's term as president, "trust and confidence" in the federal government went from an index of 52 in 1974 to 50 in 1976 for the handling of domestic policies, and from 67 to 53 for international problems (Potomac Associates, *Trust and Confidence in the American System*, p. 11). The Harris survey (March 14, 1977) reported the following percentages of American adults expressing high confidence in governmental institutions:

Institution	1974	1975	1976
The White House	18	13	11
Executive branch of federal government	28	13	11
U.S. Supreme Court	40	28	22
Congress	18	13	9

TABLE 3.3

Relationship of Debates to Increases in Confidence in Governmental Institutions, Wisconsin, 1976

Institution	First Debate	Second Debate	Vice-presidential Debate	Final Debate	Total Debates	Debates Discussion	Press Reports
Presidency	0.07	0.15	0.10	−0.01	0.10	0.13	0.15
Congress	0.08	0.17*	0.09	0.19*	0.18*	0.10	0.17*
Supreme Court	0.17*	0.14*	0.11	0.15*	0.19*	0.11	0.15*
Federal government	−0.04	0.07	−0.03	−0.04	−0.01	−0.02	0.02
Total institutions	0.09	0.16*	0.07	0.08	0.14*	0.09	0.14*

Note: Entries are beta weights (β) from multiple regression analyses, in which the postelection level of confidence in the listed institution is the dependent variable, and the predebates confidence in that same institution is the first independent variable entered in the regression equation. The effect of the debate variable listed in the column heading is then entered as a second independent variable in hierarchical regression; significant ($p < 0.05$) beta coefficients are indicated by an asterisk (*). For a more complete exposition of the data analysis, see Jack Dennis and Steven N. Chaffee, "Legitimation in the 1976 U.S. Election Campaign," *Communication Research*, vol. 5 (1978), pp. 371-394.

Source: Wisconsin Panel Survey, 1976.

This legitimating impact of the campaign and the debates may well be peculiar to the 1976 situation, in which confidence in governmental institutions began at an especially low level. In a campaign year that started with the presidency in high public esteem, debates between the incumbent and the challenger might conceivably reduce public esteem for the office. Although the general theory of democratic legitimation through electoral processes was confirmed in the case of the 1976 debates, this is always an empirical question, and the contribution debates might make to legitimation can vary from one election to another.

We have stressed in this paper a number of eufunctional results of the debates, because research findings point toward these conclusions. But other studies or other debates might have dysfunctional outcomes. For example, research has not yet focused on the proposition that the debates have a deadening effect on other phases of the campaign. Did the overwhelming concentration on the debates induce the candidates, their campaign organizations, the media, or the public to neglect other forms of communication that might also have been of value to the democratic process?

Another possible dysfunction has to do with the "star system" that is reinforced by the debates. The nation's eyes become focused on just two men, seeking a single office. All else is seemingly dwarfed: other levels and branches of government, other candidacies and issues, and, perhaps most important, the parties these men represent. Research has little to tell us about the potential effect of this overshadowing, but it seems a topic worthy of serious study. The historical tendencies toward concentration of power in the federal government, especially the executive branch, and the general decline of public enthusiasm for the major political parties seem to be exacerbated by the personalization of politics inherent in the debate format.[39] Similarly, the growing reliance on television as a source of political information is encouraged by even the occasional staging of debates. While some might welcome the tendency to formulate politics as a clash between individuals rather than organizations, we suspect that the debates overstress the role played by the generals and underplay the role of their armies.

These systemic dysfunctions could be particularly dismaying if

---

[39] For evidence on lessening public support for political parties as a device of democratic competition, see Jack Dennis, "Trends in Public Support for the American Party System," *British Journal of Political Science*, vol. 5 (1975), pp. 187–230. For a more comprehensive review of debates' functions, see Steven H. Chaffee, "Presidential Debates: Are They Helpful to Voters?" *Communication Monographs*, vol. 45 (1978), pp. 330–346.

they were studied in the context of the socialization of young people into the political system. Hawkins and others have conducted one of the few systematic studies of the debates as a stimulus to political socialization. Their data clearly show a gain in political interest as a consequence of exposure to the debates.[40] But other recent work on young voters has already shown that they tend to interpret political events in terms of persons more than parties.[41] Are these new voters also being drawn away from concern with local, state, and congressional politics by the concentration of media attention on the single office of the president, and do debates strengthen this tendency? If so, the debates, for all their valuable contributions in 1976, may foster the creation of a future electorate that will tend to neglect many elements of our multilevel democratic system that are at least as essential to its functioning as is a well-informed decision in a presidential election.

Conclusion

Many unanswered empirical quesions about presidential debates remain. This is not surprising given the small number of debates and the difficulty of investigating these phenomena from the theoretical perspectives of the academic community. Scholars have been unable to mount more than relatively small-scale research efforts because the debates are scheduled on short notice, and there is a general lack of substantial funding. Despite these difficulties, we now know a good deal about the debates' effects. There is a remarkable degree of academic consensus that the debates are exercises of potentially great importance in political communication aimed at both the elite and the masses. The tangible manifestation of this belief is the many studies, albeit modest ones, undertaken in an effort to assess their value.

One conclusion that emerges clearly from studies in both 1960 and 1976 is that the debates make substantial contributions to the process of democracy and perhaps even to the longer-term viability of the system. The research offers a great deal of support for the proposition that the debates serve important informational functions for voters. If the preferred model of individual voting behavior is one that includes such "rational" components as the individual weighing of alternatives, then the debates have been verifiably eufunctional. They

---

[40] Robert P. Hawkins, Suzanne Pingree, Kim A. Smith, and Warren E. Bechtolt, Jr., "Adolescents' Responses to the Issues and Images of the Debates," in Kraus, *Great Debates 1976*.

[41] Steven H. Chaffee and Lee B. Becker, "Young Voters' Reactions to Early Watergate Issues," *American Politics Quarterly*, vol. 3 (1975), pp. 360–385.

encourage voters to think about the nature of the choices being offered, and as an information-gathering device they have the unique virtue of allowing a simultaneous consideration of the alternatives. Voters are thus able to reduce information costs that they would otherwise be forced to bear.[42] Normally a voter must somehow compile information about the alternatives from a large series of such discontinuous, one-sided presentations as advertisements, news reports of speeches, and the party conventions. From this melange of cues the voter must discover the expected costs and benefits to be derived from various electoral choices. It is no wonder that many people short-circuit this arduous task of collecting and processing data by allowing their prior partisan identifications (and thus their selective biases) to guide their choice. In both 1960 and 1976 it was demonstrated that, given a more economical mechanism for sorting out the relevant information, a great many people will respond to what the candidates are actually presenting. Cognitive learning under such circumstances becomes both possible and actual.

In 1960 the response to this device was mainly reduced uncertainty about candidate qualifications. In 1976, however, a significant fraction of the electorate moved beyond the weighing of these simple alternatives to consider policy differences as well. Either focus represents a substantial gain over more primitive forms of information processing by the citizenry.

If we assume that the same conditions of voter uncertainty will exist in future elections, and that this will be combined with a continuing voter disposition to weigh alternative policies, then approximating the "rational voter" ideal on a higher level might be considered. For example, the candidates might be allowed to engage in a full, immediate exchange of views rather than to make side-by-side pronouncements on the same issue in formal, consecutive fashion. The debate formats have so far lacked a way to sharpen the differences through more immediate give-and-take. Such an exchange need not achieve the pinnacle of Socratic dialogue to reduce further the cost of information to voters. But with an increasingly well-educated and issue-oriented electorate, it is a direction in which future debate planning might move.

Beyond these manifest functions, the debates apparently served also to reinforce people's faith in some aspects of the national gov-

---

[42] For discussion of voter information processing within a rationalistic framework, see Anthony Downs, *An Economic Theory of Democracy* (New York: Harper and Row, 1957); and V. O. Key, Jr., *The Responsible Electorate* (Cambridge, Mass.: Harvard University Press, 1966).

APPENDIX TABLE 3.A

Correlation of Campaign Communication with Viewing of Debates, Wisconsin, 1976

Debate	Television		Newspapers and Magazines		Private Discussion	
	Prior	Subsequent	Prior	Subsequent	Prior	Subsequent
First	0.29	0.49	0.19	0.21	0.05	0.14
Second	0.38	0.46	0.20	0.28	0.23	0.21
Vice-presidential	0.33	0.28	0.33	0.23	0.04	0.06
Final	0.24	0.36	0.14	0.14	0.04	0.03

NOTE: Entries are correlation coefficients between the extent of viewing the listed debate and the extent of communication about the campaign from the source indicated in the column heading. "Prior" communication refers to the interview wave immediately preceding the debate, and "subsequent" communication means the wave immediately following it. Significant ($p < 0.05$) beta coefficients are indicated by an asterisk (*).
SOURCE: Wisconsin Panel Survey, 1976.

ernmental system. Despite being of relatively brief duration and infrequent occurrence, the 1976 debates had measurable effects on people's confidence—which in an era of low public confidence in government is an effect worth remarking. We cannot say that this impact was the result of any conscious effort on the part of the candidates and their organizations—despite the fact that both sides were aware of the generally low esteem in which the American people held the federal government. That debate-fostered legitimation applied more to Congress and the Supreme Court than to the presidency is implicit testimony to this lack of deliberate effort and to the fact that a more general process was at work.

There remain unanswered questions. On the whole, however, the studies made to date warrant the conclusions that the debates served their audiences well and that they reinforced ideas of democratic electoral competition and of the regime's legitimacy. Thus, the thrust of what we have learned so far supports the continuation, perhaps the institutionalization, of presidential debates.

APPENDIX TABLE 3.B

DEBATE AND CAMPAIGN INVOLVEMENT BY TIME OF FINAL VOTING
DECISION, WISCONSIN, 1976
(standard scores)

Involvement	Early Deciders (N = 45)	Campaign Deciders (N = 62)	Late Deciders (N = 49)
Viewing of debates	−06	+19	−10
Discussion of debates	+12	+14	−17
Attention to press reports of debates	+25	+06	−31
Attention to media's coverage of campaign	+11	+19	−24
Political knowledge	+19	+23	−31
Attention to campaign	+28	+12	−24
Campaigning activities	+23	−05	−05
Strength of partisanship	+24	−11	+02

NOTE: Entries are standard scores, calculated by scoring each group mean as a deviation from the grand mean of the total sample, and then dividing this by the standard deviation; standard scores have been multiplied by 100 for simplicity. Since each row has an overall mean of zero and a standard deviation of unity, scores can be compared from one row to another in this table. Voters were classified as "early deciders" if their vote decisions had been made prior to the debates, and as "late deciders" if they were still undecided after all the debates; those who made up their minds between these two times were classified as "campaign deciders."
SOURCE: Wisconsin Panel Survey, 1976.

Discussion

EVRON KIRKPATRICK, American Political Science Association: To what extent do your data help us in deciding between the point of view that Philip Converse [Center for Political Studies, University of Michigan] has developed in information flow and stability of partisan attitudes and the opposing position that Edward Dreyer [University of Tulsa] has taken using the same data? Converse says, "The influence of short-run factors has less impact on those who are well informed and strongly partisan and on those who have virtually no information and no commitments than on those who have some information and weak loyalties." And he later says, "Throughout these debate materials in 1960, we found that the more remote the individual's flow of information represented by the debates the more stable was his vote intention.[1]

If I understood rightly, you are saying something similar in your paper—that people with much information and high involvement and those with no information and little involvement have a high degree of stability. The floating voter is likely to have some information, and new information is likely to influence his intentions.

Dreyer takes the same data that Converse used, although a little more extensively, and comes to a different conclusion. It is on that conflict that I would like you to comment. Dreyer says:

> With the growing availability of mass media (primarily television since 1952), and the increased utilization of the media by candidates and parties, the flow of short-term political stimuli—both during campaigns and in the lengthy lulls between them—has effectively penetrated all segments of the electorate. These data also suggest that the more or less immediate circumstances that surround any given election have eroded and probably will continue to erode the stabilizing influences normally associated with the elec-

---

[1] The reference is to Philip E. Converse, "Information Flow and the Stability of Partisan Attitudes," in Angus Campbell, Philip E. Converse, Warren E. Miller, and Donald E. Stokes, *Elections and the Political Order* (New York: John Wiley and Sons, 1966), chapter 8.

torate's partisan loyalties. This weakening of the party identification–party vote relationship will be manifested across the total electorate. . . . Converse's modification of the floating voter hypothesis, while probably applicable to an earlier era of rather weak political communication, no longer seems to apply to the current situation.[2]

This is a very interesting problem, about which not much is known. Both Converse and Dreyer were using data acquired prior to and just after 1960. It seems to me that you are absolutely right in saying that we do not have many studies that effectively get at some of the problems we would like to know the answers to. I would like to hear your views about the conflict between Dreyer and Converse.

CHAFFEE: I don't want to settle that argument, although a lot of people do and will be looking at data, such as those we have presented, in hopes of resolving it. When people do that, they will probably seize on some of our data and interpretations as supporting Dreyer more than Converse; I think that is pretty clear. But they both make an assumption that we do not. Converse and Dreyer treat the electorate as a homogenous, undifferentiated whole into which the mass media pump stimuli or inputs. Our paper is based on the assumption that there are some people for whom that model does not apply. To some voters, the value of information presented on television or through the mass media is based on what they themselves do with the media rather than on what the candidates do to them through the media. In other words, there are many passive, receiver-type voters, but there are also a substantial number of voters who are active processors of data. If we look at the role of the media in the political process with this distinction in mind, I think we will come to the conclusion that the effects of the media are greater than in the past even though they are less demonstrable in a direct way. In other words, the mass media and campaign events perhaps have less direct control of voters when a sizable number of people are looking for answers and, in fairly intelligent ways, processing the information that they receive. I think our paper is pitched to a different argument than that of Converse or Dreyer.

EVRON KIRKPATRICK: In other words, if there is a decline in party commitment and an increase in the flow of information, and if the people

---

[2] The reference is to Edward C. Dreyer, "Media Use and Electoral Choices: Some Political Consequences of Information Exposure," *Public Opinion Quarterly*, vol. 35 (Winter 1971–1972), pp. 544–553.

with less commitment are more affected by the increased flow of information, then you would say that the effect of the flow of information, namely, debates, on the electorate would be greater than it has been in the past.

DENNIS: Yes, we are saying that we have a kind of contingent model of causality here. Two things combine to make the use of television more important: first, the electorate is more volatile and second, it is also more issue oriented.

THOMAS E. MANN, American Political Science Association: I am struck by the fact that you said there was no net advantage in the debates for Ford or Carter.

DENNIS: There is not if we take the three presidential debates together. If the vice-presidential debate is added, there was a net advantage for Carter-Mondale in our study and in some of the other studies.

MANN: The national surveys—the Gallup and Harris polls—made at about the time of your first survey and again at the time of the Mondale-Dole debate indicate a substantial shift: Ford was gaining and Carter was losing during that time. I am wondering if your Wisconsin sample picked up that shift. If it existed in Wisconsin as well as the nation and it cannot be attributed to the debates, to what do you attribute the shift? And how, in fact, can you separate changes caused by the debates from changes caused by other factors?

CHAFFEE: There was a very small shift in favor of Ford from before to immediately after the first debate, and a rather larger shift in the esteem in which Ford was held from before to a day or two after the first debate, because the press made much of the fact that Ford had done so well and Carter had done so poorly. After the second debate, it was just the reverse. At first there was a minuscule shift from before to immediately after the debate. Then, after Ford held a press conference the next morning and tried to explain that he did not say what he meant to say about Eastern Europe, there was a shift away from Ford.

The result of the first two debates was approximately a net gain of, say, 1 percent for Ford in terms of vote intention, according to the Gallup polls, from well before to well after both debates. In the last debate Carter picked up a little more. We tried to estimate the overall net shift by weighting the various types and directions of shifts. We concluded that Carter got probably a 1 percent net advantage—or nothing—from the debates as a whole.

JEANE J. KIRKPATRICK, American Enterprise Institute: I am interested in the research problem raised by Tom Mann: How do you isolate the effects of the debates from all other factors? Jack Dennis, if I heard you right, you said that the debates stimulated attention to campaign events, and that people with high exposure to the debates were stimulated, presumably, to pay more attention to other campaign events.

How do you know that? How do you know that people who were paying more attention to campaign events were not also paying more attention to the debates? One, how did you try to isolate the effects of the debates? This question also affects judgments about whether the debates or the election as a whole was more responsible for increasing confidence in the system. And two, on what ground do you make that causal inference?

DENNIS: One of the ways to sort this out is by measuring the responses of a panel at different times to find out, for example, what exposure people report for themselves at time one, and then at time two what sort of campaign communication of other kinds they engage in.

JEANE J. KIRKPATRICK: Did you ask them, "Do you think watching the debates has caused you to be more interested in other campaign events, or did you just watch television during the campaign?"

CHAFFEE: No, we were not particularly interested in that question, because it is self-reportive of influence. We asked them what their use of various media was at each point.

DENNIS: Because we have the different times sorted out, we can say what is different about them; this cannot be done in the usual kind of electoral study because it has no short-term process analysis. It is true we cannot control everything that happened, but we do have at least some insight from a little causal model. It is a simple recursive model that shows what doing something at time one does for doing some other things at time two. We can actually see the process of change going on.

CHAFFEE: As Jack Dennis says, our general strategy for isolating any effect of the debates or of any other intervening event is to take ad-

105

vantage of our panel design and control. The first predictor variable in any equation is the same measure at the previous time. In other words, we take a person's vote intention before the debates as the first predictor of the person's vote intention after the debates, so that all we account for is change.

4

The 1976 Presidential Debates: A Republican Perspective

Richard B. Cheney

The concept of debates between President Ford and Governor Carter was an integral part of the Ford general election campaign strategy in 1976. The decision to challenge Governor Carter to debate was based on the unique set of circumstances the Ford campaign faced in the summer of 1976 and on the experiences of the candidate and campaign staff in the contest for the Republican presidential nomination.

The Campaign for the Republican Nomination

At the beginning of 1976, President Ford began his campaign for reelection in an unusual situation for an incumbent. As a result of his having come to power under the Twenty-fifth Amendment, his name had never appeared on a ballot outside the Fifth Congressional District of Michigan. Since no national Ford organization was in place from a prior campaign, one had to be built, especially in key primary states.

Though the economy was improving, the nation was still experiencing the residue of high unemployment and high inflation after having weathered the worst recession in decades. The economic situation, the legacy of Watergate, and the Nixon pardon had served to erode the President's standing with the public. His approval rating, as measured by Gallup, had fallen sharply from August of 1974 to below 40 percent in the spring of 1975. It rose above 50 percent briefly at the time of the Mayaguez incident in the summer of that year but remained well under 50 percent throughout the rest of 1975.

In November, one year before the election, former Governor Ronald Reagan had announced that he would be a candidate for the Republican nomination for president; as events would later demonstrate, he was a formidable opponent. A nationwide poll conducted by NBC News in early December had shown that Governor Reagan held a four percentage point lead over President Ford among Republicans. Ford's private polls were producing similar results.

Thus, as the election year opened, we on Ford's campaign staff felt we had no choice but to campaign aggressively in each of the major early primaries. We simply did not have the option of staying in the White House through the primary season as previous presidents had done when seeking reelection. The necessity of campaigning actively in the spring had a direct bearing on the later decision to issue the debate challenge in the fall contest with Governor Carter.

The Primaries

In spite of the narrow victory in New Hampshire, the Ford campaign went on to win primaries by comfortable margins in Massachusetts, Florida, and Illinois. By the time of the North Carolina primary in late March, there was considerable speculation that Governor Reagan would be forced to drop out before long, and that the Republican contest would be wrapped up within a matter of weeks.

North Carolina, however, proved to be a major stumbling block for the Ford campaign. Governor Reagan's surprising victory there gave new life to his efforts and ensured that the second wave of primaries, beginning with Texas on May 1, would be hotly contested. After winning all 100 delegates in Texas, the governor went on to impressive wins in Alabama, Georgia, Indiana, and Nebraska in the next ten days. By the middle of May it was clear that the struggle for the Republican nomination would not be finally resolved until August at the Kansas City convention.

After the final primaries in California, New Jersey, and Ohio on June 8, the remainder of the summer was devoted to wooing small groups of delegates, either in Washington, D.C., or during visits to key convention states such as Missouri, Connecticut, and Mississippi. The bulk of our resources had to be devoted to the continuing contest for the nomination because of our inability to lay to rest the Reagan challenge.

One of the products of having to campaign from January through August was that the President came to be publicly perceived more as a candidate than as President. Although his active campaigning was instrumental in winning important primaries in New Hampshire, Florida, Michigan, and Ohio and in carrying important convention states such as Mississippi, the nationwide impact was negative. Instead of presidential travel to Peking and Moscow, we found it essential to arrange candidate appearances in Peoria and Miami. Instead of spending the summer as a secure incumbent watching the Democrats struggle, we found it necessary to do battle for the Republican nomination while Governor Carter sat in Plains planning his fall campaign.

In presenting this review, I do not want to imply any criticism of Governor Reagan or his campaign. While the GOP contest was obviously an important factor in setting the stage for the fall contest, the problems we encountered were due to the fact that we failed to win decisively early on. I believe it can be persuasively argued that, without a contest of some kind in our own party, the Ford campaign organization would have been in much worse shape than it was by Labor Day. We learned a great deal about our operations and capabilities as a result of having to surmount the governor's nearly successful drive for the nomination.

The Democrats

In late April and early May President Ford was still winning head-to-head trial heats with potential Democratic opponents in the polls. By early June, when it became obvious that Governor Carter would be the Democratic nominee, things changed rapidly. With the collapse of all Democratic opposition to Carter immediately after the final round of primaries, we suddenly found ourselves in the position of the underdog. By the time of the Democratic convention in July, polls by both Gallup and Harris showed Governor Carter with a lead exceeding thirty percentage points.

The governor looked like a winner. He had designed and carried out a masterful campaign. Beginning as relatively unknown, he had defeated all his competitors for the Democratic nomination by mid-June, some two months before there would be a definitive answer to the question of who would run on the Republican ticket. By midsummer, neither Ford nor Reagan appeared to have any serious prospect of overtaking Carter by November.

Planning the Fall Campaign

Some planning for the general election contest as well as for the preconvention period had been undertaken by the Ford organization in late 1975, but focused efforts to design the fall campaign plan did not really begin until June, at the conclusion of the California and Ohio primaries. Planning was delayed by the need to devote time and energy to the hunt for Ford delegates, and we were hampered by the legal requirement that money raised for the primaries could not be spent for general election purposes and by our efforts to ensure that White House personnel were not misused for campaign purposes. When planning did begin in June and July, most of the work was done by a small group of campaign and White House officials working evenings and weekends.

The draft plan was presented to the President some two weeks before the Kansas City convention. Changes were made at his discretion over the next few weeks, but many decisions were postponed until the President met with his aides and advisors in Vail during the week immediately following the convention.

The Debate Option

The possibility of challenging Governor Carter to a series of debates was first raised in mid-June in a memo prepared by Foster Channock and Mike Duval of the White House staff. The memo urged consideration of the debate option as part of a "no campaign" campaign strategy. The basic idea was that continuing to pursue the aggressive style of traditional campaigning that had been necessary in the spring would guarantee our defeat in November. As part of a package of proposals prepared after discussions with our pollster, Bob Teeter of Market Opinion Research, debates were suggested as a means of de-emphasizing traditional campaigning, maximizing the advantages of incumbency, and forcing Governor Carter to deal substantively with issues. Specifically, Channock and Duval recommended that Carter be challenged to a series of four debates on domestic affairs, the economy, national defense, and foreign policy. Although not all the recommendations in this memo were adopted, they were based on an underlying set of considerations that shaped our overall strategy.

The debate option was discussed with the President and became an integral part of the final draft of the campaign plan. The President gave instructions to keep the possibility of debates as secret as possible to preserve the element of surprise. He wanted to include the challenge to debate in his acceptance speech in Kansas City in August. To avoid any leaks, it was not mentioned in any draft of the speech. A few hours before the speech was delivered, the President himself inserted the challenge to Jimmy Carter to debate in the fall campaign.

The Ford Strategy

As serious planning efforts began in July, the outlook for the fall was fairly bleak. Our campaign strategy had to begin with a realistic appraisal of the situation. Even though the very large gap between the two candidates was expected to close somewhat once the Republican contest was resolved, we still were faced with a unique situation for an incumbent president.

No president had ever overcome the obstacles to reelection that we expected to face after the convention. President Truman's great victory over Dewey in 1948 was often suggested as a historical precedent for coming from behind. But on close analysis, the 1948 experience offered little solace. President Truman had been only eleven points behind Dewey in the polls in the summer of 1948. We expected to be some twenty points behind at the close of our convention, and the lateness of the convention meant we would have only seventy-three days in which to overtake our opponent.

Furthermore, several constraints could not be altered no matter which strategy we pursued, and they would make our task even more difficult.

1. We were the minority party. Among voters, the Democrats outnumbered Republicans more than two to one (43 percent to 21 percent). Truman's success in 1948 had been possible in part because he was building on the base of the majority party.
2. Under the new campaign laws and given the necessity of accepting federal funding, our campaign expenditures would be matched dollar for dollar by the Carter campaign. We would not be able to spend more than our opponent.
3. The GOP convention was late. The party would be divided after the struggle for the nomination, and we would have little time to devote to binding up the wounds.
4. Unlike previous incumbents, we could not campaign by wooing various voter blocs with promises of massive new government programs. Budget dollars were not available to fund extensive new spending programs, and broken promises of previous candidates had undermined the utility of such an approach. Most important, the President's philosophy and record of asking the public to make short-term sacrifices in return for long-term gains (energy proposals, legislative vetoes, and economic policies) ruled out such a strategy. Changing our philosophy in midstream would have been bad policy and would have led to widespread criticism.

Our goal had to be to win enough popular votes to carry enough states to obtain the required 270 electoral votes. To reach that objective, we would have to close a twenty-point gap in seventy-three days, while working from the base of a minority party and spending the same amount of money as our opponent.

The Carter Lead

Although the Carter lead appeared formidable in July, we were convinced that it would decrease significantly as we drew closer to Labor Day. We believed that much of his support was very soft and based primarily on his media image as a "winner." Governor Carter had risen from relative obscurity almost overnight and was suddenly a major national figure by virtue of his victories in the primaries. After the Democratic convention, we believed his popularity would decline without more "victories" to sustain it. His image as a winner would fade as his primary successes receded into the past and other aspects of his candidacy came to the fore.

A careful analysis of the results of the Democratic primaries indicated that he had not been as formidable as his presence at the top of the Democratic ticket implied. Governor Carter had never received more than 54 percent of the vote in a contested primary. He never won in a two-man, head-to-head race. Finally, he had been defeated in eight out of the last eleven contested primaries.

Thus, we anticipated that his rapid rise in the polls might well be followed by a fairly rapid decline, and that he would prove more vulnerable than most people expected in a head-to-head contest with President Ford. We believed that the governor's support was susceptible of erosion once the public came to know him better. The outlook was therefore not totally pessimistic. We believed that with the right strategy and a few breaks we could win on November 2.

Campaign Style

In spite of our optimism that the Carter lead would diminish substantially by Labor Day, we obviously still faced a difficult problem. We were so far behind that we had to conduct a very aggressive come-from-behind campaign to have any prospect of winning. Ford was not in a position to spend September and October in the White House ignoring his opponent, as had some of his predecessors. At the same time, we had ample evidence that aggressive campaigning in the past had harmed the President's standing in the eyes of the public. Survey research undertaken in the summer of 1976 had picked up disturbing, but not surprising, evidence that a portion of the public increasingly perceived the President as too political. He was criticized by some for spending too much time on politics and not enough time on the people's business. We also believed that declines in the President's popularity during his two years in office had coincided with, and to some extent been caused by, periods of active partisan campaigning.

The Ford presidency had enjoyed a very brief honeymoon during August of 1974, which came to an end with the issuance of the Nixon pardon in early September. During October and early November, after having been in office only two months, the President had undertaken a heavy schedule of campaign appearances on behalf of Republican House and Senate candidates in the 1974 elections. In July of 1975, after having been in office less than a year, it was announced formally that the President would be a candidate for reelection. The announcement was made early because of the need to build an organization and start fund-raising efforts and because we wanted to comply fully with the requirements of the campaign spending and reporting laws.

During the fall of that same year, we undertook a heavy schedule of appearances at state GOP fund-raisers. The party was in considerable disarray after the 1974 elections. Many state organizations had extensive debts, and the President's activities were instrumental in paying off those debts and raising party funds for the upcoming 1976 elections. We also knew that there would be little time to devote to such activities during the presidential election campaign itself. Finally, as mentioned above, extensive media coverage of the President's active campaign for the nomination had a negative effect nationwide and lessened the value of his number one asset—incumbency.

The problem was starkly portrayed on the cover of a weekly newsmagazine prior to the Republican convention. The cover gave equal billing to pictures of three candidates for the presidency—Governor Carter, Governor Reagan, and President Ford. In part because of extensive campaigning, the President had come to be perceived by many voters as just another candidate, rather than as President.

These conclusions played an important role in shaping the strategy for the fall campaign. One objective was to reemphasize the fact that our candidate was the incumbent. At the same time, we had to devise an approach that was aggressive without projecting the image of the President as just another candidate. Part of the answer was provided by the debates.

Public Perceptions of the Candidates

As part of the planning process, the campaign staff spent a good deal of time analyzing the strengths and weaknesses of Governor Carter as perceived by the public. In citing his positive personal traits, those interviewed described the governor as a winner, a man with strong spiritual and moral values, an honest man of character, truly concerned about government efficiency, and dedicated to making government work better. On the negative side, he was perceived as somewhat arrogant and lacking in humility; a man who tried to be all things to all men; a man about whom very little was known; a man who was fuzzy on the issues and lacked the experience to be president.

With respect to his philosophy or general position on the issues, Governor Carter had indeed succeeded in being all things to all men. When asked to locate themselves and Governor Carter on a seven-point scale ranging from "extremely liberal" to "extremely conservative," respondents tended to place the governor very close to the point they chose for themselves. Thus, Republicans tended to identify the governor as somewhat conservative, ticket-splitters moved him closer to the middle of the spectrum, and Democrats perceived him as slightly liberal. They all saw significant similarities between their own views and their perceptions of Governor Carter's views.

A separate analysis, done by Market Opinion Research, reinforced this belief that a large number of voters perceived Jimmy Carter's views much as they perceived their own. Bob Teeter and his staff developed a perceptual map that graphically demonstrated the problem. The methodology permitted voters to locate on two dimensions their own philosophical attitudes on a variety of domestic and foreign policy issues, and also to indicate on the same dimensions the voters' perception of the views of the candidates. The results indicated clearly that Governor Carter occupied a position somewhat unique among major national political figures in the summer of 1976. The voters perceived him as having views much closer to their own than had President Ford or any other national political leader.

The governor had successfully avoided getting pinned down on many issues during the primaries. To the extent that he had taken positions, we believed he had done so with a certain amount of regional selectivity, and they had not been fully communicated to those who could be expected to disagree with him. Furthermore, we believed that the public's perception of the governor's position was based in part on the fact that he was very new to the national scene.

By contrast, we believed that the President's positions on major issues were better known. After two years in office, over fifty vetoes of legislation, and numerous proposals on everything from abortion and busing to taxes, we felt that any negative impact from the President's taking a firm position had already occurred, that the public had already discounted any significant differences they felt on specific concerns. This is not to say that all potential voters had a solid understanding of the administration's policies in every area. As in all campaigns, a large portion of the electorate either did not know what the President had done on a particular problem or incorrectly identified his position. But we did believe that when an issue had direct relevance for a particular group, the President's views were much better known in most cases than were Governor Carter's views. We did not expect any significant decline in our standing in the polls as a result of restating positions already articulated in the past.

We did not overestimate the role issues had played or would play in the campaign. With few exceptions, they had been relatively insignificant during the primaries, and the Ford campaign plan clearly indicated that issues, in and of themselves, were unlikely to have a significant impact on the outcome of the election. But they were felt to be significant in terms of how the candidates dealt with them— that is, they were useful tools for displaying those personal characteristics, or lack thereof, that might qualify a man to be president. At the same time, it was hoped that trying to force a greater focus on issues during the fall would benefit the Ford candidacy. As long as the public perceived Governor Carter as holding views very close to their own, our prospects of winning in November were slim indeed. If, on the other hand, we were successful in forcing greater specificity in his positions and communicating those views to those who disagreed with them, we would have a chance to peel off key voter groups in important states. One of our key objectives came to be changing the public's perceptions of Jimmy Carter.

These considerations supported the decision to challenge the governor to a series of debates. Debates offered the opportunity to encourage greater specificity on issues and provided maximum potential impact through instantaneous communication to millions of voters via television. If Governor Carter failed to be more specific, he would run the risk of increasing the number of people who perceived him as fuzzy and indecisive. We did not believe his "trust me" approach would be very effective in a debate setting when he was asked for specific views on major national issues.

Television

Throughout our deliberations, we were well aware of the enormous importance of television. Given the size of Governor Carter's lead, we would have to change the voting intentions of literally millions of Americans by election day. No matter how extensively the President campaigned, it would have been impossible to reach enough people in person to achieve the desired result. Therefore, we operated on the assumption that personal appearances were useful only to the extent that they received extensive favorable coverage on the evening news. Whatever strategy we adopted had to take into account the reality that any activity which did not receive extensive television coverage was likely to be wasted activity.

Although television was the only vehicle which offered the potential of reaching sufficient voters to turn the situation around by election day, in past elections the networks had not devoted much time to communicating the candidates' positions on the issues. The final draft of the campaign plan cited the work of Patterson and McClure on the 1972 campaign.[1] Their content analysis of the network evening news for the seven-week period from September 18 through November 6, 1972, demonstrated that all three networks had devoted considerably more attention to campaign activities such as rallies and motorcades than they had to issues:

	ABC	CBS	NBC
Total coverage for all issues (minutes)	35	46	26
Average coverage for each issue (seconds)	80	105	60
Total for campaign activities (minutes)	141	122	130

Patterson and McClure also indicated that there was much more issue content in 1972 in the paid political advertising of the two candidates than on the evening news. This does not necessarily mean the networks had chosen to ignore issues. It could simply be a reflection of the way the 1972 campaign was conducted by the candidates. Regardless of the reason, the findings had significance for our planning efforts.

Although we had to rely on television to convey our message, we also recognized that little would be communicated about the policy

[1] Thomas E. Patterson and Robert D. McClure, *The Unseeing Eye: The Myth of Television Power in National Politics* (New York: G. P. Putnam's Sons, 1976).

views of the two candidates if we pursued a conventional campaign strategy. If we gave them rallies and motorcades, that would be the message conveyed to the public. The traditional campaign hoopla was not ignored—we undertook our fair share of riverboat rides, train trips, and balloon drops. But our objective of encouraging a greater focus on Governor Carter's policy views could not be achieved with a conventional approach.

A series of televised debates offered an opportunity to reach the maximum number of voters in a setting designed to focus attention on substantive issues. We did not expect to change the nature of the campaign in seventy-three days, nor did we believe that issues would replace the importance of the personal attributes and characteristics of the candidates. Indeed, we wanted to emphasize the President's personal strengths as well as what research told us were Carter's weaknesses. We also believed that by showing our opponent and the President responding to specific questions about their views on substantive issues, the debates would play to our strengths and to Governor Carter's weaknesses and might convince a number of voters that they disagreed with him in certain areas, something they did not believe in July.

The Arguments for and against Debates

As we developed the campaign strategy, we were very much aware that arguments could be mustered against the idea of debates. The traditional wisdom was that an incumbent president did not debate his challenger, but then this was not a traditional incumbency. The concern that debates would place President Ford and the governor on an equal plane in the eyes of the public was of little consequence. Frankly, we would have been delighted in July to have been perceived on "equal" terms.

While it was true that televised debates would give Governor Carter extensive exposure to the public, just as it would President Ford, we believed this would serve to decrease his lead in the campaign. On the basis of our analysis of his strength in the polls, the softness of his support, and his ability to seem all things to all people, we wanted the governor to have such exposure; it was thought necessary if we were to win.

We also considered the experience of Kennedy and Nixon in the 1960 debates. To the extent that physical and stylistic factors were important in public perceptions of who would "win" or "lose" the debates, we believed our candidate would come off very well. The

President's physical size and presence presented none of the negatively perceived personal characteristics which had supposedly caused Nixon to lose the first debate to Kennedy in 1960.

Substantively, the President was well equipped to enter the debates. From his service on the Hill and his two years as President he possessed a wealth of information about the functions of government. He had spent his entire professional career wrestling with the kinds of issues that were bound to come up in the course of the debates. In the past he had done very well in similar formats. In January of that year, the President had given the annual briefing on the federal budget, thus becoming the first President in nearly thirty years to do so. A format which let him respond to questions had always been more effective for him than a formal set speech.

In addition to the arguments cited above for deciding to debate, there were the President's own strong feelings on the subject. During his congressional career, he had frequently participated in debates in his reelection campaigns. The President had a strong personal desire to take on his opponent, and the whole concept of debates appealed to his competitive instincts.

The Strategy

By the time of the Kansas City convention, the broad outlines of the general election strategy had been determined, although much of the detail was left to be worked out at Vail after the convention.

The central element in the strategy was to hold active travel to a minimum until late in the campaign. When we did travel, the events would be designed to achieve maximum television impact. The centerpiece of the last ten days of campaigning, eventually developed by Bob Teeter and John Deardorff, were the half-hour specials broadcast on statewide television hook-ups in the large target states. We produced the shows ourselves, using video tape footage of the President and members of the first family campaigning in the state, and discussions between the President and Joe Garagiola of the issue in the campaign—the "Joe and Jerry Show."

When the President was in Washington we conducted what came to be known as the Rose Garden campaign. We expected our opponent to travel extensively throughout the fall, and we were confident that the news media, particularly the television networks, would cover all those events. Since the networks' measure of fairness consisted of giving both candidates equal time, whatever the President did during the day at the White House would also receive coverage on the evening news. We could therefore convey our message to the electorate, emphasizing that the President was the incumbent, and avoiding the pitfalls of too much campaign travel too soon.

To change the public's perception of Governor Carter, we relied heavily on our advertising program designed and produced by Doug Bailey and John Deardorff. The advertising campaign itself made a major contribution to our success in closing the gap during the fall and deserves far more extensive treatment than I can give it here.

The debates would give Governor Carter's policy views the exposure they had previously lacked and would perhaps help persuade several million Americans that he disagreed with them on several issues. More important, the debate challenge satisfied the need to mount an aggressive, come-from-behind campaign and provided a justification for staying off the campaign trail as much as possible. Our unconventional circumstances called for an unconventional response. We had few alternatives.

As we departed Kansas City for Vail, we felt we had achieved everything that could reasonably be expected, given the circumstances. The Reagan challenge was finally ended. We had maintained an effective, if sometimes tenuous, control of the convention, and the intraparty wounds created by the long preconvention struggle appeared to be healing rapidly. The President's acceptance address to the convention and the nation had clearly been one of the finest of his career. The debate challenge had achieved its desired result. In the opening round of the fall campaign, we had captured the initiative and gone on the offensive. The President had come out swinging, and the Carter campaign was forced to react to us in spite of their substantial lead and status as the challenger. This in turn provided time for a much needed rest and for completing detailed arrangements for the general election contest.

Preparation for the Debates

The negotiations establishing the ground rules for the debates were somewhat protracted, but once the challenge had been issued and accepted, there was never any question about going ahead with them. Our negotiating posture was based on the assumption that the more exposure provided the candidates, the better. We asked for lengthy sessions on specified subjects with follow-up questions from the panel. In return for agreement on these items, we agreed to specify no subject matter for the final debate and to take up foreign and defense matters in the second debate rather than in the first as we had originally suggested.

During the weeks preceding the first debate in Philadelphia on

September 23, the President and part of the staff devoted considerable time to preparing for the event. We obtained film of the Kennedy-Nixon debates of 1960 and reviewed them with a special focus on the supposedly decisive first debate. We also viewed video tapes of appearances by Governor Carter in debates and on talk shows during the primaries.

Extensive briefing books were prepared, including material on the policy positions of both the administration and the governor. Some of the most useful information concerned Mr. Carter's record as governor of Georgia. Much of this material was used during the first debate and later included in our advertising. We also developed questions that we expected would be asked and reviewed the published works of the panelists to ascertain their areas of expertise and interest.

We conducted several dry runs, with the President taking questions from staff people on the subjects we expected to come up in the first debate. Our preparations were as complete and comprehensive as we could make them. We did not spend as much time preparing for the second and third debates, because there was less time to do so and we did not feel it was necessary to repeat all the activities undertaken before the first debate.

Measuring the Impact of the Debates

The Ford campaign used two research methods to measure the impact of the debates. During the actual course of the debates, we collected data from an instant response analysis of a panel of registered voters. The panels consisted of approximately fifty voters from the Spokane, Washington, area. Each of the respondents had declared themselves to be undecided when asked about their voting intention prior to viewing the debate, although some of them were classified as "leaning" toward Ford or Carter. Our assumption was that the debates would have little effect on voters firmly committed to one or the other of the candidates. The composition of the panels was designed to give us as much information as possible about the reactions of voters who had not yet made up their minds.

Each member of the panel was equipped with a dial mechanism labeled from zero to one hundred. Zero indicated that the respondent was feeling much closer to Governor Carter and one hundred indicated that they were feeling much closer to President Ford. A value of fifty was an indication that the panelist was not leaning toward either man. Members of the panel were instructed before the debate to set their dial at a value that described their attitude as being closer to

Ford, closer to Carter, or in the middle. The panelists were to move the dial toward zero in response to positive feelings about Governor Carter and toward one hundred for positive feelings about President Ford.

The dial mechanisms were tied in with a computer, and throughout the broadcast the responses were summed continuously and a means calculated for the entire group as well as for two subgroups: those who at the beginning of the broadcast had been identified as leaning toward the governor or toward the President. Finally, these continuous average scores were superimposed on a video tape of the debate for later viewing and analysis. This system provided useful information on the reaction of a group of uncommitted voters to the arguments and presentations of the two candidates. It was helpful in shaping our approach to later debates and enabled us to highlight those issues on which the President scored most heavily against the governor, and vice versa.

Our second research effort involved nationwide telephone surveys conducted as part of the ongoing research program for the campaign. These surveys were not limited to measuring reactions to the debates, although questions were included that produced data on the impact of the debates.[2] Prior to the first debate, between September 10 and September 14, Market Opinion Research (MOR) conducted a nationwide telephone survey of a sample of 1,500 registered voters. Beginning on the evening of September 23, as the first debate ended, 758 of these individuals were reinterviewed. In both predebate and postdebate interviews, data were collected on the voters' perceptions of the issue positions of the candidates as well as on their personal attributes and abilities to deal with various problems, such as unemployment and inflation.

Immediately after the second debate, MOR conducted another nationwide telephone survey of approximately 500 registered voters. We did not do a predebate study in conjunction with the second debate. By the time of the third debate, we did not conduct any additional national surveys. Such a survey would have had no real value from the standpoint of making decisions about the conduct of the campaign during the few days remaining before the election, and all our resources were by then committed to tracking developments in the target states.

We of course followed the results of the postdebate polls conducted by the Associated Press and the Roper organization, but for

[2] I am indebted to Bob Teeter and Fred Steeper of Market Opinion Research for making available materials used in this section.

our purposes they provided little useful information. Responses to the simple question of who won or lost a particular debate did not, in my opinion, shed much light on the impact of the debates on the voting intentions of those who had not yet made up their minds. Their greatest significance, perhaps, lay in the convenient tool they gave the press and public to "judge" the debates and draw some conclusions about them. We had to deal with the results of those surveys because they tended to shape press reaction and commentary after a debate. But they had little relevance for assessing the progress of the campaign, especially when the two organizations produced conflicting conclusions about which candidate had "won," as occurred after the final debate.

The First Debate

The research undertaken in conjunction with the first debate indicated that we had made significant progress in several areas. The analysis of the instant responses of the Spokane panel showed the President had done very well overall, and the national pre- and postdebate surveys provided evidence that the public's information about the candidates' positions had increased and their perceptions of the personal attributes of the President had been strengthened.

According to the results of the panel study, the President had scored very well whenever he talked about taxes. On four separate occasions during the ninety-minute debate, he had raised the issue in some form, each time generating a very positive reaction on the part of the respondents. The President also scored very high when he talked about crime and when he criticized Carter's record during his term as governor of Georgia and his spending proposals. Governor Carter had been most successful on the subjects of the bureaucratic mess in Washington, the energy crisis, and the need for tax reform.

The results also indicated the importance of giving full and complete answers to each question. The instant response analysis clearly demonstrated that the President had the greatest impact on those leaning toward Carter when he took the time to explain his position on an issue and his reasons for holding that view. A fairly lengthy answer moved the "Carter leaners" a significant distance toward a pro-Ford response, but brief answers did not provide sufficient explanations to overcome their bias. At the same time, the scores for the subgroup composed of "Ford leaners" did not drop off even during a lengthy response. As a result, we altered our original belief that short, punchy answers were sometimes desirable and sought to emphasize lengthier answers in later debates.

The data generated in the pre- and postdebate telephone surveys provided solid support for the proposition that those interviewed had obtained considerable information on the issue positions of the candidates. The predebate interviews had asked about abortion, busing, welfare spending, national health insurance, the legalization of marijuana, and defense spending, but these issues were not included in the postdebate survey because they were not discussed during the first debate. On three issues, we obtained both pre- and postdebate measures of the amount of information the viewers possessed about the candidates' positions: amnesty for Vietnam-era draft resisters, the use of public funds to guarantee jobs, and the alternative of stimulating the development of jobs in the private sector. After the debate there was a significant shift from the predebate responses of "don't know" to "it depends" to identification of Ford's or Carter's stand on each issue.[3]

On the question of amnesty, the number of voters correctly identifying President Ford's position (against) increased from 40 to 60 percent between the predebate and postdebate surveys, and the "don't know" category declined from 29 to 13 percent. In the predebate survey, 53 percent indicated Governor Carter was in favor of an amnesty program; after the debates, this had increased to 70 percent, and the "don't know" category declined from 33 to 16 percent.

On the question of using federal funds to guarantee jobs, there was similar movement. Those citing President Ford as being opposed to such guarantees rose from 35 to 58 percent; the "don't know" category declined from 43 to 22 percent. The number citing Governor Carter as being in favor of federal guarantees increased from 44 to 71 percent, and the "don't know" category declined from 45 to 22 percent.

Changes in the amount of information the public possessed about the candidates' position on the question of stimulating jobs in the private sector were not as pronounced but were still significant. Before the debate, 46 percent believed President Ford supported this proposition, 8 percent said he was against it, 43 percent said they did not know what he thought. After the debate, 63 percent said the President was for the concept, 16 percent against, and 21 percent said they did not know. Those citing Governor Carter as being in favor of

3 Andrew Morrison, Frederick Steeper, and Susan Greendale, "The First 1976 Presidential Debate: The Voters Win," paper presented at the annual meeting of the American Association of Public Opinion Research, Buck Hills Falls, Pa., May 1977.

stimulating jobs in the private sector increased from 39 to 45 percent, those saying he opposed the idea increased from 12 to 27 percent, and the "don't knows" declined from 46 to 28 percent.

The postdebate survey also indicated we had improved the respondents' perceptions of President Ford's leadership qualities and his ability to deal with specific problems. During the interviews, registered voters had been asked to identify which of the candidates they most trusted to make the right decision, which was most effective in dealing with tough problems, and which demonstrated the most concern for the average citizen. On the question of trust, President Ford had the edge before the debate (45 percent to 36 percent for Carter). After the debate, the President had increased his lead somewhat to 48 percent with only 35 percent citing Governor Carter as being more trustworthy. Before the debate, both candidates had been viewed as being equally effective in dealing with tough problems—39 percent for each. After the debate, President Ford had a slight advantage: 44 percent viewed him as more effective, compared with 41 percent for Governor Carter. On concern for the average citizen, Governor Carter clearly had the edge (Carter 46 percent and Ford 28 percent) in the predebate survey and maintained it in the postdebate survey (48 to 31 percent).

The voters were also asked to indicate their perception of the relative capabilities of the two candidates to deal with problems such as inflation, unemployment, holding down taxes, reducing crime, running the federal government, handling foreign affairs, and maintaining a strong national defense. On all seven items, perceptions of President Ford improved between the predebate and postdebate surveys from two to nine percentage points. For Governor Carter, the maximum gain had been two percentage points and in one instance he suffered a decline of six points.

On five of the seven issues, President Ford had the advantage going into the debate. Governor Carter had a clear advantage on the issue of reducing unemployment, and there was no significant difference on the seventh issue, combating crime. The debates did not reverse any of these advantages, but the number of voters citing President Ford as being more capable of handling these problems increased, and the percentage taking a "don't know" or middle ground position had declined from two to five percentage points on each item.

Obviously, some caution is in order in interpreting these results. A definitive judgment about the impact of the debates would require a far more rigorous analysis than is possible here or can be supported by the data we collected during the 1976 campaign. Our predebate and postdebate surveys did not permit us to separate out the influence of other factors, and many other developments over the ten-day period separating the surveys could have accounted for some of the changes observed. For example, even though foreign policy and defense were not discussed during the debates, we observed changes in the voters' perceptions of the candidates' ability to handle these issues. The administration's diplomatic efforts in southern Africa could have had an impact, or changes in the President's perceived ability to deal with domestic issues could have rubbed off on public perceptions of his ability to function in the area of foreign policy. In addition, Governor Carter had been actively campaigning around the country, and President Ford had appeared repeatedly in the Rose Garden to comment on issues and developments in the campaign.

Our research effort was not designed to generate a rigorous and definitive judgment of the relative impact of the debates on the public. The intent was to measure progress toward our goal of winning on November 2 and to gather information that would be useful in running the campaign and implementing the campaign strategy. Data focusing on the debates were useful in highlighting which aspects to emphasize in the future and in making relatively minor adjustments in our approach. But at that point, late September, the strategy was set and could not be changed significantly. The only data of any relevance were those that might affect how we implemented that strategy.

On the basis of the information available, we judged the first debate a success. We believed the President had scored well on a number of key points, that we had enhanced the voters' understanding of the candidates' issue positions, strengthened the President's image as a leader, and gained ground on the question of his ability to deal with difficult problems. It was clear we had reached a large portion of the electorate. According to our surveys, some 89 percent of all registered voters had seen or heard the first debate.

The Second Debate

A good deal has been written about the impact or lack of impact of the second Ford-Carter debate on the outcome of the 1976 election. Most attention has focused on the President's misstatement concerning the degree of Soviet influence in Eastern Europe. My own view is that it was not as decisive as some have suggested.

There is no question that the second debate was less successful from our standpoint than the first had been. In my opinion, however, its impact was more significant on the press than on the public at large. This in turn had an impact on the public after the fact and became a problem which had to be dealt with. But I do not believe the Eastern European statement determined the outcome of the election.

I viewed the second debate on a television set in the President's holding room backstage at the theater in San Francisco. My initial reaction, before seeing any results from our research, was that the President had done well on substance. I was aware that his response to the question on the Soviet role in Eastern Europe had not been accurate, but I also knew what he meant and hoped that the public would also. I felt Governor Carter had improved his style and the way he handled himself since the first debate. But I also believed that substantively he had made a weak showing. Admittedly, I was not then, and may not be now, totally objective about the relative ability of the two men to conduct U.S. foreign policy.

My view at the time was based on a feeling that the President had been very effective in discussing U.S.-Soviet relations, SALT, the defense budget, China, and our arms policy in the Middle East. Governor Carter, on the other hand, had been vague when asked which elements of U.S. foreign policy he disagreed with. I did not believe his comments had demonstrated any deep understanding of the problems the United States faced in the world. When he had scored rhetorically, I felt his comments had focused on the form rather than the substance of national security concerns.

The seriousness of the problem was brought home by the press corps shortly after the second debate ended. As we had done after the first debate, Brent Scowcroft, the President's national security advisor, Stu Spencer of the campaign committee, and I met with the press to respond to their questions. We knew we had a problem when the first question put to us was, "Are there Soviet troops in Poland?"

As mentioned previously, the research efforts for the second debate were less extensive than for the first. We did not do a pre-debate survey, but we conducted an instant response analysis in Spokane and a nationwide telephone survey of some 500 registered voters that began immediately after the debate on the West Coast and continued through the next evening.

The Spokane panel analysis, when compared with the results for the first debate, showed generally lower (that is, more pro-Carter) scores for the second debate. Part of this may have been due to the predebate inclinations of the respondents. They had set their dials at a value reflecting how close they felt to either of the candidates before the debate began, and the average score was some five points below that for the first debate.

Nonetheless, it was clear that the governor had scored better than in the first debate. The President had scored well at the outset on the question of Communist involvement in the Italian government and again toward the close in discussing the Mayaguez incident and the Arab boycott. In the central portion of the debate, the President's remarks on negotiations with the Soviets, his opposition to selling arms to the Chinese, and his comments about Korea had generated positive responses. Governor Carter, however, had generated more positive responses in his criticisms of secret diplomacy and arms sales to Iran, in his call for fireside chats to discuss foreign policy, and on his comments about nuclear proliferation, the Arab boycott, and the Panama Canal.

The panel study showed virtually no immediate impact with respect to the President's comments on Eastern Europe. Average scores during the debate swung from a low of 29 (pro-Carter) to a high of 64 (pro-Ford). During the exchange on Eastern Europe between Max Frankel and the President, the average score held fairly stable between 44 and 48. It was clear the comments failed to generate any positive response, but neither was there any immediate negative reaction.

The nationwide postdebate survey also indicated a delayed re-action to this portion of the debates.[4] At the time, we had immediate access only to the raw data collected in the interviews. On October 6, the night of the debate, 101 interviews were conducted on the West Coast. Because of the lateness of the hour in the East, however, inter-viewing there took place the following day between 9:00 A.M. and midnight (EST), when 397 respondents were questioned. Care had to be exercised in evaluating the data over time, because we did not have matched national samples. But there were substantial shifts in voter perceptions between Wednesday night and Thursday night, even allowing for the built-in bias of having all of the interviews on the first night conducted in the West.

The first wave of interviews showed that President Ford was perceived as having done the better job in the debate by a margin of nine percentage points. The interviews taken the next night showed a drastic reversal, and Governor Carter had taken a substantial lead on this item. Throughout the twenty-four-hour period there was a de-cline in pro-Ford responses and a corresponding increase in pro-Carter responses. Morrison's paper, mentioned above, corrects for the built-in bias of using only results taken from subgroups of the total sample and validates the basic conclusion of serious erosion over time.

Respondents were also asked to specify what they felt each

---

[4] Morrison and others have covered this material in some detail (ibid.).

candidate had done well and not done well during the debates. On Wednesday evening, immediately after the debate, not a single respondent mentioned President Ford's comments on Eastern Europe. Yet by the next evening, 20 percent of the 121 interviews conducted after 5:00 P.M. mentioned this statement as one of the things he had not done well. In my mind, the data indicate that for much of the viewing public, the misstatement about the status of Eastern Europe was not a significant item until it received extensive comment and coverage in the press after the debate. Regardless of whether the public perceived it as a problem immediately or only after being told it was by the media, we still faced the task of clarifying the situation over the next several days.

The second debate obviously was not a plus for the Ford campaign. It created difficulties in several areas. The debate and the commentary afterward generated a negative reaction from the public. It cost us time as the issue ran its course and placed us on the defensive for the next several days as we clarified the President's position. Furthermore, the intense focus on Eastern Europe meant that little or no attention was paid to what I felt were substantive weaknesses in the Carter presentation—specifically his denial of ever having advocated a $15 billion cut in the defense budget, and his charge that the Ford administration had been responsible for overthrowing a democratically elected government in Chile. (The Chilean coup had occurred during the Nixon years.) Finally, I did not believe the governor had demonstrated any broad understanding of U.S. foreign policy. But all of this proved to be of little consequence as we tried to cope with reaction to the statement on Eastern Europe.

Another problem that affected our campaign during the same period was the publicity given the investigation by the Watergate special prosecutor into allegations that President Ford had misused campaign funds while he was a member of Congress. We were able to correct the difficulties stemming from the second debate by making clear the President's views on Eastern Europe and meeting with political leaders of the relevant ethnic groups. But there was absolutely nothing we could do to alleviate the impact of extensive coverage of the special prosecutor's activities. We were confident that we would ultimately obtain a clean bill of health when the prosecutor found there was no substance to the charges, but we had no way of knowing when that would be. All we could do was to deny the allegations, but such statements are hardly designed to win over voters in the midst of a come-from-behind presidential campaign, especially in light of the track record for previous White House denials of allegations being investigated by the special prosecutor. For the Ford campaign, the latter problem was more serious and difficult to cope with than was the controversy over the second debate.

The Third Debate

As we prepared for the final debate October 22 in Williamsburg, circumstances improved considerably for the Ford campaign. The special prosecutor had closed his investigation, the flap over Eastern Europe faded, and the polls showed continued erosion in Governor Carter's lead. In the major target states, our polls showed us moving to within striking distance.

The third debate took on less significance for us than the first two. We had less time to prepare, and by then debates between the candidates had become somewhat routine, not only for the public but also for the campaigners. The debate itself turned out to be routine, generating no real surprises for either side. Our own research activities were shifted to tracking developments in the handful of big states which we felt would determine the outcome of the election.

Our primary focus during the last ten days of the campaign moved away from the debates and onto our advertising campaign and a heavy schedule of travel in the large electoral vote states. One of our more successful efforts was the television shows we produced ourselves in six of those states. They permitted us to reach the maximum number of people at a very low cost. To the extent we were able to close in on Carter in those final days, I believe these activities were more significant than the third and final debate.

Conclusion

A year after the election, with the benefit of hindsight, I still believe the decision to include the debate option in our 1976 campaign strategy was the right one. Given the circumstances we faced in the summer before the convention and the size of our opponent's lead, we had few alternatives. The debate challenge satisfied our need to mount an aggressive campaign without having to spend all our time on the road throughout the months of September and October.

Beyond the dynamics of the campaign itself, I believe it is very difficult to separate out the debates from other activities and determine exactly their impact on the election day result. It seems clear that the debate challenge gave the Ford campaign the initiative at the close of the Kansis City convention and that the first debate was a major plus for the President. The second debate clearly went to Carter in the public mind and threw the Ford organization off stride for several days. There appears to be a consensus that the third debate was somewhat anticlimatic and did not have much impact one way or the other.

I believe the evidence supports the contention that the debates did increase public awareness about the positions of the candidates on issues, although some of that would certainly have occurred without the debates. It would be a mistake, however, to conclude that this was their only impact. Although we did not collect much information on this point, it seems clear that the voters also judged the candidates in the debates on general perceptions of their personal qualities and competence.

While the debates did provide a means by which candidates could communicate directly with the voters via television, the role of the news media was substantial in interpreting the events after the fact. After both the first and second debates, we believed the press commentary served to magnify the actual outcome and to shape voter sentiment even though the voters had seen the event themselves.

In the end, we were unable to overcome the Carter lead, and from that perspective our strategy was unsuccessful. But in the light of our July deficit of more than 30 percent, we felt we had run a successful campaign. I believe the debates were an important part of that success and would recommend them again under similar circumstances.

Discussion

STEVEN H. CHAFFEE, University of Wisconsin: The paper is fascinating, and I am going to use it and quote you a great deal. I want to ask you about something you rather glossed over. In the period between the convention and the debates, Ford picked up a lot of votes. Immediately after the convention, Ford issued the challenge. Did you get any data to indicate that the issuance of the challenge produced new support? Ford seemed to pick up a lot in that period, and yet you state that "the debate challenge satisfied our need to mount an aggressive come-from-behind campaign." Do you have any evidence on that?

CHENEY: No, I don't. The only data I have seen on the subject would be the work Bob Teeter did in connection with the campaign in 1976, and I don't believe he has anything that would indicate specifically why we closed as fast as we did in September.

I would not overemphasize the role of the debates. From the standpoint of the Ford campaign, we had really two general targets or areas of concern. One was the impact of the debates on the voters. The other was the impact on what I have generally referred to as "campaign dynamics." Ford's acceptance speech in Kansas City clearly was a major plus for the campaign. We thought it was good enough that we paid to rerun it again later on television. Other positive factors were that we left Kansas City having maintained effective, if somewhat tenuous, control of the convention; the acceptance address was a success; the Reagan challenge was over; and Jimmy Carter spent his time, in July and August, down in Plains planning the fall campaign and draining the fish pond.

All those things were working for us as we moved into September, so that we got the result we had anticipated at the outset. But I could not say that the closing of the gap between late July and early September, or even late September, was due specifically to the debate challenge. The debate challenge was important because it let us acquire a posture of going on the offensive as we came out of Kansas City, even though we were some thirty points behind and even though

131

Governor Carter was the challenger. That is what I would refer to, in general terms, as "campaign dynamics." Governor Carter was forced to react to us rather than the other way around.

How that is translated into impact on the voters, I don't know. The press as much as anything influences the immediate impact. Several things happened in September. Carter's campaign got off to a rocky start. The *Playboy* interview came out later in the month. The Rose Garden campaign that we pursued through most of September was very effective, I think, because it let us emphasize the fact that the President was the incumbent. It was based on the assumptions that Governor Carter would travel extensively, that he would get extensive coverage in the press when he traveled, and that the networks' measure of fairness was equal time. No matter what the President did during the course of each day, we knew we were going to get an equal amount of time on the evening news as long as Governor Carter was on the road. We went out into the Rose Garden and into the press briefing room and the Oval Office and conveyed our message. I think that had an important impact during those weeks in September.

MARGITA E. WHITE, Federal Communications Commission: I realize the main issue here is the presidential debates, but I am curious about the vice-presidential debate. Did you seek to monitor that debate also? What kind of coordination was there, and what are your thoughts about the merits of vice-presidential debates?

CHENEY: I don't have any data on the vice-presidential debate. We didn't make the kind of research effort there that we did on the others. My view is that it was not very important. Jack Dennis and Steve Chaffee may have picked up some information on the vice-presidential debate. As I recall, they said it was more decisive in terms of a public perception of who won or lost than any of the presidential debates. The vice-presidential debate was something we agreed to and we had to go through with, but it really was not crucial to what we were trying to do as we managed the campaign.

LOYE MILLER, JR., Chicago *Sun-Times*: Clearly there was a feeling among at least some of us who were covering the campaign that the vice-presidential debate probably had more to do with the outcome of the election than a lot of other big things that happened in the fall. And, accepting your premise that when you went into it you gave it no strategic weight to speak of, did you afterward pick up any blips? Did either you personally or the brass of your campaign collectively pick up any feeling that it had had an effect?

CHENEY: My view is that its impact has been overrated. Some of the results in the 1976 elections cast a lot of doubt on the idea that the vice-presidential question was a key. We have to look at where the votes came from. For example, in northeastern and urban Ohio Governor Carter ran roughly equal to Hubert Humphrey's 1968 totals in a three-way race, and fairly poorly for a Democrat. But he ran up around Lyndon Johnson's totals in that southern tier of counties along the Ohio River. So it seems to me we have to consider *where* the vice-presidential debate would or would not have had an impact. I don't think that those southern Ohio counties went the way they did because of the vice-presidential debate or the candidates for vice-president. My own belief is that the debate did not have much impact. People who think it was decisive—I refer specifically to columnists and commentators after the fact and to voters who cited that as a reason (though I don't think there were many)—such people would have had some reason to vote the way they did with or without the Dole-Mondale debate. That is my own personal view, but I really cannot support it with data.

WALTER MEARS, Associated Press: To belabor Eastern Europe a bit, there was a story at the time that never got published (to my knowledge, anyhow) that Ford went to bed believing he had won the second debate. When either Scowcroft or you or someone else was sent to tell him, "We've got a problem on our hands, and we may have lost this one," he got his back up and therefore did not make what, at that point, would have seemed to be an easy correction. It got more difficult as time went on, and he backed off for about four days. What happened when that problem was raised with him? You talked to him about it at breakfast on Air Force One, if what I heard is correct.

CHENEY: Well, I do not really have any data on that point. [Laughter.] The President has been asked that question directly, as I recall; it is addressed fairly extensively in Jules Witcover's book on the campaign.[1] As I have said, I had the feeling when I left the hall that night that he had done very well in the second debate. I felt that, substantively, his performance had been good, that he had been more in control of the situation than he had been in the first debate, and that Governor Carter had not done well on substance .

It turned out that my assessment of the ultimate political impact of that second debate was faulty. I think the President felt he had

---

[1] Jules Witcover, *Marathon: The Pursuit of the Presidency, 1972–1976* (New York: Viking Press, 1977).

done well. He has since said that he had thought the allegation was that somehow the U.S. government, his administration, had a policy of conceding Soviet domination of Eastern Europe, and his response was geared to that question, which wasn't really asked. The question was whether or not the Soviets do, in fact, dominate Eastern Europe.

Like a great many individuals, he felt fairly strongly about it. It wasn't until about noon Friday, California time, that we convened the press conference and he spelled out clearly his views on Eastern Europe—he was aware there were Soviet divisions in Eastern Europe. We followed that up when we got back to Washington on Monday morning by meeting with a group of political leaders from ethnic groups from Eastern Europe and pretty well put the thing to rest.

MEARS: The thing had been blown out of proportion. Why wasn't there a clear statement saying, "I misspoke. What I was trying to say was this"? That would have settled it right there.

CHENEY: That is what we finally did on Friday, but it took us a while to get there.

CHARLS E. WALKER, cochairman of the 1976 Debates Steering Committee: I think this is one of the most significant aspects of the debates and the media. If you won't criticize the media, I will. One of the reasons for the debates was to get the media out of the way as the filter between the candidates and the public. I came down from the balcony that night after the San Francisco debate and a leading so-called print journalist grabbed me and said, "Charlie, who won?" I said, "I think Ford won hands down," and I ticked off various points such as those you mentioned. And he said, "Yes, but what about Eastern Europe, what about Eastern Europe?" In this instance, even though we had debates, we had the media playing a very significant role.

CHENEY: I can't argue with any of that, Charlie. That is a fact of life and something we have to deal with in managing a campaign. I still stand by the original decision we made to debate; we did not have very many options in the summer of 1976, and I think we got out of it everything we could reasonably expect.

Although the debates are a device that lets a candidate communicate directly with the voter and lets the voter watch the candidate perform under pressure, or respond to questions, or debate his opponent in the classic sense, the fact of the matter is that the media do have a big role in interpreting the results. Look at the delayed reaction. Even though people watched the second debate themselves—saw it with their own eyes—the media played a big role in how people responded to the debate two days after the event; no question about it.

MICHAEL ROBINSON, professor of political science, Catholic University of America: I have done a content analysis of your remarks today, and five times you have said, "I don't want to get down on the media about this."

CHENEY: I think that's important when they are present. [Laughter.]

ROBINSON: I mentioned to someone else in the room that it sounds to me very much like Marc Antony saying Brutus is an honorable man. I would like to know why you don't want to get down on the media. Do you feel that they are doing a job as you expected they would, that you knew from the start how they would behave, and that there is no point in complaining?

CHENEY: I guess it cuts both ways, and we probably benefited from that same phenomenon at other times during the campaign. Jimmy Carter's comments in *Playboy* probably did not have a great deal of relevance to the question of who should be the next president of the United States. We benefited considerably from the fact that for several days the press corps followed him around and asked him about lust.

Where do fairness and equity lie? In managing the campaign, I think we have to look at it in a pragmatic sense: that is the way our system works, and we have to deal with it on those terms. If the question becomes whether there should be some sort of institutionalization of debates, the impact of the media has to be considered in deciding the answer and in making recommendations. But I also may, at some point in the future, want to become active politically, and therefore I do not want to get myself in hot water now.

GEOFFREY SMITH, London *Times*: I wonder if I may ask a question from the standpoint of a British visitor. You referred to press monitoring of the debates as being on occasion more important than what actually happens in the debate itself. Does this apply only to presidential debates, or does it also apply to other current affairs programs, such as "Meet the Press," for example? In Britain, we do not have anything that corresponds directly to your presidential debates, but we do have a great deal of current affairs television during election campaigns. There, what happens on the screen is supposed to be more important

135

than the press reactions to them. And yet, that does not seem to be the case here.

CHENEY: I suppose we would have to measure relative impact to answer that, but I think there is no question but that the press does play an important role in interpreting an event even though the public has seen it with their own eyes. Throughout the course of the campaign, most of the events or happenings other than the debates are conveyed to the public through the media—statements by President Ford in the Rose Garden, the shows we did toward the close of the campaign, Governor Carter's campaigning, the *Playboy* article, or the resignation of Earl Butz. A presidential candidate all by himself has absolutely no impact on the public until he begins to deal with the press and the media, and they, in turn, convey his message to the public.

Debates are different, in the sense that the two candidates do not communicate through the press corps when there is a debate, and 89 percent of the electorate see the debate with their own eyes. In reality, what does happen is that, after the fact, that event gets interpreted by the media.

5

Did the Debates Help Jimmy Carter?

Stephan Lesher
with
Patrick Caddell and Gerald Rafshoon

In commenting on the close election of 1976, Jimmy Carter said flatly that "if it hadn't been for the debates, I would have lost. They established me as competent on foreign and domestic affairs and gave the viewers reason to think that Jimmy Carter has something to offer." Carter's assessment raises a series of questions:

- Did he "win" the debates in the sense that he was superior to President Ford?
- Did the debates change the minds of voters; that is, did they shift votes from Ford to Carter?
- If Carter would have lost the election except for the debates, what may we infer about their value for the future?
- If they helped Carter, did they hurt Ford?
- Did they provide a service to the electorate of sufficient magnitude to institutionalize debates?

Opinion research available to Carter as a candidate and assessments of Carter's closest political advisers lead to several conclusions.

1. The debates helped *both* candidates by diminishing, if not eradicating, the general public's negative perceptions of each.

2. Carter was the greater beneficiary because his likely presidential performance was less "known."

3. "Winning" or "losing" the debates had an insignificant impact on the electorate for both candidates.

4. The outcome of the debates changed few votes; in the Carter campaign, the debates were planned to shore up perceived weaknesses among likely supporters rather than to expand support.

5. Although Carter undoubtedly is right that he would have lost the election without the essential forum of the debates, the debates

did not "hurt" Ford in the sense of eroding his support in the electorate. Because of the political reality of Carter's vast lead at the time of the presidential nominations, Ford was required to try to make some dramatic incursion, and the debates provided that opportunity. Because Carter knew his numerical lead was "soft" in the sense that it included armies of voters who normally voted Democratic, he was required to demonstrate that he merited their confidence.

6. The debates provided a valuable service to the electorate by enabling voters to view the candidates unimpeded by media interpretation and uninfluenced by the stagecraft of paid commercials; whether they shed significant light on the differences between the candidates' or not they shed significant light on the differences between the candidates' views, they at least enabled voters to formulate opinions on the personalities of the two men.

7. Because of severe federal limitations on campaign spending, candidates are limited in the amount of television time they can buy. Debates carried by the networks as news events therefore furnish the electorate its greatest exposure to the candidates. Although pressure to debate will be greater than ever on future presidential candidates, the decision to have them and the formats they may take will remain political decisions that will differ from campaign to campaign.

The debates clearly helped both candidates for president improve their images in 1976. Hurting Carter was what his aide, Hamilton Jordan, termed "the weirdo factor"—the public perception that because of Carter's outspoken religiosity and his unusual candor (which, more often than not, hurt him with voters), he was somehow out of step with the American majority. Hurting Ford was what one aide termed "the 'dumb' issue"—the public perception that good old Jerry Ford could not, as Lyndon Johnson once said, walk and chew gum at the same time.

The media must be faulted for these obviously erroneous public concepts. For one thing, few among the correspondents covering the 1976 presidential campaigns were familiar with southern Baptists. This denomination has always prided itself on its openness and outspokenness—so much so that it always has washed its dirty laundry in public at its state or regional conventions. As a result, a stereotype grew of southern Baptists as antediluvian racists and Neanderthal social thinkers. To be sure, the denomination does include people like Lester Maddox, but it also includes men and women in universities and in pulpits who provided leadership in effecting racial integration with minimal violence.

Further, most readers of national newspapers and magazines

probably lean toward more sophisticated religions and remain some-what suspicious of evangelical faiths. There even may be a hint of racism in those who find the chanted sermons of Martin Luther King, Sr., touching, but who feel vaguely uncomfortable with a white, middle-class businessman and politician who admits readily that he regularly falls to his knees in prayer. The reporting of Jimmy Carter's conversion did little to dispel stereotypes in the minds of readers; questioners, for example, wanted to know if Jimmy Carter thought God spoke to him. Such questions clearly indicated reportorial ig-norance and suspicion, which were reflected in many of the reports.

While it is true that much of Carter's campaign revolved around his projected personality as a man of honesty and impeccable integ-rity, the media nonetheless focused so heavily on a couple of his ran-dom comments—"ethnic purity" during the primaries and "lust" after his highly publicized *Playboy* interview—that voters scarcely could ignore the "weirdo factor."

As for Ford, much of the media ignored his Yale law degree and concentrated on his unfortunate accident-prone nature. Though some-times amusing—and always pictorial—Ford's penchant for slipping on airplane ramps or bumping his head on helicopter doors began to take on a media life of its own. Ford could not escape the "dumb" issue. Whenever the President would mispronounce a word or forget the name of a town in which he was campaigning, it became part of the story.

Thus, the debates offered Carter the opportunity to appear for uninterrupted chunks of time before the electorate and discuss matters of substance—and thereby demonstrate that he was neither weird nor fuzzy on the issues. For Ford, the debates gave him a chance to demonstrate he had a command of the presidency and of the issues. "He didn't play Chevy Chase," said Carter adviser Gerald Rafshoon.

The debates opened at a time when Carter had begun to fall in the polls. In the *Playboy* interview Carter had spoken of lust in his heart (in the context of his belief that he should not judge others by his personal standards) and had used vulgar terms such as "screw" and "shack up." Advance publicity of the interview did nothing to assure voters who remained somewhat suspicious of the candidate's self-pronounced integrity and competence. It also added to the general belief that Carter had not addressed the issues confronting the nation.

"Jimmy Carter had been talking issues for more than a year," says Rafshoon,

> but it was being filtered through the press. For example, in a major speech he addressed the subject of detente. But the

story on the TV news shows that night featured people standing outside the auditorium carrying anti-abortion placards. At the end of the first debate, one of the commentators said the news of the event was that Carter had said should there be another Arab oil boycott, he, as president, would respond with an economic boycott against the Arabs. Carter had been saying that since Iowa, and we had a sixty-second TV spot on the subject—but it had never been picked up. With the debate, Carter talked issues for ninety minutes— and no one could edit what he said.

"The debate also was a great leveler," Rafshoon continued. "It presented both men in the same context and removed Ford from the trappings of the presidency."

Carter understood the importance of using that "leveler" despite his early, apparently insurmountable lead in the polls. His aides had wanted to prepare a telegram to Ford congratulating him on winning the Republican nomination—and adding a challenge to debate. But Carter vetoed that idea as "tacky," according to Rafshoon. Instead, a news release was prepared in which Carter would challenge Ford to debates after the President's acceptance speech. Ford beat Carter to the punch, however, by issuing the challenge during that speech. The Carter lead, apparently, had persuaded him that he needed debates at least as much as Carter did.

When the subject of debating Ford was discussed by Carter aides between the nominating conventions, Carter pollster Patrick Caddell relied on a study by Samuel Popkin of the University of California and Robert Abelson of Yale which demonstrated that the historic Nixon-Kennedy debates of 1960 had changed very few votes. "An historical misconception had grown over the years," Caddell recalls, "that those debates led to a massive shift of votes from Nixon to Kennedy. But what they had done was to serve as a reinforcing mechanism for those inclined to vote for Kennedy but who had doubts about his ability to be president." According to Caddell, the exercise gave the public a sense of confidence in Kennedy's ability to run the government. "Any 'unknown'—that is, any candidate who has not occupied center stage in foreign policy or governmental decision making—has to solve the 'competence problem,'" Caddell says.

Thus, it was clearly to our advantage to debate. We were not going to "kill" Ford or knock him out of the race with a crushing blow. For one thing, our polls showed that despite the press, people did not perceive Ford as inept or stupid. They did not think Ford was a leader of great vision—but they did not think he was dumb. <u>People expected him to win the debates, in fact.</u>

The object for us was to shore up the growing defections from Carter to Ford. From the start, our analysis was that it would be a very close election. For example, the people who said they would vote for Carter—and at this time they were favoring Carter by wide margins—nonetheless awarded Ford very high marks in terms of their personal views of the man. While Carter was leading by more than thirty percentage points in our polls, Ford was rated as doing a good job by 57 percent of those polled. Therefore, it was obvious to us that the Ford vote—which at the time was lower than George McGovern's vote four years earlier—would rise dramatically.

We were seeing defections from Carter even during polling interviews. We would begin by asking the person for whom he intended to vote. At the time, most answered they intended to vote for Carter. But after we came to the questions about whether they intended to vote for Carter even though he might be a risk or unknown quantity, compared with Ford who might be less effective but who would not hurt the country, people would say, "Well, now I'm not sure. Maybe I'll vote for Ford after all." With these kinds of defections, we could anticipate considerable erosion. Carter had the benefit that any Democrat has—strength in numbers. But he had an unknown personality and was believed to be fuzzy on the issues and was perceived as being too religious to avoid suspicion.

In the absence of burning issues in a campaign, the voter's perception of a candidate's personality is the most crucial factor in determining a wavering vote. Because so many votes were wavering, our strategy was clear. We had to debate to reinforce those people who intended to vote for Carter. Debates would give him exposure in depth, would demonstrate his competence in the same arena with an incumbent president, would retain his solid vote—and keep reinforcing it.

Winning or losing debates, whatever that means, does not change votes. It has been viewed aptly as a football game. A fan roots for his team, but if it does not win he does not stop being a fan of that team.

People leaning toward Carter watched the debates wanting to be assured that the candidate was not some latter-day Rasputin but rather that he possessed the calm confidence and knowledge that would merit the vote they planned to give him.

In preparing for the debates, the Carter camp sought to minimize as much as possible the difference between the President of the United States and a previously unknown former governor from a southern state. They wanted all the debates to be general in nature rather than to cover specific areas. They wanted the candidates to be seated rather than standing; the informality not only would lessen the presidential atmosphere but also would play to Carter's strength of communicating best in relaxed circumstances.

Clearly, these were opening gambits by the Carter aides. When they retreated to their fallback positions, they got essentially what they went for: equal footing, no presidential seal or special deferential treatment of the President, and, most importantly, the focus on domestic affairs for the opening debate. "Domestic affairs was our obvious strong suit," Caddell says, "considering the general Democratic social programs and the domestic economic problems. We expected we would win that rather easily. So much for expectations."

According to the polls, Ford "won" the first debate rather handily. Carter appeared to be nervous. "I don't know whether it was nervousness," Rafshoon recalls, "or just the accumulation of years of respect for the presidency. But it took him a while to hit his stride." When he did, technical difficulties interrupted the debate for nearly half an hour—just as Carter was sailing smoothly into his summation.

Nonetheless, Carter—who had been sliding as much as six or seven percentage points a week in the preference polls—was able to halt his slide after each debate. Caddell's polls found, in fact, that while Carter dropped another point immediately after the first debate, he gained two points later that week. The importance of the debates for Carter was that each time one was conducted it halted serious slippage of his support.

Caddell's findings showed that Carter clearly had "lost" the first debate in people's minds, but his natural constituency hardened and he remained in the lead. The debate had occurred shortly after widespread publicity on the *Playboy* interview. As it turned out, the ensuing debates also were marked by preceding events so that the debates themselves became watersheds or breaking points in the campaign.

Before the second debate, Secretary of Agriculture Earl Butz caused a mini-scandal for the Republicans by telling a joke with racial overtones in the presence of Watergate figure John Dean, on special assignment to the Republican national convention for *Rolling Stone*. Dean published the joke, and soon demands for Butz's resignation besieged the President. Ford's decision to allow Butz to resign gracefully rather than to dismiss him summarily was viewed by the media as indecisiveness.

Meanwhile, Carter had been advised that he had to "win" or at least be counted as "even" in the second debate. Although he had previously eschewed coaching by his aides, his shaky performance in the opening debate persuaded him to seek basic coaching on presenting a relaxed appearance. Further, the second debate would concentrate on foreign affairs—conceded to be Ford's strong point. With Ford the overwhelming favorite in this area, Carter had an opportunity for a stunning upset.

Caddell advised Carter to avoid positions on foreign affairs that Ford could label as either liberal or conservative. "Hit him from the left and from the right," Caddell counseled. What he meant was to talk about human rights on one hand, and then condemn the administration's handling of the Chilean government; to talk about the inept handling of SALT agreements on one hand, and the problem of world hunger on the other.

In the course of the debate, Ford made his notorious remark about Eastern European nations not being under Soviet domination; Carter responded to that deftly by saying that Americans of Eastern European extraction would be surprised to learn that from Mr. Ford. Again, it took several days for Ford to clarify what he meant to say; by that time, Ford's slip had been the subject of massive media exposure.

After the second debate, Carter told Caddell he was just warming up to do battle with Ford; he had made the conscious decision after the first debate that it was he and not the format that showed excessive deference to the President. "You haven't seen anything yet," Caddell recalls Carter telling him. But though Carter had gained a significant advantage after the second debate and showed signs of increasing his lead, which had been narrowing, he lost this advantage by trying to destroy Ford. He attacked Ford on the campaign trail in harsh terms—and the ploy backfired.

Caddell's polls showed more slippage nationwide. The Carter camp took heart, however, when the polls showed that Carter had a stable showing in the large electoral states in which the election would be decided. While Ford was closing in the South and making gains in the West, the large industrial states—while close—were showing no changes.

Still, Caddell did not understand why Carter suddenly began showing more slippage. Then he realized that the *Playboy* interview, publicized before the first debate, was just coming on the newsstands with considerable advertising. It reintroduced the importance of the "weirdo factor," especially among housewives. Caddell's polls indi-

143

cated as much as a ten-point difference between Ford and Carter from this crucial group of voters. "We came sliding into the third debate," Caddell says. "Somehow, we had to stop our slippage again and try to provide some momentum for the closing days of the campaign; we had to reinforce our support; we had to shore up the women's vote."

Carter decided the best way to achieve those goals was to keep the debate in a very low key. He decided to confront the *Playboy* problem directly. When he had a chance to mention it, he explained what he had meant but added that he would not again provide an interview on his religious beliefs for that kind of publication. After Ford answered a question about the investigation into his tax affairs, Carter responded with "no comment." The polls showed the final debate was perceived as a narrow Carter victory—but it served the candidate's purposes. In the election, Carter did almost as well with women as with men.

Each debate was an "event" for three or four days, accompanied by considerable advance publicity and postdebate analysis. They took the focus off the campaigns and therefore tended to limit the trivia that dominates media coverage of almost any presidential campaign: stories about slips of the tongue, off-color jokes, use of vulgarities, placards carried by demonstrators, which candidate was waffling most on the abortion issue. That Carter was the greatest beneficiary is clear.

A challenger to an incumbent cannot answer the questions in people's minds about what kind of risk he might be as president except through heavy exposure. That the debates were judged as "dull" by most of the people who watched them worked to Carter's advantage. (Senator Robert Dole, the Republican vice-presidential nominee was anything but dull in his debate with his Democratic counterpart, Senator Walter F. Mondale. Dole might have titillated the party faithful, but he offended most viewers.) The unknown candidate must be given greater exposure for voters to get an in-depth sense of his personality. Carter knew that serious debates with no cross-questioning by the participants themselves could do him no harm and might do him a great deal of good.

As a rule, debates like those in 1976 allow people to resolve questions in their minds about the personalities of the candidates. Marginal voters are much more influenced by their perceptions of the character and leadership qualities of candidates than by issues—especially in a year without any of the searing or emotional issues that existed in 1968. If the election had been conducted on issues alone, the Democrats—with the advantages of difficult economic problems confronting the Ford administration and their vast superiority of numbers of registered voters—would have won handily. But the election finally revolved on the question of character. It was a close race between an incumbent perceived as a decent man though no great leader, and a challenger exuding calm confidence in his leadership qualities but not really known for his personal integrity.

Contrary to many people's belief, presidential debates do not resolve candidates' positions on issues and thus do not resolve who will vote for whom. Rather, they provide a reinforcing mechanism, a forum in which voters may test the assumptions they already hold about the candidates.

The format of the debates in 1976 was satisfactory. To conduct such confrontations with a single moderator would raise questions of who that moderator would be and whether one person could develop a series of fair questions to keep the debate on a high level. To permit cross-questioning would open the door to a shooting match in which one candidate—likely the one trailing in the polls—might simply seek to embarrass his opponent rather than to shed light on problems. Furthermore, unless the equal time provision of the Communications Act is changed, an outside sponsor such as the League of Women Voters is needed so that the debates are covered by television as news events. That is merely a ruse, but it works.

Most proposed changes would serve the end of sensationalism, which is exactly what the debates should avoid. The nature of campaign coverage by the media is to seek out the startling; debates are designed for dull solidity. Debates are a valid part of the system of elections just as free media coverage is. People should be given an opportunity to hear and see candidates with a minimum of interpretation and media exaggeration. While no one would condone an American election without free-wheeling media coverage, the voters' perceptions of candidates should not be formed solely by press and television reporters and by paid advertising. Debates, speeches, news conferences, paid advertising—all are part of the synergism of an American presidential campaign and should remain so.

If debates clearly help the "outsider," however, will any incumbent risk strengthening his opponent in future debates? It happened in 1976, to be sure, but the circumstances were exceptional in that the President had not been elected to that office. The circumstances will vary from election to election. To pass a law requiring debates would be extremely difficult, and to limit debates to two candidates would pose the question of a conflict with the Constitution which Congress would be hard put to solve.

Debates must therefore remain the product not of government

but of the people. And if an incumbent wishes to avoid the confrontation, it would be up to the people to decide if that action alone would affect their votes. There was relatively little publicity in 1964 and 1972 when the incumbent presidents ruled out debates with their challengers. But that was before Watergate and before the electorate became suspicious of the government. To avoid debates in the future will not be easy for an incumbent—certainly not in the near future.

Discussion

GEOFFREY SMITH, London *Times*: Did Carter concentrate, in the first debate at least, on pumping out factual information to the viewers as a deliberate tactic to try to overcome what you have termed the "weirdo factor," or was this a style that he and you believed to be most appropriate to this kind of debate?

LESHER: As to the first part of the question, it was a deliberate tactic of Carter's, and that is why, instead of having coaching or dry runs, he locked himself up with his books. He did want to spew out lots of facts as an indication of what a good grip he had on difficult questions, especially economic questions. Whether it is part of his normal style —well, you see him as much as I do now.

SMITH: I did not mean to ask whether it is necessarily part of his normal style, but whether it is his belief and your belief that such a style is especially appropriate to televised debates?

LESHER: Let me put it this way: It is my associates' belief that Mr. Carter is one of the smartest presidents in terms of his knowledge and general intelligence that we have had in many years. They say that he understands issues, that he has a good grasp of them, that he does not merely spit back summaries at press conferences. Therefore, I would think that, in following his normal style of discussing things rather broadly and with significant information—or facts, if you will— Carter would think that is the way to show himself to best advantage.

NELSON W. POLSBY, University of California, Berkeley: My perception of the first debate was that, in fact, Carter was not following his normal style; he was simply spitting out large numbers of irrelevant facts, and it was quite uncharacteristic of the way he normally deals with issues, at least by hindsight. This leads me to question the extent to which he was explicitly following the Kennedy model. Everybody who replays the 1960 debates notices that Kennedy crammed himself with "factlets" and then laid them on the viewers, come what might. And since Kennedy "won" (that's not really true, but we all know it anyhow), that is supposed to be how Kennedy did it.

My question is: To what extent was the Kennedy model in Carter's mind? I noted a similar tendency in Gerald Ford; maybe Dick Cheney has something to add about the extent to which Ford's planning was affected by the ostensible Kennedy win and the Kennedy style of hyperfactualism. I remember a general question to Ford that went something like this: "Do you think you spend too much time or not enough time up on Capitol Hill explaining things to Congress?" And the answer was, "Seventeen and a half hours was spent by me and Secretary Kissinger." [Laughter.] In other words, he could not answer yes or no or even maybe; it had to have a spurious number attached to it, which reminded me, I must say, of Kennedy.

LESHER: Let me clarify what I was saying. In being nervous before that first debate, Carter was not, in fact, following his usual style. He had, as I indicated before, told his people he did not want any coaching; he wanted to know the facts. But, instead of discussing them in a relaxed fashion, as he tends to do and did in the ensuing debates, in that first debate he did exactly as you said, and it worked against him.

He began to hit his stride toward the end of the first debate and in his summation, which was interrupted by the technological breakdown. Before the first debate he did not take coaching, but he did watch the Kennedy-Nixon debates. I was told that he concentrated on their first debate, which was supposedly the knock-out debate, and that may well have been a cause of his initial nervousness. Because he was not following his usual style, he could have been uncomfortable and nervous.

RICHARD CHENEY, former Ford chief of staff: As soon as we began to think about the debates, we were extremely conscious of the 1960 precedents. They were the only precedents we had. I personally watched reruns of the first 1960 debate—supposedly the decisive one —three or four times as we prepared for our first debate. President Ford himself saw it at least once that I can recall, and possibly even more. We were very much aware not only of the supposed impact on the viewer of the televised picture of Nixon's discomfort, but also of the statement that has often been made that the people who heard the first Kennedy-Nixon debate thought Nixon won, while the people who saw it thought Kennedy won. That kind of information was in all of our minds as we looked at it.

It wasn't a matter of trying to shape the candidate's conduct in a way that was "Kennedyesque" rather than "Nixonesque." Looking at it, though, before we made the decision to debate we made the judgment that those physical and personal characteristics that were negative factors for Nixon in the first Kennedy-Nixon debate were not a problem for Ford. In the process of negotiating the format the Carter people were very much concerned about the setting, as we were. We were eager to get the two podiums as close together as possible, because our man was taller than their man, and we thought that was an asset that should be exploited. We insisted on standing up rather than sitting down. It was part of the political negotiation process, and we were very sensitive to such factors. The President's inclination to cite numbers is just part of his character. He has always done that and still does. And it probably was an accurate number.

JAMES KARAYN, director of the 1976 debates: I'd like to mention a number of things that happened in the second debate in 1976. Throughout the whole first debate Carter was very nervous, and this resulted from being in the presence of a president. That should never be minimized. A candidate can go around and campaign all over the place; he can call his opponent the biggest dummy in the world; but when he gets face to face with the man who is president of the United States, it has an effect. I remember standing next to Ford when he walked out on stage, and Carter was physically nervous shaking hands with him. He was in the presence of a president. But all through that debate he was very careful never to call him Mr. President; he called him Mr. Ford. He also referred to the Republican party, and that whole debate was on party lines, not personalities, which was very unusual; it was getting back to party things. And Ford responded about the Democratic party. They got to talking on party lines rather than on the personalities because the incumbent was one of the debaters.

Another thing was the great discussion about those stools. We negotiated until 3:00 A.M. about whether there would be stools on which the candidates could sit down. The Ford people did not want a stool and the Carter people did. It became a great issue. We said we would provide them, and if they wanted to sit down, they could, and if they didn't, they didn't have to. A great issue in the Carter camp for the second debate was to make Carter look more relaxed. As a calculated stunt, he was to sit down when the President was answering a question.

He also smiled a great deal during all of Ford's answers. At some points, to some people, it looked almost as if he were sneering at the President. This was a calculated move, part of creating an image. The one thing he got out of the Kennedy debate was that Kennedy never answered any questions. If Kennedy were asked a question about avocado raising in California, he would say, "That's very interesting, but I want to talk about peaches in North Carolina," and would proceed to do so.

The first question that was posed to Carter in the second debate was by Max Frankel, and Carter made a statement. He caught himself later in an answer when he said, "In my opening statement tonight," although we had had no opening statements. One of the reasons we decided not to have opening statements in the format was that in that first debate in 1960 many people felt the outcome had nothing to do with Nixon's performance or his makeup or anything like that; the opening statements were decisive. Each candidate had an eight-minute opening statement, and Kennedy drew the first opening statement. People forget that Kennedy was little known—far less known on television, certainly, in 1960 than Carter was in 1976. And Kennedy's eight-minute statement was such a sales pitch, so powerful, it didn't matter what happened after that. The first eight minutes was the end of those debates.

MICHAEL ROBINSON, professor of political science, Catholic University of America: Mr. Cheney said earlier that the longer a candidate speaks, regardless of what is said, the more positive the response of the viewers in the room. That seemed to be something that the candidates might have learned from the kind of research that was done. Did the candidates, as it appeared, learn that the more they ignore the question and simply say what they have to say, the better they will do? It seemed that by the third debate the candidates had really decided that they would, with impunity, simply ignore the question and say whatever they felt. Did they learn that over three debates? And if they did, would it perhaps help from the point of view of citizenship to have the candidates ask each other questions, in an attempt to keep them to the questions?

LESHER: I don't believe that politicians really have to be told that the basic "Meet the Press" technique is to respond somewhat to the question and quickly move into the area that you want to talk about anyway. Second, the reporters on the panels were free to suggest, and in fact on one or two occasions did suggest, that the question had not been answered. To that extent, I think the format worked rather well, as well as it can with politicians.

On your second question, no; I like the format the way it is. I think that most changes—especially having candidates ask one another questions—would result in a shooting match, with charges leading to sensationalism, with much more heat than light. And I think the present format, while hardly perfect—like democracy itself —works better than any other I can think of.

AUSTIN RANNEY, American Enterprise Institute: It is a matter of record that the format and the rules established in both 1960 and 1976 were agreed upon after negotiation between the two candidates. The networks in 1960 and the League of Women Voters in 1976 had a certain input in making the rules, but fundamentally nothing was done to which either candidate strongly objected in either year. We all understand why that was so, and it may be that that is how it will always be. If that is the case, the rules will always depend upon the nature of the candidates and what they think are their personal pluses and minuses. But I wonder if it would be better for the nation if the rules for the debates were set by someone other than the candidates, and set well in advance of the debates. In such a situation the candidates would have to adapt themselves to the rules as best they could. Otherwise the debates will always have this ad hoc nature that many people deplore.

KARAYN: As long as there are debates, it does not matter who the candidates are. In 1960 there was a split among the four networks— the fourth being Mutual Radio. CBS wanted an Oregon-type debate, a university-type debate. Dr. Stanton really fought for that. NBC did not; they wanted, from the very beginning, a "Meet the Press" format, which is exactly what they called it.

The Nixon-Kennedy advisers immediately saw the conflict. In their second meeting with the networks at the Mayflower Hotel, the representatives of the two candidates sent the network people out of the room and proceeded to write up a format. Then they invited the networks back in fifteen minutes later and said, "That's the format we'll go with and nothing else." And the networks took it.

This time, we thought we would be a little smarter, and worked out a format to take into negotiations. The one I proposed would have been a combination of some face-to-face discussion and some questions from a panel. I still think somebody has to get some material out on the table, or else, as Steve Lesher says, it will get into a shooting match and there will not be enough material on the table. I think at some point in the debate the candidates can be allowed to go at each other. In all debates, at the halfway point the moderator could have said, "Now, President Ford, would you like to ask Governor Carter a question," or something like that. It would have worked perfectly.

Regardless of what the candidates said publicly, this time neither wanted face-to-face questions. As one of Nixon's people said in 1960, "We want a third party to ask the dirty questions." What would have happened in 1976 if, in the third debate, Governor Carter had said to President Ford, as Joe Kraft did, "Mr. President, don't you think that's a rotten economic plan you have?" The whole question might have backfired, regardless of what the President said. I have a feeling it would have backfired on Governor Carter as an insult to the President of the United States. But it's all right if Joe Kraft does it, because he is not running.

LESHER: I don't think we can artificially create a format for an unknown set of candidates, nor should we. The President of the United States was Mr. Ford, and I don't believe there should have been laws —because of the constitutional problems if for no other reason—to tell the President of the United States whether he should debate or, if he does, how he is going to do it. And I don't think the candidate of any major party, even if he is not an incumbent, should be told that either.

If the candidates have input it is going to minimize the physical advantages of one over the other. Obviously, they were not going to have a Mutt and Jeff show with Ford versus Carter. It would not have been accepted, and then there would have been no debates. I dare say that if it had gotten out that for that reason there were to be no debates, most people would have said, "Why don't Carter and Ford agree to stand six feet apart? What's such a big deal about that?" Or it might have been suggested that Governor Carter was afraid of standing next to a man taller than himself. But the candidates obviously worked out all the wrinkles; they jockeyed around for different stylistic advantages, and it came out about equal for both sides. I think the debates were successful.

No, I would not like an outside group saying, "This is the way the debates will be." Then, perhaps because of a perceived height difference, Mr. Carter might have lost a great many votes, or perhaps because they were seated, Mr. Ford might have lost a great many votes.

STEVEN CHAFFEE, University of Wisconsin: I agree with both of your conclusions about the future. But I am left with a third question, and

I wonder how you would answer it. On the one hand, you see a value in having debates, but on the other hand, you don't think they should be legislated, with everything written in stone and with very little flexibility. But what should be done, what feasibly could be done?

LESHER: I think what should be done is exactly what is going to be done. I suggest that in 1980 the Republican challenger will challenge the incumbent to debate. I dare say that the incumbent is going to be under rather heavy pressure to accept, partly because of the 1976 debates in which he participated, and partly because of some of the post-Watergate suspicion of government that will attend an incumbent who refuses to debate.

I also suggest that by that time Mr. Carter's lead will either be so narrow that he will figure he is better off debating and shoring up his weak points or, conversely, it will be high enough that he will not be concerned about debating and its possible ill effects for his campaign. If he has a good lead, he will probably not want to debate, but I suggest that he will be forced into it by public pressure. If he chooses not to, people like Mr. Miller [of the Chicago *Sun-Times*] and Mr. Mears [of the Associated Press] will let folks know. In 1980, it's not going to be so easily forgotten.

JACK DENNIS, University of Wisconsin: As a social scientist, it seems to me most interesting that important decisions—indeed, what seem to be quite momentous decisions—are being made about the format and the rules, on the assumption that these things make a great deal of difference. But, from the studies that have been done both in 1960 and 1976, there is really not much evidence to support such theories. Very often when I listen to Mr. Cheney and Mr. Lesher, I see them hanging their decisions on very thin reeds, as far as relevant research is concerned.

At some point somebody needs to do something about designing more comprehensive research so that we can test some of these variables that are thought important. Now such factors are not necessarily the variables that social scientists would think important, but at least we need to field better studies so that they will be more useful in campaign decisions. Unfortunately, there has been essentially no funding for this kind of research. It has been self-generated and therefore more limited than it should be, given the importance of the decisions that are being made.

CHENEY: First of all, politics is a much less exact discipline than political science. In the course of trying to make campaign decisions, we rarely have time to test our assumptions. We rely on hunch and judgment and political lore. Second, the distance between the podiums may seem equally important to the question of whether there will be a prescribed subject for a particular debate or whether there will be a debate. But obviously there is a great difference in the relative significance of those kinds of things in the course of the campaign.

For us, however, especially since we were behind, we could not afford to leave any stone unturned. It could conceivably be, for example, that in 1960 the Nixon people had no idea of, or apparently paid little attention to, those factors that people thought afterward had made the difference. In 1976, frankly, we did not know what was going to make the difference. Therefore, we negotiated over whether the candidates would sit or stand and what the camera angles would be, which was another subject of great debate.

Obviously, some things are far more important than others. But you are right, there is very little evidence, and an awful lot of judgments are based primarily on gut feelings.

6

The Case for Permanent Presidential Debates

James Karayn

The late Walter Lippmann, reflecting upon the 1960 debates between John Kennedy and Richard Nixon, said they were so significant to the political process that he saw no way they would not become a permanent part of the political process.[1] Despite his assessment, sixteen years passed before such debates occurred again.

Today, two conditions of American society make the presidential debates imperative. First, the public gets most of its information via television. Televised debates offer a dramatic and enlightening presentation which the voters may compare and contrast with the political advertisements and brief news clips. In fact, if the television coverage of candidates consists only of spots and news clips, it is incomplete, reflecting only the images fabricated by the candidates' media advisers or the conduct of the candidate in a controlled situation without spontaneity. That coverage would also preclude the face-to-face meeting of candidates which is one of the most desirable elements of the debates. Second, the media and American politics are inextricably joined. The political process has been so accelerated and its impact so widely extended by the media that it is virtually impossible for a candidate to wage a successful campaign without television.

The Ford-Carter "Great Debates" are acknowledged by both sides to have been the essential factor in the 1976 campaign. It was estimated that about a quarter billion people watched those debates

---

[1] Specifically, in his syndicated column that appeared in the fall of 1960 following the debates, Lippmann said: "The TV debate was a bold innovation which is bound to be carried forward into future campaigns, and could not now be abandoned. From now on it will be impossible for any candidate for any important office to avoid this kind of confrontation with his opponent": New York *Herald Tribune*, September 29, 1960, p. 26.

on worldwide television,[2] including nearly 160 million Americans.[3] Perhaps no other event since the walk on the moon has had so vast an audience.

Those debates, and the events which accompanied and followed, have been the subject of investigation and evaluation from all sides. There have been controversy and criticism, and there have been many attempts to assess their effect on the electorate. These exercises began even before the actual plans for the debates were officially announced, and they continue apace even now. It is necessary to examine the successes and failures of those encounters and the extensive analysis they fostered if we are to formulate a positive plan for future presidential debates.

The 1976 Presidential Debates

The 1976 presidential debates illustrated emphatically the power and the promise of television in a campaign. They made history, they made enemies, and, to a large extent, they made the race an exciting and vital experience for the candidates and the voters alike. For the first time in American political history, an incumbent president debated his challenger, and the vice-presidential candidates also shared a history-making confrontation. In the process, the commercial networks and public broadcasting relinquished nearly six hours of prime-time programming and spent hundreds of thousands of dollars covering the four debates. It was estimated that the commercial networks lost nearly $16 million in revenue over those four prime-time telecasts.

The logistics involved were staggering. The candidates devoted precious hours and days to rearranging their already hectic schedules and preparing for their appearances. Planeloads of journalists moved across the country to the four sites of the debates, lugging along literally tons of equipment. The newspaper space they devoted to coverage of the debates would fill volumes. It is clear, to judge by the time, money, and effort expended on them, that the debates are a milestone in American political life and history.

Criticism of the debates came from all quarters. Insiders, journalists, and others associated with the media claimed that the debates

---

[2] From a letter sent by Eugene P. Kopp, acting director, U.S. Information Agency, December 21, 1976, to the Honorable Frank Thompson, Jr., chairman, Committee on House Administration of the U.S. House of Representatives.

[3] A. C. Nielsen Co., Nielsen Plaza, Northbrook, Illinois. In a release dated November 5, 1976, Nielsen reported that 64.1 million households tuned in one or more of the debates, on average viewing 2.8 of the possible four debates. Nielsen figures 2.5 viewers per household; hence the 160 million figure.

had more to do with style than substance. Indeed, many political reporters who had covered the candidates throughout the campaign suggested that the debates produced no revelations new to them regarding either candidate. However true that may have seemed to them, the important thing to remember here is that the general public had no easy way of obtaining information about either candidate's position on the issues before the debates, and likely would not have sought it out even if such information had been handy. To a political reporter traveling with the candidates, the questions and answers of the debates may have seemed "old hat." To the viewing audience, on the other hand, the debates provided their first opportunity to see and hear the candidates addressing themselves to the critical campaign issues.

In that context, the debates were greatly substantive. The first debate, for example, showed that Mr. Carter was presenting himself as a conservative in fiscal matters. There was a marked contrast between the two candidates as to whether combating inflation or combating unemployment would be given priority. The defense budget, amnesty for draft resisters, national health care plans, aid to beleaguered cities, the environment—all these issues came up for discussion. The reporters may have heard it before, but it was fresh, new, and revealing to the massive audience which was taking a first long look at the two men from whom a president was to be chosen.

Sadly, neither the press nor the public took full advantage of one important facet of the debates. The subject matter of the debates and its treatment by the candidates should have spurred both press and viewer to further investigation of the candidates' positions. The press decided to place much of its emphasis on "horse race" analysis—who won or who lost—rather than on the issues and their ramifications. That emphasis was passively accepted by the public. It seems to me in retrospect that both press and public squandered an opportunity to enlighten each other about the campaign.

Other critics suggested that the debate format was misleading in that it asked the candidates to display qualities which had little to do with being president. Columnist Joseph Kraft said that the debates "put a premium on . . . quickness, the capacity to articulate something in a hurry, the appearance of being confident—very, very superficial qualities." NBC's Edwin Newman, moderator of the first debate, shares Kraft's basic view. But Newman went on to say, "The great advantage of the so-called debate format . . . is that it appears to be dramatic and leads people to watch. . . . And it does enlighten them somewhat about the candidates and the issues." Kraft also commented that "the debates were probably the best thing going in terms of giving the American people the best available view of the candidates in the flesh."[4]

Still other critics argued that the 1976 debates served no real purpose because many voters were already committed to their candidates and parties. A Roper poll showed, however, that late in 1976 nearly 56 percent of registered voters were uncommitted and were actually waiting to see the debates before making up their minds.[5] Half the electorate is a significant segment of the population to be uncommitted. A University of Wisconsin study by Steven H. Chaffee and Jack Dennis revealed that the voters who saw little or none of the debates cast their votes on candidate image, and that voters who saw part or all of the debates voted instead on issues.[6] The debates served to reinforce the convictions of committed voters and were a critical part of the decisions reached by uncommitted voters. In all cases, the debates forced viewers to watch and evaluate the opposition candidate; that result could not have been reached through any other form of comparison.

It was suggested that the 1976 presidential election was facing a meager voter turnout because of a lack of genuine controversy and emotion in the campaign. Before the debates, some observers were predicting a voter turnout as low as 40 percent of the electorate, one of the lowest in American history. But the debates breathed new life and fire into the campaign. The actual turnout was 53 percent, and the margin of increase can be directly attributed to the Ford-Carter television debates. In the case of Gerald Ford, the debates allowed him to close a seemingly insurmountable gap in popularity between himself and Carter. In Jimmy Carter's case, before each debate he had a prob-

---

[4] "Just How Great Were Those 'Great Debates'?" *Broadcasting*, January 3, 1977, p. 56.

[5] *Roper Reports* (New York: Roper Organization, 1976), vols. 76–79. A Roper Organization poll conducted during the week of August 28–September 4, 1976, showed the following:

	Percent
Strongly favor Carter	28
Strongly favor Ford	14
Total indicating strong preference	42
Slightly favor Carter	18
Slightly favor Ford	14
No preference	24
Total indicating slight or no preference	56

One conclusion which can be drawn from the Roper data is that approximately half the electorate was undecided or capable of being influenced by the debates.

[6] See Chapter 3 in this volume.

lem which the debate allowed him to resolve. In both cases, it was the independent or uncommitted voter who was watching closely and whom the debates finally convinced.

Perhaps the most telling fact about the 1976 debates is that as early as June of that year both camps were discussing the advisability of participating in the debates. Gerald Ford's decision to challenge Jimmy Carter to debate was apparently made on his way to accept the Republican nomination.[7] That decision was an attempt to half the Carter momentum which was building in the wake of the Democratic convention nearly a month before.

Gerald Ford found himself at the helm of a party in disarray. His challenge to Jimmy Carter served to galvanize the Republican forces behind their leader. Jody Powell, then Carter's top aide, insisted that the Carter camp had prepared the same challenge on the very day that Ford issued his. As Powell reflected later, a broken duplicating machine at Carter headquarters prevented a simultaneous exchange of challenges.

The "Great Debates" were a spectacle to some, an exercise in futility to others, *sine qua non* to still others. Amid all the retrospective analysis, one fact about them stands out clearly: they altered immeasurably the character and conduct of the 1976 presidential campaign and demonstrated the high desirability of making them mandatory in future campaigns.

The Case for Mandatory Debates

The case for mandatory debates is a two-part proposition, based on two interpretations of the imperative involved.

In the one sense, mandatory debates would mean that every candidate for the presidency would be obliged to present himself to the public for their inspection—for a "presidential job interview." It is not too much to ask the men who are applying for the highest job in the land to confront one another in a public forum on the issues and on their qualifications to serve. As I indicated before, the public receives perhaps their most comprehensive impressions of the candidates from television, and without the debates, the voters' decisions would be based primarily on the ad campaigns and the news clips.

It is said that Jimmy Carter, at one point during the 1976 campaign, called the debates "the surrogate campaign."[8] Although the

---

[7] See Chapter 4 in this volume.

[8] During the week of October 15, 1976, on the Carter campaign airplane, Jimmy Carter made this remark to Joseph Albright, Washington Bureau chief for Cox Newspapers. Albright related the conversation to me.

debates were never intended to substitute for the traditional campaign activities—whistle-stopping, "pressing the flesh," speaking engagements, and the like—they did indeed supplant some of those activities to the benefit of both candidates. Both Ford and Carter knew that the debates provided them with a unique opportunity to present themselves and their positions to the widest possible audience. Whatever points they may have lost or scored with the voters, they had the chance to present themselves as best they could.

Not only is there a need for the debates but the voters have an inalienable right to have them. The period between the debates of 1960 and 1976 saw the rise of the issue-oriented voter, an electorate more politically sophisticated and aware. That heightened awareness was created by the tumultuous events of those sixteen years: Vietnam, the Mideast, Watergate, the Chicago convention. Those crises and others made voters more aware of the need to gain access to candidates on all levels and to elicit from them their responses to problems facing the nation and the world. I advocate whatever steps may be necessary (short of a constitutional amendment) to ensure that televised presidential debates happen every four years. My own suggestions regarding such steps will be presented in the next section.

The second interpretation of the imperative relates to the necessity of making the preparations for and the staging of the debates as nonpartisan as possible. The debates should be developed and designed to preclude any input from any candidate which would weight the situations or content disproportionately.

In 1976 both Gerald Ford and Jimmy Carter expressed eagerness to debate. Yet both refused to agree to participate until each was satisfied that it was to his individual political advantage to do so. Even after the debates were agreed upon, intense and exhaustive negotiations were necessary among the two factions and the League of Women Voters, sponsors of the debates. These negotiations concerned moderators, locations, content, staff, and even set decoration. Beyond the negotiations with the candidates, there were lengthy discussions between the league and the networks about the television arrangements and format.

By the time the debates had become a certainty, but before the actual telecasts, some nine months' work had to be crowded into a scant five weeks. That late in the campaign, there was simply too much work to finish confidently and a great deal of pressure from the candidates to modify the debates according to rapidly developing trends in the campaign itself.

I propose, in light of the experiences of 1976, that a specific agenda of events be prepared and announced at the very beginning of the election year, and that all candidates be bound by it. In that way, the candidates' campaigns can be arranged to accommodate the debates, instead of the converse as in 1976. Announcing the agenda of events at an early stage in the campaign will also ensure sufficient time for full preparations for the telecasts.

A further reason for mandatory debates, and a persuasive one, is that three days after election day 1976 Jimmy Carter said that he could not have won without the debates. Since that statement, he has refused to commit himself to debate in the event that he runs for a second term. I consider it unlikely that any incumbent will willingly agree to debate his challengers. Further, Barry Jagoda, President Carter's media adviser, told me recently, "We won't participate in debates in 1980 without having a lot of input into the format and all other arrangements." Likewise, members of the Ford camp said that Gerald Ford would not have debated if he had not been forced to try to overcome a thirty-point deficit in the political polls.

These debates are too important to the voters to have to rely on the candidates' willingness for their existence. From the examples of 1976, it is clear that candidates, especially incumbents, are disposed not to debate unless pressured. Mandatory debates would make it necessary for the candidates to confront the electorate and each other face to face and would absent them from all influence on the form and content of the debates. This would make for an impartial forum that would enable the voter to choose on the basis of more and better evidence.

The Agenda of Events

The agenda of events that I propose is a carefully planned succession of televised political activities that should augment the campaign and serve the electorate in a logical step-by-step manner. This agenda would be announced at the very beginning of the election year to allow each party and candidate to incorporate it into the entire campaign strategy and schedule. The major events of the nine- to ten-week period from Labor Day to election are:

Week 1: Back-to-back addresses by the two candidates
Week 2: First presidential debate
Week 4: Second presidential debate
Week 5: Separate interviews with the presidential candidates
Week 6: Vice-presidential debate
Week 7: Third presidential debate

Week 8: Minority candidates debate

Last week before election: Fourth presidential debate.

In addition, at some time during this period, television should allow the public to hear from the major advisers to the candidates on domestic affairs, foreign affairs, fiscal policy, and other matters. We have all learned lessons about the president's men; we deserve a chance to assess them with the same scrutiny we apply to the presidential hopefuls. Although I have designated no specific event involving these advisers, I urge that attention be given them in some television forum during that period.

To take a closer look at each of the events on the agenda, in Week 1 the candidates would begin the climatic ten-week race to the election with open and unhindered public statements regarding their positions on issues, their policies, their priorities, and their qualifications. These statements would be presented on the same night, and the question of who goes first can be settled with the mere flip of a coin.

For the first debate, in Week 2, the subject matter, format, and questions to be posed would be predetermined, as for all subsequent debates. After approximately two weeks, the second debate would take place in Week 4.

In Week 5 the candidates would be interviewed separately, away from the debate format and atmosphere. This would be an opportunity for each candidate to assess the debates to that point, to clarify or explain any questionable areas of the debates, to update the electorate on the progress of their campaigns, and to address themselves to new or sustaining issues.

In Week 6 the vice-presidential candidates would be brought face-to-face in their own debate. This is the electorate's look at the men who may become, as the cliché goes, "a heartbeat away from the White House." In 1976, over 55 million people watched the Dole-Mondale debate.

In Week 7 the third presidential debate would take place, followed in Week 8 by a significant variation from the 1976 schedule: appearances by the minority candidates. This matter remains the Gordian knot of political predicaments. In 1976 there were 106 candidates for president legitimately registered with the Federal Election Commission at the time the debates began. Beyond the bare fact of a candidate's eligibility, there exists no equitable way to determine which of the minority candidates are "viable." The League of Women Voters was subjected to pressure and to legal action by the forces of Eugene McCarthy and Lester Maddox. Though the two were recognizable national figures, there remains a question as to their viability as presidential candidates.

The problem of minority candidates is further complicated by Section 315 of the Federal Communications Act, the so-called equal time provision. I advocate permanent repeal of Section 315 as it applies to presidential and vice-presidential races, and possibly throughout the entire political spectrum, including Senate, congressional, gubernatorial, and local elections. I think flagrant abuses of equal access to the media would be contested by public interest groups. Further, the cautions exercised by broadcasters regarding license renewal would keep political broadcast coverage balanced.

According to the proposed agenda, the final presidential debate would occur in the last week before the election.

Before we enter election year 1980, there will be many suggestions on how best to handle the events in such an agenda. The basic structure is flexible, however, and this or any other suitable agenda involves three critical factors: a format which guarantees direct meeting and exchange between the candidates; repeal of Section 315; and announcement of the agenda in January of the election year.

The National Debate Commission

To establish and enforce the agenda I have proposed, I further advocate the creation of a special National Debate Commission. It is essential that there be a formal body invested with the clout to oblige the candidates to debate. To judge by the league's experience in 1976, their months of intense background preparation might have been completely ignored had not Gerald Ford cast down the gauntlet to Jimmy Carter. Future debate might be jeopardized if the candidates cannot be forced to put aside any unwillingness they might feel.

The National Debate Commission should be chartered by Congress and include representatives from an extensive cross-section of society. Political associations, broadcasters and journalists, business and union officials, civic groups, nonpartisan interest groups such as the League of Women Voters, and individuals familiar with the negotiations and production of the debates should all be represented. The commission should be relatively small (no more than nineteen members) and must remain autonomous and immune to political interference. It should be funded by Congress or the Federal Election Commission.

If "debate fever" becomes contagious in this country, the commission could extend its influence throughout the entire election

163

process. A regulatory and advisory body such as the commission would be of tremendous value in revitalizing America's election process at the grass roots. It could establish a workable format for debates, formulate guidelines to be followed by candidates and broadcasters alike, and contribute immensely to the importance and effectiveness of political debate across the country. The commission could become the institution that fosters more and greater dialogue between candidates and the electorate. Such dialogue is necessary in a nation of politically sophisticated and aware voters. The most efficient and effective way to bring about permanent presidential debates is through the creation of the commission and the enforcement of a workable agenda of events that is mandatory for all candidates.

Throughout my approach to the agenda, I have made debates the pivotal events. Despite the various criticisms of the debate-type encounter, I maintain that it is the most favorable of settings. It has the irresistible appeal of a contest; it offers the only certain opportunity for immediate confrontation and exchange between the candidates; it is predicated upon spontaneity, a factor which has proven to figure strongly in the viewers' evaluations of the candidates; and it can offer (and I urge that it be provided) the opportunity for the candidates to cross-question each other directly. The participants in both the 1960 and 1976 debates denied themselves and each other the opportunity for cross-examination, but such exchanges would have been spirited, revealing, and healthy for both sets of candidates and their campaigns.

The Reason for It All

Above all considerations, and on the assumption that presidential debates will be mandatory, the reason for proposing these procedures is plainly to avoid repeating the chain of events which surrounded the 1976 debates. The Great Debates were like the little girl with the little curl: when they were good, they were very, very good, and when they were bad, they were horrid.

The League of Women Voters began the debates project amid adverse conditions. There was skepticism, maneuvering, and wariness on the part of both candidates' staffs. In the end, four peculiarities of the 1976 elections gave impetus to the league's dogged determination to promote the debates.

First, there was the widespread feeling that, in the wake of a decade or so of political scandal, the people wanted to know much more about their elected representatives. Independent surveys had shown that seven out of ten voters favored debates, and that public pressure could in fact be brought to bear on the candidates to commit themselves to them.

Second, a Federal Communications Commission ruling in the fall of 1975 left the candidates with no legal or legislative grounds on which to avoid the debates. The ruling stated that nonbroadcast groups could stage political debates as public events, and that radio and television covering them would be exempt from the equal-time rule.

Third, it looked as though Jimmy Carter was to be the Democratic nominee, and he would need the public exposure offered by the debates. Carter's campaign had made him relatively well known as a personality, but his positions on the issues were vague. It was thought that he would welcome the opportunity presented by the debates to assert his candidacy.

Fourth, and most significant, Gerald Ford needed the debates desperately. He had not been elected, and he was struggling to secure the nomination of his own party, which was bitterly divided. He was running well behind the possible Democratic nominees in the polls, and whoever was chosen as his opponent would be the standard-bearer of a party twice the size of his own.

In addition, the 1976 elections fell under the Federal Election Campaign Act and were federally funded. The ceiling placed on campaign spending negated the traditional Republican strategy of making up deficiencies in popularity or campaigning by simply outspending the opposition. Ford would need the debates in order to achieve campaign parity.

The league's preparations began in late April with meetings with each commercial network. The results were dismal. Each network emphatically rejected the notion of televised debates, particularly since they would be allowed limited influence in planning them. In the face of such opposition, the league mobilized a far-reaching campaign to build up interest in the project. Endorsements were sought from a cross-section of groups—civic, political, professional, union, and business. A major nationwide petition was launched by the league through its local chapters in an effort to enlist backing for the debates at the grass roots. An editorial campaign was promoted in the daily press to draw the attention of the public to the debates and the need for them. A series of polls was commissioned through George Gallup, Jr., a member of the league's steering committee. One such poll indicated, as I have stated, that seven out of ten voters wanted the debates and thought they would bring the presidential campaign into sharper focus. The last phase of the preparations involved working with the candidates themselves. As has been indicated, the candidates and their staffs were reluctant throughout.

On the morning of August 19, 1976, I sent a message by telegram to both candidates simultaneously. That message invited them to participate in the proposed series of debates sponsored by the League of Women Voters Education Fund. I sent the message on behalf of the Debates Negotiating Team, which consisted of League President Ruth Clusen; Executive Director Peggy Lampl; and Co-Chairmen Rita Hauser, Newton Minow, Charls Walker, and myself. The message contained many details which we knew would undergo alteration in the weeks to come, but it would serve as the practical basis for our agreement and all further negotiation. We urged both candidates to recognize the shortness of time and to designate a negotiating representative to meet with us as soon as possible.

Later that morning we held a press conference to disclose the contents of the invitation and to foster among the press a supportive and attentive posture toward the debates. It was as though we were announcing plague. A mere eleven reporters attended. A scant eleven weeks from election day we were unable to convince key people (press, networks, campaign staffs) to take the project seriously. It took President Ford's dramatic challenge to thrust the concept into the center of public and media attention.

Those immense difficulties—apathy and skepticism on the part of the candidates, the oppressive time restrictions, the complex and often frustrating negotiations, the extensive research and background preparation, the mobilization of literally thousands of people, and the coordination of their activities—were patently beyond the scope of even so vast, well-organized, and competent an institution as the League of Women Voters. It is a tribute to the devotion and single-mindedness of all concerned, not only that the debates happened at all, but also that they were on balance a success.

These difficulties and their resolutions are the province of a commission such as the National Debate Commission which I have proposed. That body could be empowered to perform all the necessary creative and logistical activities aimed at bringing about the debates. It could develop an agenda of events such as the one proposed earlier, and make it an integral part of campaign activity. Announcing that agenda early, perhaps January 1 of election year, would serve several purposes. It would likely promote earlier and more lasting interest among the voters in the campaign and in the candidates. In addition, there would be less anxiety—on the part of the candidates, the press, and the public—about the "sudden-death" significance of the debates, that is, the negative effects of blunders, disclosures, or theatrics. An early start and an extended period over which the events of the agenda would be scheduled would minimize these effects and allow sufficient time for the candidates to correct errors and false meanings. (Would Gerald Ford's candidacy have been different if he had been able to clarify his disastrous blunder about Eastern European freedom in the second debate?)

The commission could also develop for each event on the agenda a format that is equitable to all candidates. It could decide on the proper mix of unchallenged declaration, question and debate, and cross-examinations between the principals. The commission would have the latitude to invite carefully chosen moderators and panel members, to formulate issues to be addressed or questions to be asked, and to deal with the participants liberally without coercion from either candidate or the networks. In such an atmosphere, the candidates can be made to feel unrestrained in their approach to each other and to the issues at hand.

Perhaps the most forcible argument for the creation of the National Debate Commission is the Federal Election Campaign Act. Primaries and general elections are now federally funded. With predictable ceilings on the expenditures of candidates, many traditional campaign activities will be severely curtailed or even eliminated. The debates offer an attractive substitute for activities which become unaffordable. At the same time, the need for candidates to reach diverse voter blocs and growing numbers of uncommitted and independent voters will not diminish. The knowledge that their campaigns are being fueled by tax dollars may increase pressure on candidates to become more visible and more accountable to the public concerning national issues and their own political stands.

Debates such as the 1976 encounters are becoming more and more popular as a campaign element. Of 252 members of Congress who responded to a recent poll, nearly 70 percent said they had met their opponents in debate during their last campaign.[9]

Debates offer the electorate a necessary alternative to the media images so carefully projected by candidates through their media advisers. Political commercials can be revealing in that they show

---

[9] Poll of Congress by the Campaign '78 Debate Survey Project for the Aspen Institute, September 1977; Jim Karayn, project director; Douglas Frost, project coordinator. The project sent questionnaires to sitting members of the Senate and House. Of the 252 who answered, 176 of them, or 69.8 percent, said they met their opponents in debate in their last campaign. Of those who debated, 114, or almost 65 percent, said they felt that debates "contribute significantly to the electoral process."

the voters what the candidate wants them to notice. The self-image implicit in them can be important in helping the voter form a comprehensive portrait of the candidate. But nothing can replace or even approach the value to the voter of a candid, spontaneous, face-to-face meeting in which the voter has the advantage of immediate comparison and contrast.

I am firmly convinced that the best interest of America's voting public is at stake in the concept of the National Debate Commission and its activities. In this age of growing voter apathy and less than candid political campaign activities, the possibility of direct communication between candidates and the public cannot be dismissed. In the face of weakening party affiliations and fuzzy definitions of issues, candidates, and their policies, the benefits and potentials of televised debates are immense.

The Great Debates of 1976 were a demonstration of American democracy at its best. President Carter, in writing about the debates, said, "There will never be any way of knowing for sure which of us gained the most from the debates. The polls do not present a clear picture. The only certain winner was the American voters, to whom the debates afforded an invaluable chance to examine the candidates in intimate detail."[10]

---

[10] From a letter from Jimmy Carter to Dr. Sidney Kraus, director of communications, Cleveland State University, April 8, 1977.

Discussion

AUSTIN RANNEY, American Enterprise Institute: You have said public pressure is the way to make incumbent presidents engage in debates. I don't quite see how this public pressure would make them debate if they really don't want to. Can you speak to that?

KARAYN: I believe that the only thing we had going for us in 1976 was public pressure, and we found an incumbent who wanted to debate as well as a challenger who knew he was going to have to debate. But public pressure is the only tool we have. We cannot leave it to the prospective nominees; we need a commitment from the Democratic national chairman and the Republican national chairman that whoever their parties nominate has to debate.

RANNEY: You might get such commitments out of the two national chairmen, but how are they going to make their candidates live up to those commitments once they are nominated? Surely there is no way the national chairmen can make the nomination conditional on accepting the obligation to debate.

RICHARD CHENEY, former Ford chief of staff: Especially in light of the fact that the first order of business for the nominee is to decide whether or not to keep the incumbent chairman or replace him. As I said earlier, I am still reluctant to let anything other than the candidates' own judgment govern whether or not there should be a debate. It seems to me that in general terms we should advocate the process. But binding commitments that take away the candidates' control over their own campaigns make me very uncomfortable.

KARAYN: Everybody worries about the rights of the candidates, but we impose certain conditions on being a candidate. By law we say that a

NOTE: James Karayn's case for permanent presidential debates was presented to the conference in a form somewhat different from that of the preceding chapter. The discussion is still relevant, however, since it concerned the substance of his position rather than the manner of presentation.

president has to be thirty-five years old or older and has to be born in America. A candidate has to accept certain limitations on what kind of funding he can take and on how much funding he will have.

I think debating becomes even more of an obligation when candidates take federal money, and I do not think it should be left entirely up to the candidates to decide all by themselves how they are going to campaign before the public. Maybe debating should be regarded as an obligation they have to the public and they have to fit it in. They can campaign any way they want, using speeches, commercials, or anything else. But they also have to do debates because, with all of their flaws, the debates are the most purely voter-oriented events in a campaign. I'm not against campaign commercials. They give a lot of information, but I don't think they should be the only thing.

CHENEY: Are you suggesting that debates should be mandatory?

KARAYN: Yes.

CHENEY: Should they be made a condition, perhaps, for receiving federal funds for campaigns?

KARAYN: That is one way of making them mandatory. I don't think it should be left to each candidate to decide whether to debate. He can campaign any way he wants; this is not taking away his right to campaign. But he has to come to a "job interview," and the people who "own the company"—the voters—make the conditions of when, where, and how they want to conduct the job interview.

Dick Cheney, let me ask you this: In a practical sense, if Gerald Ford had been ten points ahead after the convention, and if the economy had not been a problem at the time, do you think your people would have debated?

CHENEY: I can't speak for President Ford on this point. In terms of what I would have advised—and obviously we are talking about a hypothetical situation—I'd have to say I would not have been very eager to enter into a debate.

You have talked about the public pressure that was built for debates. We did not feel any pressure. We made a cold, hard, calculated decision that the debate option offered us something we felt we needed in our strategy. If we had concluded that the debate option didn't make any sense, we would not have had any problem saying, "Sorry, we aren't going to debate." Especially for an incumbent president, it boils down to a situation where he has to make the call himself. Unless debates are made mandatory and required by law, the decision is going to be made on an essentially political basis. My judgment would be that trying to build some other kind of structure to guarantee that an incumbent will debate simply will not work.

CHARLS E. WALKER, cochairman of the 1976 Debates Steering Committee: I think we would have a good chance of pulling it off by repealing Section 315 and creating a high-powered blue-ribbon commission. I wouldn't go so far as to make it mandatory. But make them an offer they can't refuse. If the incumbent, in particular, does refuse he would put himself in a very difficult situation and possibly lose a lot of support as a result.

When the commission lays out the dates and the schedule, it is known in advance what the dates are going to be. Then, when the time for the debates comes, it would be very risky, in my judgment, for the incumbent to back out unless he had a tremendous lead. As I said earlier, I don't believe that any president of the United States is going to have that sort of tremendous lead, given all the problems that confront him.

I would like to see a move made in Congress along those lines. The real problem, it seems to me, is political. If Mr. Carter is very much against it, the Democratic Congress will not move against his wishes. Having said that, as a Republican-type lobbyist, I will be glad to donate the services of my firm for lobbying for setting up a commission.

KARAYN: We did a pretty good job of organizing public pressure. We had something like fifty-seven major newspapers in this country, well in advance of the Republican convention, favoring debates. We even had editorials on the networks supporting debates before they became concerned about who was going to sponsor them. We had Gallup polls which showed that eight out of ten people in America wanted the candidates, whoever they were, to debate. The League of Women Voters got a lot of publicity over a petition drive. We had people like you lobbying at the White House. And yet Dick Cheney says they really didn't feel the pressure. Does any president? Maybe we are being terribly naive.

WALKER: I agree with Cheney. I don't think the pressure was there now that I have learned from his fascinating paper that the decision had been made considerably earlier. I had been basking in the light of the memo I sent to the White House in August giving all the strong reasons for the debates—but the decision had already been made.

HAL BRUNO, *Newsweek* magazine: I don't like the idea of a mandatory government commission, but I think that in the very natural course of events an incumbent president who refuses to debate is now going to spend the entire fall campaign explaining why he won't debate. If I were the campaign manager for his opponent, I would simply buy TV time and put the empty chair on the platform. I think the debates are going to become institutionalized, almost by force of public opinion.

CHENEY: Circumstances may have changed, given what happened in 1976, but I still would advise the current incumbent in 1980 to sit down and look at the possibilities. Is it going to help or hurt him to debate? If it's going to hurt him, don't do it. If it's going to help, do it. It is basically that kind of a judgment, and the question is whether circumstances have changed enough so that there is no way at this point that he could avoid a debate in 1980, because of the political cost.

MARGITA E. WHITE, Federal Communications Commission: I would like to go back for a moment to Jim Karayn's comment about the power of television. Doesn't that logically lead to some follow-up steps? For example, would the president be required to have press conferences, or would congressional meetings have to be televised, or would local congressmen have to appear on local television and be accountable once a month?

KARAYN: Yes, I think presidents should hold regular press conferences, but not by law. I think that broadcasters should do everything in their power to get mayors and governors to hold regular press conferences. And I think local broadcasters should be chastised if they don't carry the press conferences.

WHITE: Are you talking about a law or a mandate by law?

KARAYN: I don't like laws any more than anyone else. I hope these things would come about because people feel an obligation and, if they don't do it, because a lot of pressure will be put on them. But I would almost say that there should be a law, if they are not going to do it on their own. I feel these appearances are due the electorate.

GEOFFREY SMITH, London *Times*: On the basis of British experience I put forward a suggestion earlier of having candidates appear incessantly within the confines of one program. I press this point because most of the arguments that you have used to justify debates seem to me to be relevant to the case for candidates for president submitting themselves to scrutiny by independent examiners on television during the course of a campaign. There are different ways of doing that. The debate is one of those ways, but it is not the only way.

KARAYN: That is why I call my whole proposal an agenda of events. The debates are the centerpiece of it, but there should be some exploration of candidates alone. I propose that midway through the agenda there should be a one-on-one interview with each candidate. At the beginning of the agenda, each candidate would take, say, a half hour to explain why he wants to be president, what he thinks of the problems of the country, how he thinks he will go about solving them.

I feel that the debates are still the main item on this agenda because they get a great audience. They are contests, and that is important. Two people are pitted against one another, and that makes it interesting to the public.

If we had put Carter on for fifteen minutes and then Ford for fifteen minutes, I don't think we would have gotten half the audience. We might have for the first one, perhaps, because everybody felt obliged to see it; but not for the others.

It is a fact that people watch. It is a contest, a confrontation, and that, frankly, makes good television. It is playing to the masses, yes, but it gets information over—and without sacrificing much information. I am willing to do a debate or a confrontation format to get more of the public to watch. Maybe some people are not.

Perhaps I have been in public television too long—I know how to bore people. One of the worst things we could do would be to create a magnificent program and have no audience. We would not have done a thing, if we put on two presidential candidates and only the aficionados and their families watched them.

There is something about two men coming together in the same room, even if they are not debating each other face to face, even if there is a third party in between asking questions. They are playing to a world audience, and they are very conscious of being together.

At the first debate in Philadelphia the Carter people insisted that there be "parity"; that was always their line. When we got down to how many people could be backstage, we finally arrived at ten people for each candidate, plus three extra for the President: his physician, the White House communications operator, and the President's military aid. And still the Carter people complained. So I said,

"We'll hire you a nurse and a guy from the phone company, and we'll go to Woolworth's and get you a phone and put it in a black bag so you can have parity plus three also."

It is important that the candidates come together. Otherwise we will not get the audience. Maybe we should have three one-on-one interviews, and maybe only three debates. I don't know the magic formula there. But in the agenda of events the centerpiece should be debates, because they will get the largest audience.

Some people have argued that there should not be debates because in this country we do not have a parliamentary system; and since party leaders do not debate issues in parliament, debating is not a skill a president needs. I don't know. A president, from the day he is inaugurated, is under constant pressure. Those debate situations with his opponent create some of the conditions that he is going to face as president, some of the tension that he is going to live under.

It is foolish to say that the way a candidate responds, his glibness, his ability to think on his feet, are not important qualities for anyone who is trying to be president. If a president is not prepared to appear on television two or three times a week, in one form or another —then he is not going to make it. I don't care how good a president he is otherwise. He needs to keep his credibility with the public, and a lot of that comes from his ability to conduct himself well on his feet, with television looking over his shoulder and picking up everything he does, every gesture he makes. Those are the facts of life, and debates help us understand them.

7

Debatable Thoughts on Presidential Debates

Nelson W. Polsby

Are presidential debates a good idea? Embedded in this deceptively simple question are several others, not so easy to formulate or to answer. When we discuss presidential debates, are we discussing some idealized notion of presidential debates, or presidential debates of the kind we are most likely to get? Is the implicit model the Ford-Carter debates or the Kennedy-Nixon debates or perhaps even the Lincoln-Douglas debates? What sorts of constraints, controls, or conditions should govern presidential debates? Who should monitor or impose these conditions? If presidential debates are a bad idea, should they be prohibited? If they are a good idea, should they be made mandatory?

The contribution that presidential debates in some idealized sense are supposed to make to American politics can be stated compactly. They are supposed to contribute to public enlightenment in at least two ways: (1) By exhibiting the main presidential candidates in a situation in which they relinquish control over the agenda, and hence must react spontaneously, it is thought that candidates' real capabilities and limitations can be discovered. (2) By subjecting the candidates to similar stimuli, any differences in the responses can be attributed to genuine differences in their basic characters or personalities or philosophies and hence can be considered reliably predictive of real differences in their likely conduct of the presidential office. Debates are therefore to be regarded as an especially useful form of public discussion, without which, as democratic theory instructs us, public choice is uninformed and irrational. Rationality, the conscious adaptation of means to ends, is a necessary condition of choice processes in which citizens get approximately what they want in the way of public officials and public policy. Debates, therefore, can be seen at a minimum as useful adjuncts to the deliberations through which citizens make their most important contribution to the proper functioning of democratic government and as potentially helpful in assisting an intelligent and effective choice.

The Ideal versus the Probable

This, at any rate, is how presidential debates ought to contribute to electoral decision making, and in an ideal world they would certainly do so. But to what extent are these ideals reflected in actual practice? Is the argument in favor of debates founded on empirical premises that are well established in historical experience? At two key places in the argument outlined above, the verdict must be negative.

Spontaneity. Political candidates, while not averse to appearing to be spontaneous, are in general loath to let go of the agenda when exposed to the public. Typically, they seek rather tight ground rules establishing a limited subject matter for their joint appearances. In the presidential debates of both 1960 and 1976, the classic debate format —in which antagonists address one another—was discarded in favor of "parallel play." In the latter format nobody needs to play the "heavy," and the incidental presence of an opponent in the room is subordinated to the requirement that both candidates respond to the questions of a panel of journalists. This format maximizes the opportunity for campaigners to key their responses to rhetorical formulas already in use in their campaigns and to avoid saying anything new.

Observers of the first Ford-Carter debate could see what happened when a genuinely unplanned and unforeseen event interrupted the flow of campaign slogans. The failure of a small piece of electronic equipment shut off the broadcast sound for twenty-odd minutes. The candidates seized the opportunity for spontaneity by standing in their places, zombie-like, acknowledging neither the presence of one another nor the respite from their ordeal. It was as though they had been wrapped in aluminum foil and frozen for twenty minutes, an appalling demonstration of their utter reliance on preprogramming.

A student of rhetoric might well ask: To what extent did the candidates make use of the presidential debates to introduce fresh ideas, fresh thoughts, fresh language into the discussion? To what extent did they fall back on the rhetoric they had already tried out on hundreds of audiences and used in countless more stereotyped campaign situations? Casual observation suggests that both Carter and Ford scored as close to zero on a freshness scale as it is humanly possible to do.

In a sense, they were ratifying the political judgment that John Kennedy and Richard Nixon made before them. The following passages give the flavor of these two candidates' attitudes toward the opportunity their debates afforded for the spontaneous revelation of their talent for governing. The first is from Nixon's *Six Crises*:

> All the previous week I had used every spare minute preparing my opening statement and studying the issues that might be raised by the panel of newsmen. I got up early Sunday morning and worked through the day, without interruption. . . . For five solid hours that afternoon I read through the digested materials which my staff had prepared, on every issue that might conceivably be raised during the course of the debate. . . . I had crammed my head with facts and figures in answer to more than a hundred questions which my staff suggested might be raised.[1]

The second passage is from Theodore Sorensen's *Kennedy*:

> [Kennedy] directed that his schedule be arranged so as to allow him the maximum time for briefing, preparation and rest before each encounter. . . . Prior to the first debate, we reduced to cards and reviewed for hours the facts and figures on every domestic issue, every Kennedy charge and every Nixon countercharge. We threw at the Senator all the tough and touchy questions we could devise. One session was held on the sunlit roof of his Chicago hotel, another in his sitting room, the last in his bedroom after he had confidently napped for nearly three hours in the midst of a bed full of file cards.[2]

Stuffed like Christmas geese with "facts and figures," the candidates went before the camera. As we all know, Kennedy "won," mostly on appearance, not substance, and mostly because of the first debate— although the influence of the debates overall on the electoral outcome has never been established to have been substantial. But in a close election, every feather on the scale assumes great weight.

The Kennedy-Nixon debates sanctified certain political verities that have subsequently aided thinking about the real value of the debate format. "Winning" is a matter of subsequent interpretation and occurs in two categories. Honors for general appearance, poise, fluency, good manners, lack of perspiration, good posture and so on, the

---

[1] Richard M. Nixon, *Six Crises* (New York: Giant-Cardinal Edition, 1962), pp. 362–363.

[2] Theodore C. Sorensen, *Kennedy* (New York: Harper and Row, 1965), p. 198.

"smile and shoeshine" qualities immortalized by Willy Loman, are within the gift of the general populace as measured by commercial poll takers. Kennedy worried about being too youthful and cut his hair. Nixon worried about being too menacing and (after a careless beginning) pancaked his five o'clock shadow. Ford's seconds worried about baldness, Carter's about shortness and about the presidential seal.

There is no way to sweep the field in this category; the goal for each candidate is to look presentable and inoffensive. Strangely enough, at the second level of competition, in which elite observers—the press and professional political handicappers who have independent access to the media—judge the substance of the candidates' presentations, the same fatuous rule applies. Mistakes, misstatements, miscalculations, contradictions, slips, and errors are all that matter. No particular credit is given for originality or thoughtfulness, and the revelation of a complex mind is just as likely as not to be interpreted as indecision or vagueness and lack of capacity for leadership.

In this context, the debates are best understood not as an occasion for the ventilation of ideas or the exploration of genuine disagreements about the future course of events, but as a trial by ordeal, pure and simple. Whoever holds his hand over the fire for the prescribed period without flinching survives. There are no winners, however, just losers—those who say something that sends the press baying like a pack of beagles into the next week or ten days seeking after clarifications, revisions, apologies, or concessions. It is no wonder that the candidates themselves are so fixated on preparation, on control over the setting, on elaborate ground rules, and are so little inclined to emphasize the potential of the debates to encourage spontaneity.

Inferences about the President in Office. The same forces are at work nullifying inferences about the candidates' probable conduct of public office. In a setting such as the debates, no sane presidential candidate will attempt to defend a course of action that seems vulnerable to attack, even though he knows perfectly well he will follow it. Nobody who heard the Ford-Carter debates—and who knew nothing about the conduct of foreign affairs—could doubt that neither possible subsequent administration would tolerate secrecy in foreign relations. The actual outcome has been quite different, as knowledgeable observers knew it would be. In reality, both candidates knew perfectly well that the conduct of foreign affairs is impossible without a high degree of secrecy, but neither was willing to defend the proposition on nationwide television, especially with his opponent nearby and ready to adopt the more easily defended position. The debate format is certainly no guarantee against the raising of fake issues, and, as in the case of secrecy, may actually hinder the process of civic education on any issue that presents problems of public relations.

This, however, merely involves an unwillingness on the part of candidates to disclose their likely behavior if elected. A more fundamental problem is their inability to do so, since in the American politi- K cal system the capacity to debate is of negligible relevance in actually governing. At most, candidates can say—with greater or lesser degrees of truthfulness—which of an array of policy alternatives they would pick, and perhaps in an especially revealing discussion they might disclose their capacity to think of or to formulate alternatives. On the whole, however, the ability to stimulate a bureaucratic apparatus to bring forth alternatives while no doubt related to an ability to imagine alternatives in the first place, requires a large panoply of talents and disciplines that are not so easily revealed by the debate format. The capacity to pick correctly among alternatives, to understand the reasons for picking one alternative and not another, the capacity to see whether the selected alternative is being pursued by a government agency—these managerial talents are quite inexpressible through debate. It is rather like judging the ability of a comedian to get good results from his writers by watching him ad-lib a routine.[3]

Talents for administration of a bureaucratic apparatus, or negotiation with constitutional equals, patience and tact under fire, the capacity to motivate others in day-to-day contact, even the willingness K to do homework over a long period, all are hard, if not impossible, to infer from the way in which even the most skilled politicians debate. One difficulty is the fact that debates are far more ritualistically antagonistic in their structure than is the general run of a president's day-to-day administrative experience. Even when dealing with congressional adversaries, the goal, quite unlike that in the debate situation, is to find common ground, not to sharpen differences of opinion. This is, of course, a feature of any system of separation of powers and contrasts sharply with the parliamentary tradition where bashing the opposition in oral debate is still considered a useful attribute in a leader. The latter talent is frequently a hindrance in the sort of legislative bargaining or foreign affairs discussion in which a president must engage.

My conclusion is that presidential debates do not reveal the un-

---

[3] A famous illumination of the different skills involved is Fred Allen's observation about Jack Benny, a master editor of comic writers, that he "couldn't ad-lib a belch after a Hungarian meal."

guarded inner man nor do they disclose the caliber of his intellectual equipment most relevant to the conduct of the presidential office.

Some Residual Advantages

The foregoing argument is meant to knock presidential debates off their pedestal rather than to characterize them as utterly useless. Viewed in a light less exalted than the rosy glow cast by democratic theory, debates may have advantages. For one thing, they are extremely good advertising. As long as campaign expenditures are limited as a condition of federal subsidy for presidential campaigns, the advertising value of debates cannot be ignored. Debates get people's attention—especially the first debate in a series. They alert the television-watching population to the advent of an election, and they provide elementary information about the main contenders. One of the chief effects of expenditure limitations in the 1976 election was to dry up voluntary efforts and to restrict local advertising for the national ticket. Televised debates, themselves suitably advertised, can take up some of the slack, help pass the word around, and increase the interest and attention of the general population in the upcoming election.

Candidates can to some extent use a debate series to speak directly to voters without the mediation or interpretation of the press. This opportunity is not unqualified, since television commentators have their say before and after the candidates speak. If the 1960 and 1976 format is followed, some attention has to be paid to the subjects raised by the panel of journalists. As I have already suggested, however, and as the experiences of 1960 and 1976 have amply demonstrated, candidates can easily evade the point of questions put to them and simply respond to key words in the question, thus delivering whatever message they like—whether preprogrammed or not. Their major problem is to avoid the pitfall of making some untoward or unguarded remark that will require a damaging subsequent admission of mistakenness, or imprecision, or lack of clarity. The press can be relied on to pursue any such opportunity for embarrassment that candidates provide, and this greatly circumscribes the candidates' own chances to use the debate format to make an unmediated presentation of their own views.

Although it is not always good politics to do so, the debate format can provide an opportunity for candidates actually to sharpen the issues between them, thus illustrating at least crudely to voters the policy consequences of a vote in one direction or another. In general, for example, Democrats worry more about unemployment than inflation, Republicans more about inflation than unemployment. Presumably, candidates can make such points in a debate situation, although this general exercise in line-drawing may be misleading as a guide to governmental policy once a president is in office. Lyndon Johnson, had he debated Barry Goldwater in 1964, would certainly have pursued a theme that was prominent in his campaign, accusing Goldwater of an itchy trigger finger. Yet this would have misled the voters about what Johnson himself would do after the election. Many people who followed the career of Richard Nixon with care and approval were bitterly disappointed by his Chinese diplomatic initiative. Jimmy Carter's desire to balance the federal budget will make it difficult for him to display the compassion toward the unemployed he accused Gerald Ford of neglecting. Yet it may be true that Johnson was indeed a more pacific choice than Goldwater, that those who voted for Nixon did correctly calculate the odds against rapprochement with China as compared with what Humphrey or McGovern would have done, and that Ford is a far less probable friend of the unemployed than Carter. For what it is worth, debates do give candidates a chance to display genuine (as well as to advertise false) differences between themselves, even if they lead to no difference at all in the ultimate conduct of governmental affairs.

Finally, although highly contrived and artificial, and not particularly helpful for predicting administrative behavior, debates offer a situation in which both candidates occupy more or less similar and similarly exposed positions. For viewers who can find some intellectual sustenance in seeing both candidates under corresponding conditions of stress, debates afford an opportunity to make whatever direct comparisons they think appropriate.

Thus, of the four residual advantages of debates—the opportunity to get the attention of the voters, the opportunity for candidates to speak directly to large audiences unmediated by journalistic interpretations, the opportunity to sharpen issues, and the opportunity for viewers to compare candidates under roughly comparable circumstances—only the opportunity to advertise seems to me to emerge as an unqualified benefit.

Inferences for Policy

If the benefits of debates are dubious, there seems no compelling reason to insist on them as a matter of public policy. I am aware of no evidence demonstrating that presidential electorates which have been edified by debates are very much better informed than electorates in years when no debates have occurred. A general propensity on the part of some voters to expose themselves to debates no doubt correlates strongly with a receptivity to all sorts of political information, and so while it may be true that enthusiastic debate-watchers are better informed than most of their fellow citizens, in all likelihood this would be true even in the absence of debates.

It may be argued that while debates cannot be shown to do much good, neither do they do much harm, and therefore obstacles should not be put in their path. This argument is certainly unexceptionable as far as the interests of the vast majority of the general public is concerned. The issue is a bit more clouded, however, when we contemplate the interests of candidates of nonnegligible minor parties and the protection of their rights to proselytize among the general population as easily as do major party candidates. In the past, debates between the two major candidates have been facilitated by legislation temporarily suspending FCC requirements of equal access to radio and television for all candidates for a given public office. Without legislative sanction, station managers, at best a notoriously skittish lot, would feel vulnerable to complaints from parties of all sizes that equal time was being denied them. Certainly there is a general public interest in providing ample opportunity for people to glimpse the most likely next incumbents of high public office, and this suggests that the legislative decision to facilitate debates, when the major parties have agreed to have them, is the correct resolution of the problem, as far as it goes.

There remains, however, some difficulty over the question of the standing of minor parties, and on this account one hesitates to recommend that the major parties receive substantial or additional forms of assistance or incentives to conduct debates that are restricted to their candidates alone. It is hard enough to organize politically outside the two major parties in this country. Recent rules providing for federal subsidies have awarded very substantial advantages to the major parties. To press their advantage even further seems on the face of it to be questionable public policy.

Where does this leave the matter of presidential debates? The wisest course, it seems to me, is neither to require nor to prohibit them; they should be legally possible but unsubsidized. Under such circumstances, I would expect that in some presidential election campaigns there would be presidential debates, and in some years there would not.

I do not know of any exhaustive list of strategic contingencies that purports to enumerate all the factors controlling the probability of debates taking place. Among the considerations involved, I should think would be the following:

1. In general, incumbent presidents running for reelection ought not to want to debate. This would give their opponent too big a target to shoot at and invite making their record the primary campaign issue. It may well be that an incumbent's record in office ought to be the main issue of a campaign, but there is no reason to expect an incumbent willingly to offer up such a juicy prospect to an opponent. In addition, sharing a platform with an adversary tends to waste the asset of incumbency by dissipating the aura of mystery that clings to the presidential office. Seeing a challenger and a president debating on equal terms may put in people's heads the notion that either one might well occupy the presidency, an idea that it is in the interest of the incumbent to discourage.

2. Conversely, anyone who challenges an incumbent should want very much to debate, since a debate in these circumstances is a free ticket to parity in the eyes of many observers.

3. An incumbent president can be regarded as a special case of a larger class of candidates, namely, people who are for one reason or another extremely well known as compared with their opponents. It is, in general, not in their interests to aid in advertising the competition.

For example, in the California gubernatorial election of 1974, the Democratic candidate, Edmund G. Brown, Jr., had reason to believe his name was well and favorably known. Many prominent California politicians have carried the name of Brown, including the young Mr. Brown's father, Edmund G. (Pat) Brown, Sr., the former governor. When Brown's Republican opponent, Houston Flournoy, proposed debates, Brown was faced with a tactical dilemma. It was unwise to give Flournoy an opportunity to go about the state proclaiming Brown's cowardice and debating an empty chair. It was also unwise to give Flournoy a lot of free exposure by agreeing to a series of well-publicized debates. Brown's managers solved this problem by agreeing to several debates but demanding that they be shown only to narrowly restricted audiences. Thus, they felt they could avert the stigma of avoiding debates but at the same time retain many of the advantages of having refused to debate at all.[4]

4. In general, Republicans should want to debate, and Democrats should want to avoid debates. Two axioms of American politics lead to this conclusion. One is that Democrats outnumber Republicans by

[4] Mary Ellen Leary, *Phantom Politics* (Washington, D.C.: Public Affairs Press, 1977) pp. 94–111.

a substantial margin in the presidential electorate. The other is that people tend to pay more attention to the messages sent by their own party. Thus, the task of a Republican candidate for president is, in part, to find ways of wooing potentially disloyal Democratic voters, a task which entails, in part, getting their attention. Since debates mobilize large audiences from both sides, if a Republican can conduct himself in a way that does not polarize sentiments but appeals to a bipartisan audience, the debates give him his best chance to make his case.

5. Conversely, Democrats should be extremely wary of a debate situation, since their chances of converting Republicans are in general far less than the chances that Democrats will defect. Republican voters are on the whole very loyal to their party and are less easy to dislodge than Democrats. So, the net effect of a debate under ordinary circumstances is that both candidates will be targeting Democratic viewers. Democratic candidates must decide, in calculating whether or not to debate, the effects of giving their opponents a chance to work the Democratic side of the street.

I know of no compelling reason to take calculations of this kind away from politicians and to demand that they debate or require that they not debate. If debates themselves could be shown to be an overwhelmingly informative sort of civic education, it might be worth asserting a general interest in their favor. But no such thing can be shown, and consequently the way in which candidates handle the question of whether or not to debate can properly assume its place as one more piece of information that sophisticated observers can use in taking the measure of candidates.

Improving Presidential Debates

Most of the comments I have made so far refer to presidential debates of the kind we had in 1960 and 1976. Both sets of debates were notable for their intellectual barrenness and suggest the possibility that debates are most likely to occur when there is the least to debate about. This ought to be a sobering thought to those familiar with how Abraham Lincoln and Stephen Douglas used the possibilities of the debate format in 1858. That notable series took place in several county seats in Illinois. The opening speaker customarily held forth for one hour; his opponent replied for one and a half hours, and the first speaker wound up for a half hour. Spectators streamed from far and wide to witness one or more of these debates, and it may be supposed that a fair number of those present came away with an enlarged understanding of the most pressing issues of the day.[5]

Nobody sits still for three hours of political oratory these days, and given the general level of American political oratory, it is no wonder. Yet there is a nagging temptation to ask if something might not be done to improve the potential for civic education of an event like presidential debates. A large number of Americans will watch, and a substantial proportion of them will be genuinely eager to learn what they can about the future conduct of their affairs.

What is required at a minimum is something that candidates are most unlikely to grant, namely, a change in format that would open up the possibility of more spontaneous consideration of issues and that would permit better inferences about the way candidates would actually behave in office. Confrontations between candidates can be ruled out as a method for producing either of these desiderata, even if candidates were willing to participate in confrontations, which they evidently are not. Likewise, I wonder if the panel of captive "neutral" journalists has not had its day. One very great difficulty with this format, hallowed by thirty years of Sunday afternoons with Lawrence Spivak and his imitators, is the severe constraints that interrogating journalists have been required to observe. One follow-up question seems to be the limit beyond which interchange between candidate and questioner is forbidden.

This is altogether unsatisfactory. The spontaneous capabilities of a candidate's mind can be discovered far more successfully in conversation, where entitlement to the floor is subject to tacit negotiation, moment by moment, where interruptions are possible, and where all parties to the interaction are responsible for its content, and the straightjacket of question and answer gives way to a more freely flowing discussion. Skill at this sort of conversation is far more relevant to the conduct of the presidency, because a president must stimulate and participate in this sort of interaction in order to do his job.

It is not beyond the reach of human ingenuity to design a format that captures some of these qualities. A presidential debate on economics could be scheduled for, say, a Sunday from 3:00 to 6:00 P.M. By lot, the two major candidates would decide who gets the first hour and a half and who gets the second. From 3:00 to 4:30, the Democratic candidate would discuss economics with two economists of his choosing and two economists chosen by his opponent. From 4:30 to 6:00 the

<hr>

[5] See Harry V. Jaffa, *Crisis of the House Divided: An Interpretation of the Issues of the Lincoln-Douglas Debates* (Seattle: University of Washington Press, 1973).

Republican candidate would have his economics seminar with two economists of his choice and two chosen by the other side. Observers could watch each candidate's silences as well as his interventions; they could judge how well he learns from his allies as well as how he meets the challenges of his opponents. They could also get a sense of how well he is able to participate in discussion pitched at a high level— since it is in the interests of his opponents to set a fast pace. Opposing experts would presumably be people of standing in their field, whose own reputations, as well as that of the candidate they favored, would be at hazard if they indulged in discourtesy or demagogy.

In principle, any number of paired conversations could be arranged on foreign affairs, military problems, agriculture, welfare, and so forth. The pressure, as well as the limelight, would be diffused and shared by all participants, and this feature alone might well make this proposal intolerable to candidates. But, if we are ever to tame the myth of the imperial presidency, it may not be a bad idea to start with the imperial candidacy.

Conclusion

I have argued that in their present format presidential debates are uninteresting, uninformative, and unedifying. They are not worth preserving and they are not worth prohibiting. The potential for civic enlightenment in audiences such as debates typically command is so great, however, that it is worth trying to figure out how to transform them into something more real and more eventful. Candidates should, in the last analysis, decide whether they want to participate, and they should be permitted to negotiate any deal they can get. This may well lead to a Gresham's law of presidential campaigning, in which bad talk drives out good. It is a risk Americans have been taking since the mid-nineteenth century when mass political campaigning began. There is no practical alternative, since a Food and Drug Administration for the mind trespasses on First Amendment rights. Thus we are reduced, or elevated, to exhortation in the hope that the informativeness of presidential campaigns can somehow be enriched by improvements in the ways in which presidential debates, or transformations thereof, are conducted.

Discussion

JACK DENNIS, University of Wisconsin: The first point Polsby makes against debates is that though the candidates are supposed to exhibit in a spontaneous fashion their own personalities and their own abilities, this does not, in fact, happen. I am glad that there is *not* too much spontaneity, that the candidates prepare themselves seriously for their appearances and spend a lot of time trying to memorize material relevant to what it is they stand for. I am glad that their views are not thought up on the spur of the moment and that they do represent themselves as people with well-developed views that they have presented before in other contexts.

POLSBY: Would you speak briefly on the spontaneity issue to the comparative advantage of debates over other forms of public presentation? It seems to me that your position is perfectly defensible, but it is also a critique of debates. If you want the candidates to be well prepared and preprogrammed, then what you really want is the prepackaged programming that they now have. Isn't that the case?

DENNIS: I am not glad it is all preprogrammed, because I do not believe it is all preprogrammed. I think there is a good deal of give and take and extension of existing views. There is even some new content occasionally. But the candidates are presenting themselves to people who do not have much information about what they stand for. What they have to say may have been said before, but it is novel for the audience.

You thought the twenty-six-minute gap was very revealing of their personalities. I am wondering if that really is a revelation of personality or, rather, a revelation of how they are constrained by a situation.

POLSBY: The latter is what I meant. If people believe that debates are spontaneously revealing of personality, they have to confront the very strong negative evidence of that twenty-six-minute gap.

JAMES KARAYN, director of the 1976 debates: Can I give an answer to that? When the audio went out, nobody believed it could happen. Everything was double-miked, double-cameraed, and double-cabled. It shocked everyone that it lasted so long. I don't think any of us, even the panelists or the candidates, will ever believe that we sat there for twenty-six minutes, even though the records show it.

Carter and Ford kept quiet because they know the great danger of an open mike. If they were talking and no one told them they were back on the air, they might have been heard saying something they didn't want heard. What would have happened if Ford had turned to Carter and said, "Well, I just read *Playboy* and it's real interesting that you have lust in your heart," and Carter said, "Well, yes, I really have been lusting for Betty Ford," or something like that? A quarter of a billion people around the world would have heard it, which is why they stood silent.

NORMAN ORNSTEIN, Catholic University of America: Nelson Polsby mentioned both the debate format itself and the questioners. On the matter of questioners, early in the preconvention campaigns there was a series of debates on public broadcasting among the Democratic candidates, and the participants included economists and other professionals. I found these programs far more enlightening, far more interesting, and far more challenging to the candidates than the later debates using journalists only. That left me with the impression that it is not so much the debate format itself as the types of questions and the questioners.

All the papers deal with the preparation candidates go through, the tough questions that are asked in practice sessions. From what I have read, I conclude candidates are generally prepared for journalistic questions, things that they have heard in press conferences. The preconvention debates with the economists asked very different kinds of questions. They challenged the data sources and statistics that candidates were using and made them appear, in fact, much less prepared and more likely to move to spontaneous responses than when questioned by journalists. I think questioners may have a great deal more to do with it than the format has.

POLSBY: I think this is getting us into interesting territory. My notion is that if we can invent a format in which the candidates can go beyond whatever formulas they have been using to advertise themselves, maybe we can, in fact, learn something about how good their minds are and how well they put them to use. The last part of my paper was an attempt to imagine a way in which we might use the debates to learn more about how good the candidates are and how they cope with complex material.

The difficulty is that a president has to deal with very complex material. The world is a very complicated place; presidents have very heavy responsibilities. The paradox is that the formulas of rhetoric they allow themselves to use in order to get elected president are far more one-dimensional and less complex than are the realities of the job. My view is that it would be nice to find some way of moving toward a better understanding of how candidates would behave as president. That, it seems to me, would be the highest and best use of the time dedicated to public debate.

KARAYN: Ornstein was talking about the prenomination forums put on by the League of Women Voters. In those, questions were taken from the guests of the league and from the public, and experts were used in the debates as resource people. The one in Boston had economists; the one in Florida had people who deal with social programs; the one in New York had urbanologists; and the one in Chicago had foreign policy people.

One practical problem with that format was that even in the primary it was very hard to find authorities who were not already committed to particular candidates. In Boston, about fifteen leading economists were approached, but they were already committed to candidates. It is difficult to get an economist who won't be challenged as too partisan.

POLSBY: You don't need neutrality, in my view, under those circumstances.

KARAYN: All right, if you want to have people from both sides. A second problem is that experts like that may be too expert for the general public to comprehend. I was arguing earlier that the debate format is better than a lot of others because it attracts an enormous audience. It is a form of horse race, a boxing match; there is confrontation. But experts sometimes go way beyond what the public can understand. The other danger is that if they are experts they have egos too, and they want to talk about *their* theories. At every one of those sessions, I would sit down with the experts for an hour or so and say, "Nobody here wants to hear what your favorite theory is: We have seven candidates coming on; we have only got ninety minutes for everything, and we don't have time to hear your theory." On the Boston program one economist held forth on his own favorite economic theory, and he did not let any candidate talk. By Chicago we had it worked out, and the people we had as experts in the foreign policy area acted as resource persons.

My theory has always been that the questions should come from the floor and the experts should be merely resource people. Elie Abel was the moderator, and if he did not pick up on a flaw, or if a candidate gave the normal answer out of the rolodex in his brain, one of the experts could stop and say, "Now just a minute, Senator Jackson, that won't work. That is just not true. Those figures don't add up." It is very hard to get them to do that.

POLSBY: Particularly since you took the experts aside ahead of time and, in effect, told them to shut up. That is always the big fight between the media people and the experts. The media people are always saying, "Now the public, whom we represent, wants to see movie stars." And they have the figures to prove it. The public wants to see movie stars, and the experts have to shut up. I want to balance things a little differently.

KARAYN: No, the point was that we were trying to get the public to understand more about the candidates. We were not doing an economic seminar; we were not doing a foreign policy seminar. The experts were there only to challenge the candidates. Some of them were very good; the ones in Florida became much better. They really went at Carter and said, "You don't have enough money in the budget to do a national health care plan."

POLSBY: Actually, Elizabeth Drew did ask the question about the budget, I recall, in one of the debates, and she pursued it. But the ground rules were such that it was impossible to fix it so that Carter would have to respond. She asked her question; he gave his nonanswer. She asked it again; he gave a nonanswer again, and then the buzzer went off.

KARAYN: Nelson, whether this is done with experts or journalists, with a one-to-one interview or with a panel, a man running for president of the United States is well equipped to evade a question he does not want to answer. They all do it. If Liz Drew had taken the next ninety minutes and kept going at him from forty-two different angles, he still would have evaded it. But that is revealing to the public too.

8

Presidential Debates: An Overview

Jack W. Germond and Jules Witcover

The 1960 Debates

In the 1960 presidential campaign, two nonincumbents—John Kennedy and Richard Nixon—agreed to debate the issues before a nationwide television audience because each felt, on balance, that the confrontation would be in his self-interest. Kennedy looked upon the debates as a means of demonstrating that at the age of forty-three he had the experience, qualifications, and bearing to be president. Nixon, against the advice of President Eisenhower and other Republican leaders, agreed out of a conviction that he could beat Kennedy, on foreign policy questions particularly, and that by declining to debate he would hand Kennedy an exploitable issue. When Congress passed a resolution suspending the Federal Communications Commission's equal time provision, Eisenhower signed it, clearing the way for the Kennedy-Nixon debates.

Of the two candidates, Kennedy grasped the importance of the debates much more fully than did Nixon, and he prepared much more carefully and intelligently. Kennedy arrived in Chicago the day before the first debate was to be held in a CBS studio there. He got a good night's sleep and spent the next morning going over likely questions with his aides. According to Earl Mazo, the former political reporter for the New York *Herald-Tribune* and a Nixon biographer, tapes of Nixon speeches were played for Kennedy "to help put him in a properly aggressive mood." Then, after making a short speech to a union convention, Kennedy took a nap, had another question-and-answer session with his aides, had a leisurely dinner, and went to the studio. Nixon, by contrast, arrived in Chicago late the night before the debate, was up early to address the same union group, returned to his hotel shortly after noon, and went into seclusion to prepare for the debate by himself. On arrival at the CBS studio, Nixon hit his knee, hurt in a previous accident, on the edge of his car door while getting out. He looked tired and nervous, and because he was told Kennedy did not use any makeup—Kennedy was, as usual for him, sporting a Florida tan—Nixon decided to use only a very light shaving stick over his perpetual five o'clock shadow.

In both appearance and style, Kennedy beat Nixon in that first debate. He took the offensive from the start, charging that the nation had been stalled by an ineffective Republican administration. He looked vibrant and confident. Nixon, though, seemed bent more on combating his old image as a political hatchet man than on besting Kennedy on the issues. He was exceedingly defensive. No fewer than five times in his opening statement, Nixon expressed agreement with Kennedy rather than going on the offensive himself. Most of those who watched the debate on television thought Kennedy had "won." The Gallup poll just before the first debate had Nixon ahead, 47 percent to 46 percent for Kennedy; after it, Kennedy led, 49 percent to 46 percent. Many of those who heard the debate on radio, however, thought Nixon had prevailed, or at least had held his own—an indication of how much Nixon's appearance had hurt him with the television audience.

The difference in public reaction between those who watched the debate on television and those who heard it on the radio seemed to underscore a view later enunciated by pollster and political consultant Joseph Napolitan. To gauge the impact of a television performance, Napolitan said, he always turned off the sound and watched only the image. In this way, he contended, he was able to anticipate the public consensus on the performance—because to most viewers the image had more influence in shaping opinion than what the "performer" said.

There were three more debates, with Nixon faring better in each, but they were held before progressively diminishing audiences, and as time passed only the first was generally remembered. Poll takers calculated that 70 million persons had watched the first debate, compared with "only" 48 million for the fourth. The impact, however, was such that Walter Lippmann wrote: "The TV debate was a bold innovation that is bound to be carried forward into future campaigns, and could not now be abandoned. From now on it will be impossible for any candidate for any important office to avoid this kind of confrontation with his opponent."[1]

---

[1] New York *Herald-Tribune*, September 29, 1960, p. 26.

But Lippmann was wrong. He overlooked the single condition that had to be met for the debates: they had to be perceived as being in the self-interest of both participants. In 1964 incumbent Lyndon Johnson was running so far ahead of challenger Barry Goldwater that Johnson calculated he would not be harmed politically by refusing to debate, and he was right. (Johnson's old colleagues in Congress saw to it that no exception to the FCC equal time provision was approved. Under that provision, all fringe candidates for president would have had to be invited to participate or given an equivalent amount of television time.)

Nixon in 1968 and 1972 was equally evasive. Although he barely defeated Hubert Humphrey in 1968, Nixon was leading him by twelve percentage points in the Gallup poll in early September and was confident he could weather Humphrey's taunts that he was afraid to debate the issues. And in 1972 Nixon, now the incumbent, ran against a candidate, George McGovern, so politically wounded by his own missteps that there was no serious loss in refusing to debate him.

The 1976 Debates

Not until 1976 did the two major-party candidates again see the debates as being in their self-interest. Gerald Ford, the country's first unelected and hence politically untested president, was trailing Jimmy Carter by about fifteen percentage points at the time a decision on debating had to be made, and Ford had to gamble. Carter agreed because he was still not well known by millions of voters. Besides, he could hardly reject Ford's challenge, made before a huge television audience in his speech in Kansas City accepting the Republican nomination. (Carter had a debate challenge ready but Ford beat him to the punch after word of Carter's plans leaked out.)

The FCC equal time provision was sidestepped by the fact that the sponsor was not the networks but an independent nonpartisan body, the League of Women Voters Education Fund. The fund made all arrangements for the debates as a bona fide news event that the networks were then invited to cover. Independent candidate Eugene McCarthy and third-party candidate Lester Maddox both sought redress in the courts but were turned down.

In their preparations for the debates, both Ford and Carter learned the lessons of 1960. Carter had briefing books prepared by Stuart Eizenstat and his issues staff, and the candidate pored over them in seclusion in Plains before the first debate. Ford's staff, leaving nothing to chance, built in the family theater of the White House a mock-up of the actual set to be used in a Philadelphia theater. The podium was identical and the television angles were checked so that the president's TV adviser, Bill Carruthers, could recommend which position Ford ought to assume. As Ford stood at his lectern answering questions from a panel of White House aides, others held up cardboard placards indicating how much time he had left to answer each question, placards similar to the electric timing devices that would be used on the actual set. Each round of questions and answers was videotaped so that Ford and his advisers could evaluate his performance and make adjustments. At one session, a television set was placed on Carter's lectern and old tapes of Carter answering questions on network panel shows were run off over closed-circuit TV so that Ford could familiarize himself with Carter's style. It went like this: Ford would be asked and would answer a question from his "live" panel, and then Carter, on tape, would get his "turn." Ford's aides wanted the President to rebut each taped Carter answer, but debating a television image was a little too much for Ford; he drew the line at that.

Despite this elaborate preparation, according to one of the participants, Ford was treated too deferentially by his aides. They would ask tough and even impudent questions, but when Ford answered them in less than the most effective way, nobody would tell him so. "He would get asked the questions," this aide said later, "but if his answer was off target, nobody seemed to want to say so." While Ford's answers were never completely wrong, this aide added, "it was clear that his mind does not work in a way to take political advantage of every opportunity." In other words, there was no preparation in tactics, in how to direct the course of debate to put Carter on the defensive.

Still, by most accounts Ford "won" the first of the three presidential debates, mainly because Carter, usually a man of supreme self-confidence, uncharacteristically was thrown off stride at the beginning by the knowledge that he was debating the President of the United States before an audience of more than 100 million Americans. Carter's lead in the Gallup poll dropped from eighteen points at the time of the first debate to eight. Later, however, Carter shed his nervousness and restraint and went on the attack, and by most reckonings either held his own or bested the incumbent in their two later confrontations on television.

Determining the "Winners" and "Losers" in Presidential Debates

The whole question of who "wins" and "loses" in political debates is complex and vexing. Editorials and political scientists seem generally to deplore the sports-page approach in the press and among politicians to what is supposed to be an exercise in the edification of the electorate. But the voters, as well as the press and the politicians, do tend to see winning or losing as the ultimate end in election campaigns, and they insist that the score be kept as the game goes along.

Scoring, however, is not as simple as it may seem. In the first debate of 1976, for example, conventional polling techniques agreed generally that Ford had won and Carter had lost because the challenger seemed ill at ease at the start and, as Carter himself had feared in advance, "excessively deferential" to the incumbent President. In another sense, however, it might be said that Carter gained more from the debate even if he lost the decision on points. The confrontation came just a few days after the controversy over Carter's "lust in my heart" interview with *Playboy* magazine had reached a boil. Continuing private polls taken for both Carter and Ford showed that Carter's stock was plunging rapidly with each passing day. It was, apparently, not so much what Carter had said about sex as it was his judgment in making the comments, particularly through such a medium. After the first debate, however, the curve downward began to flatten out, probably because Carter, although "losing," had been able to demonstrate that he was a rational, credible candidate. The debate, rather than the *Playboy* interview, became the focus of political discussion. Carter may have "lost," but at least he had succeeded in changing the subject.

The truth is that campaign debates are likely to be measured in terms of their political effectiveness, not their substance. One candidate or the other may make the most telling arguments on issues of genuine significance, but in the political community his success or failure will be measured by the impression he has left with the electorate. The central question is whether a candidate comes away from a debate having, in the politician's phrase, "helped himself" or "hurt himself" with the voters.

This pragmatic standard, of course, increases the hazards of debating for a candidate. He recognizes that eighty-five minutes of effective discussion on the issues can be destroyed by a single lapse—at least in terms of political perceptions. There is no better evidence than what happened to Ford in the second debate.

Just as conventional wisdom ruled that in the first of the 1960 debates Kennedy's aggressive performance and Nixon's defensiveness and appearance had produced a victory for Kennedy in the election itself, the second of the three 1976 debates led many to say later that a Ford blooper was his ultimate undoing. In that debate, the incumbent in response to a question about the Helsinki agreement with the Soviet Union said that "there is no Soviet domination of Eastern Europe, and there never will be under a Ford administration." Questions seeking to clarify the answer only inspired Ford to repeat the same conclusion.

What made Ford's answer so damaging was that it seemed to many of the press, and eventually the electorate at large, to reinforce the nagging image of the President as an intellectual lightweight. Robert Teeter of Detroit, Ford's pollster, said later that a quick telephone survey immediately after this debate had Ford "winning" by eleven percentage points. Later polls, however, after the press and television commentary on the remark, finally showed Ford "losing" by an incredible forty-five percentage points! In his polling, Teeter began with calls to the West Coast the night of the debate (held in San Francisco, where it was three hours earlier than in the East), and the following day calls were made in the Midwest and then the East. Voters in the Midwest, by the time of Teeter's calls, had been exposed to one cycle of analysis in the press, and those in the East to two cycles on radio and television and in local newspapers.

Ford's blooper—and his refusal for nearly a week to apologize publicly and admit error, which his strategists implored him to do— arrested the forward motion of the Ford campaign at a critical time. It reinforced the view that debating in a presidential campaign carries a very high risk—though in an election as close as this one turned out to be, no one occurrence or issue could be said to have been *the* decisive one.

Determining the Future of the Debates

In any event, the five presidential election campaigns from 1960 through 1976 established that in the absence of legislation or agreement between the two major parties, debates would take place only when they were seen by both candidates as worthwhile or, at least, politically unavoidable. The first question is thus whether the public interest, as opposed to the narrower interest of the candidates, is served by this criterion for conducting the debates. It seems quite clear that the public interest is not thus served. Televised debates in 1964, a year in which Johnson won election with 61 percent of the vote, probably would not have changed the outcome. But they might have led to a more pointed airing of Johnson's decisions and plans concerning the war in Vietnam. And in 1968 Humphrey might have been forced by television debates to break more cleanly and earlier with Johnson's Vietnam policies—a move that, in our opinion, could have won the election by gaining the active backing of supporters of the defeated Gene McCarthy and of the late Robert Kennedy. It is inconceivable that Nixon would have been able in 1968 to stonewall on his own "secret" plan to end the war and in 1972 to say virtually nothing about the war or anything else in coasting to reelection over the hapless McGovern. A law requiring televised debates in 1972 probably would not have altered the result, but at least it would have helped in getting the incumbent to defend his Vietnam policy more fully before the American people.

Perhaps even more important, debates in 1972 might have significantly changed the entire course of the Watergate affair. Although many of the disclosures about Watergate and all it came to signify did not come until after the 1972 election, some of its dimensions were beginning to suggest themselves during the campaign. But neither McGovern nor the press was able to take the issue to Nixon effectively —or to focus any serious public attention then on what finally was to be exposed as the most outrageous political scandal in our national history.

But how realistic is it to expect a Congress dominated by the Democrats to pass a law locking the incumbent Democratic president into a requirement to debate? Not very realistic, probably, unless the president himself would take the lead in steering the proposal through both houses. President Carter, who most people think was helped in his candidacy by the 1976 debates, has been unwilling to commit himself unequivocally to debate as the incumbent in 1980, let alone to lead a fight for the debates in Congress.

The other possibility—have the two major parties agree to require their nominees to debate—seems only slightly more realistic. Still, pursuing both avenues could produce the desired results on one track or the other. The parties, the Democratic party in particular, have been very protective of their prerogatives in the business of elections. The last Democratic national convention, for example, pointedly urged Congress to take no action concerning primary dates or any other matters touching on the internal affairs of the party. The introduction of a bill to require debates conceivably could spur the parties to agree to hold debates and to make the candidate's willingness to debate a condition of presidential nomination.

Malcolm Moos, a former Eisenhower aide and political scientist, proposed after the 1960 debates that Congress call upon the networks to allocate time to the major-party candidates, stipulating that if either candidate failed to appear, his time would be made available to his opponent. That provision would surely dramatize one candidate's refusal to confront his opponent and might make it nearly impossible for either candidate to decline. Sponsorship by the League of Women Voters or some similar group, making the debates news events as in 1976, would circumvent the need to go to Congress.

The Desirability of Presidential Debates

Just how valuable are the debates? That is hard to say. A woman in Pittsburgh in 1976, when asked by a reporter whether she was watching the Ford-Carter debates, replied: "Oh, I watched a few minutes of the first one and then I turned it off. I don't want either of them influencing my vote. I want to make up my own mind." The sheer size of the television audience for the debates, however, suggests that they must have a considerable impact. For many millions of voters, the debates in 1976 constituted the best or even the only opportunity to examine the knowledge, the quick-wittedness, and the style of the two candidates in a situation of considerable stress. Very likely the debates may only reinforce an opinion already held, or create uncertainties that finally are resolved in terms of surface impressions or party affiliation. But they can have, undeniably, a major, if not a decisive, influence.

The other side of this coin is the danger that the debates might be allowed to become a substitute for a traditional campaign, rather than simply an important element in it. There were already signs last year that many voters thought themselves to be "doing their duty" by watching the debates, and thus didn't feel obliged to pay attention to what was going on in the campaign week after week on the stump. And if the voters are tempted by apathy and inertia into giving too much weight to the debates, so are the candidates tempted to devote more and more of their effort to television. Presidential politics, however, should require something less sterile than three or four ninety-minute confrontations in a television studio. The candidates, although they sometimes do not realize it, can be educated about problems in the society by face-to-face contact—by walking the streets, by turning up at plant gates at 6:00 A.M., by making off-the-cuff speeches to audiences that may include annoying hecklers.

In 1968 Nixon ran for president in near isolation, following a carefully conceived schedule that avoided any spontaneous events. At that time, the nation was coming to a boil over Vietnam, yet the programmed Nixon seldom was in a position to hear the voice of the American people who were against the war. When the antiwar protest erupted, he failed as president to gauge its scope and impact.

In 1972 as well, he ran as if he were in an isolation booth, while George McGovern thrashed about in full view of a press corps that found itself, for all practical purposes, having only one candidate to cover. That may have been sound political tactics for Nixon, who by this time did not seem to care much about what the public thought, but it was, in a very real sense, cheating the voters. To a lesser extent, the same strategy was used off and on by the Ford campaign in 1976 and was dubbed the Rose Garden strategy. The President campaigned from the White House to emphasize that he was "presidential," in part because polls by Bob Teeter showed that when Ford went out on the stump he helped his candidacy in that locale, but hurt himself nationally because he seemed less "presidential." By contrast, Carter in 1976 won his party's nomination by an unprecedented job of "retail" campaigning—meeting the people where they lived and worked. In doing so, he could honestly say he knew what was on people's minds. The public, in turn, had a better chance to judge Carter by hearing him speak from the steps of the nation's town halls and perhaps by engaging him personally in a discussion. That the voters often came away saying Carter was fuzzy on the issues did not contradict the importance of such personal contact; in truth he *was* fuzzy on a number of issues, and knowing that was in part, at least, knowing Carter.

It could be said, of course, that retail campaigning from Iowa to New Hampshire to Massachusetts to Florida to Illinois to North Carolina and so on exacts too much from the candidates in the presidential primary season. But those early weeks and months of stumping are valuable trials for the candidates, under conditions that can measure their mettle. By observing them living under pressure day in and day out, the press comes to know them well. Although the stamina to survive the campaign is not necessarily a valid test of a potential president, it is surely as good as the ability to get through three ninety-minute debates without self-destructing.

Too great a focus on the debates can also mean that too much weight is given to any blooper of the sort Ford made on Soviet domination of Eastern Europe. That episode deserved close examination because it seemed to underscore one of Ford's biggest problems—the public impression that the President was a lightweight not really smart enough to hold down the job. Carter's attempt to exploit the Ford gaffe afterward, however, proved to be just as revealing of Carter as the gaffe was of Ford.

Therefore, we would not argue that debates should be abolished because they may distort a campaign, nor would we argue that they should be allowed to dominate a campaign and thus present a distorted picture of the dynamics of political competition.

Improving the Debates Format

Having concluded that the debates are worthwhile and somehow should be made a mandatory part of the process of electing a president, we must examine how they can most effectively provide the electorate with information on which to base an informed vote.

News reporters and analysts were used as panelists in 1960 because CBS proposed the debates and obliged the other networks to join in. The panels for the first and fourth debates were therefore composed entirely of television and radio reporters; for the second and third debates, two print reporters, picked by lot, were included. In 1976, when the sponsorship passed to the League of Women Voters Education Fund, the panelists were selected by the fund's board, with each candidate entitled to recommend panelists but with the board making the final decision. The criteria in 1976 were more restrictive than in 1960 and produced a better mix of television, newspaper, and magazine representatives. The sponsors leaned away from reporters who were covering the candidates on the campaign trail, however, out of a conviction—wrong in our opinion—that those reporters were too close to the candidates and too involved in daily spot coverage to be likely to pose the kinds of broad questions that would shed real light on the character and the vision of the candidates.

This fear that "the boys on the bus" would not focus enough attention on the "important" and "substantive" issues of the campaign is in line with the purists' desire to see votes cast solely on the basis of issue positions of the candidates. It seems to us, however, that there is just as much reason to try to gauge the character and the personality of the candidates, since that is precisely what millions of voters do in deciding between the two.

In the first debate of 1976, for example, an excellent panel did an admirable job of probing for the differences between Ford and Carter on the issues of unemployment and inflation. But they did not force Carter to explain just why he felt obliged to adopt the vernacular in talking to *Playboy* magazine, which is still not well understood. Nor did they try to get a justification from Ford for, in effect, hiding out in the Rose Garden, attempting thereby to spoon-feed the news media. Indeed, all through the 1976 campaign there were questions raised by the conduct of both candidates that cried out for thorough examination in the debate format. And that, in turn, cries out for including on each panel at least one questioner who has been intimately involved in the revealing day-to-day dynamics of the campaign.

The televised debates have one great advantage over daily in-person coverage of the candidates. Hard, specific questions can be asked in such a way that the candidates must respond. They cannot run away from interrogation as they can, and often do, on the campaign trail. Of course the candidates can use the old dodge of answering a question that has not been asked. But if follow-up questions are permitted by the panelists, reporters can pin down the candidates to a degree that they cannot often do when covering the campaign on the run.

In both 1960 and 1976, the questions asked were adequate to provide the viewers with a fairly well-rounded portrait of each candidate, though it was clear from the start that a candidate could steer the discussion into any area he wanted, if he were deft enough. Thus, in the first 1960 debate, designated as a discussion of domestic issues, Kennedy, said to be inexperienced in foreign policy and too young to deal with Nikita Khrushchev, conveyed his toughness in his opening statement: "We discuss tonight [domestic] issues, but I would not want . . . any implication to be given that this does not involve directly our struggle with Mr. Khrushchev for survival." Kennedy then went on to offer his proposals for "getting this country moving again" in terms of impressing the Russians and Chinese of the soundness of the American society and economy at home.

In the final debate of 1976, when Carter was determined to make a public apology for his remarks in *Playboy*, which had hurt him among women voters, he simply took the first opportunity—a question about how much responsibility he took for the low-level campaign —to say that although other national leaders had given interviews to *Playboy*, he would not "had I to do it over again." And he added: "If I should ever decide in the future to discuss my deep Christian beliefs, I would use another forum besides *Playboy*."

A pertinent question to be raised, indeed, is whether interrogators —from the news-gathering community or from academia or anywhere else—are necessary or desirable. If the objective is to have the two candidates debate, and to enable voters to gauge from that exchange the abilities, the resourcefulness, the knowledge, and the vision of the candidates, why not have them go at each other without a panel, but with a moderator to keep the dialogue within a set of ground rules? If that format were used, the candidates might be less willing to participate, because such an exchange might have too much riding on it, in terms of voter reaction. If panelists are therefore deemed necessary, their selection by the sponsoring nonpartisan body, the League of Women Voters or some other, would be preferable to choice by lot, if only because the news-gathering community—like any other field—has its share of lightweights whose participation could detract from the whole undertaking.

Another alternative to a simple candidate against candidate or candidate-panel-candidate format might be to have each candidate and his staff prepare in advance a series of questions for the other candidate, to be posed by a moderator. A panel might be present to ask follow-up questions not anticipated by the candidates in their advance preparations. The selected panelists would also have a heavy responsibility to pose questions that would cut new ground on the candidates' stand, particularly on those issues that were evaded in the frenzy of the campaign. It is easy, and not very revealing, for the candidates to slip into rhetoric used repeatedly on the stump.

In perhaps a better variation the other candidate would have an opportunity to ask the follow-up questions himself. Such an approach could well assure that any candidate's weaknesses—whether of style or substance—would be explored fully. There are few better, tougher critics of any politician than his opponent. In this case, strict ground rules would have to be adopted to make sure the debaters stayed on the issues and did not by their questions allow the debate to sink to an exchange of wild charges and smears. With so much riding on the debates, one would expect voter backlash against any candidate who started slinging mud—as in Republican vice-presidential nominee Bob Dole's discourse on "Democrat wars" in his debate with his Democratic counterpart, Walter Mondale—and that danger alone would persuade the debaters to keep it clean.

Whether in the panel format or in direct debate, the 1976 formula of three presidential debates of ninety minutes each, one on domestic issues, one on foreign policy and defense, and a third on unspecified topics, seems about right. In this era of increasing interest in the vice-presidency, the debate between the two nominees also should be retained. Although it cannot be proved that the outcome of the 1976 election hinged on the choice between Mondale and Dole and their performance in debate, the exercise was worthwhile as an indication of their reactions under stress. Dole's rather incredible insouciance at the start of the debate ("We'll be friends when this debate is over—and he'll [Mondale] still be in the Senate") his stand-up comic manner (running for vice-president was "indoor work with no heavy lifting"), and finally his biting sarcasm (George Meany "was probably Senator Mondale's makeup man") and his reference to "Democrat wars" demonstrated either an insensitivity to the public's heightened concern over the vice-presidency or a thinly veiled uneasiness veneered with bluster.

If the vice-presidential debate proved to be revealing on one level, it failed on others. Perhaps because it was only one hour long it was not noticeably more penetrating than a half-hour program such as "Meet the Press" or "Face the Nation." For example, neither Mondale nor Dole was questioned as closely as each deserved on his record in the Senate and on possible areas of conflict with the presidential candidates with whom each was running. It might help if more than one vice-presidential debate were held, and for longer than an hour. But though there is undeniably more interest now in vice-presidential nominees, the public probably is not ready for a larger dose of them.

The Problem of Third-Party Candidates

There remains one other problem that requires more serious consideration than it has received to date—how to deal with third-party or independent candidates. The debates of 1976 allowed no provision for such candidates. Clearly, it would have been a distortion of the political realities and an inhibition to the dialogue between Ford and Carter to have included independent candidate McCarthy and third-party candidate Maddox. But the cards are heavily stacked against such candidates already, and the restriction of televised debates only augments the favored treatment given to the major-party candidates, just as the federal campaign subsidy provisions do.[2] Although there would be no way to assure a viewing audience for minor candidates even remotely as large as that attracted by the major-party candidates, some consideration should be given to their legitimate need for television time. To protect the networks from the demands of crackpot candidates, arbitrary decisions would have to be made, perhaps by the Federal Election Commission or some independent panel, to determine which minor-party or independent candidates would receive the free television time.

Conclusion

As the first priority, the decision of whether to participate in televised presidential and vice-presidential debates should be taken out of

---

[2] The federal campaign finance reforms of 1974 make it exceedingly difficult for third-party or independent candidates to qualify for federal subsidies, which are paid only as reimbursements after the election if a candidate wins 5 percent of the vote.

the hands of the candidates and away from their yardstick of self-interest, and the debates should be given institutional status. The most direct way to accomplish this is to lobby the incumbent President, publicly and privately, to include mandatory debates in his election reform package, which still awaits congressional approval. With or without White House support, leading figures on Capitol Hill involved in election reform, notably Senator Birch Bayh, chairman of the judiciary subcommittee on the Constitution, should be recruited to sponsor and push the necessary implementing legislation. At the same time, appeals to the Democratic and Republican national committees to agree between themselves to commit their 1980 standard-bearers to participation in televised debates would at least help focus public awareness. Another alternative is the proposal by Malcolm Moos that in effect would force the candidates to debate, since if either one stayed away his opponent would collect a windfall of prime television time.

If Walter Lippmann were alive today, he probably would be more cautious in predicting, as he did after the 1960 Kennedy-Nixon debates, that the TV debates "could not be abandoned" and that it would be "impossible" for any candidate to beg off. If Carter as the incumbent in 1980 declines to debate, and if no legislation or party agreement has been reached, and if the Moos scheme is not adopted, there will be little anyone can do to force a debate. Nevertheless, there will probably be more public sentiment to continue the debates in 1980 than there was in 1964, when Johnson's race against Goldwater generated more laughs than demands for a serious TV exchange of views. Holding debates in 1980 could be crucial in any attempt to lock them into institutional status. If they can be arranged, and then again in 1984, a pattern could be established that would make it harder for any presidential nominee to refuse to debate.

As presidential candidates spend ever larger shares of their campaign funds ($21.8 million each to Ford and Carter in 1980 under the federal subsidy) there is an increasing need to hold the debates. At a time the airwaves are being bombarded with slick television and radio advertisements that are effective with millions of voters—voters do not even recognize they are paid commercials—a thorough examination of the candidates and their views is badly needed.

By the same token, the debates should not be allowed to become a substitute for all the elements that now comprise a presidential campaign. In 1976, when Ford and Carter each used more than half of their campaign funds for paid television, grass-roots politics was severely cut back. There were few old-fashioned neighborhood storefront headquarters to provide a sense that a campaign was in progress, to involve many people in volunteer work, and to send ripples of interest into the neighborhood and community. But the fate of grass-roots politicking is a separate matter, one that could be handled by increasing the federal subsidy and earmarking an adequate amount of money to put the presidential campaign back into the nation's neighborhoods. The central problem here is to develop ways to make certain self-interest of the candidate is not the deciding factor in whether there will be debates. Ideally, they could be assured if Carter would express a commitment to debate and then put the influence of his office behind the idea. That, however, may be too much to hope for.

Politicians are prone to change their feelings about televised debates once they move into the White House. One such man said in an NBC interview in early 1962 that "debates between the presidential candidates are a fixture, and in all the elections in the future we are going to have debates between the candidates." He was the man who declined to debate in 1968 and 1972, and his name was Richard Nixon.

Discussion

JAMES KARAYN, director of the 1976 debates: I don't know where the idea came from that we excluded from the panels reporters who were traveling with the candidates. In 1960 the networks wanted to use only network correspondents as questioners. The Nixon and Kennedy people said they couldn't live with the political heat of that, so the networks agreed that in the second and third debates they would also allow print journalists. They told the two candidates' organizations, "You pick them; we don't care how, but you choose them." Pierre Salinger and Herb Klein said, "My God, we don't want that problem." So they put the names of everybody who was traveling with the two candidates into a fishbowl and drew for who would be on the panels.

In 1976 we felt strongly that the panels should not be limited to people traveling with the candidates, but we never excluded anybody traveling with the candidates. Somehow that impression got out, but it was never the case. We merely did not want to keep out all the other journalists.

GERMOND: Our point was that maybe the panel needs to be more structured, and that at least one of the reporters with the campaigns should be there to ask those hard questions about the *Playboy* interview, the Rose Garden campaign, and the like.

KARAYN: I was very careful not to get involved in what the panels were going to ask, but obviously the *Playboy* thing came up in the discussions before the debates. Elizabeth Drew was certainly informed enough to think about that, and certainly so was Frank Reynolds. It was their choice not to bring it up, and I really don't know why they chose not to.

It is easy to forget that out of all the reporters in this country, there were twelve people picked: three moderators and nine questioners for the three presidential debates. Each of those debates averaged about fourteen questions, that is, forty-two questions in three debates, and nine questioners. The big problem is more what to discard and what not to ask or who not to choose than it is what to choose. All the big subjects have to be covered, and one of the problems all the panels faced was whether to ask about the subject that was most current in the campaign at the moment or whether to leave that job to the day-to-day press. Should the debates be limited to the big, broader issues the president will face during the following four years?

GERMOND: To get to the heart of the problem, there is nothing more meaningless than a "Meet the Press" broadcast. Everybody asks three or four questions and the answers make a lead on the AP story the next day. The debates avoided that, but they also left the impression that the substance of the campaign was a discussion of the issues, when, in fact, that was not the substance of the campaign. That is why I think the panels ought to have included one or two people like Curtis Wilkie with the Boston *Globe*, who traveled with Carter a long time, and someone out of the White House press corps who traveled with Ford the whole time. They knew that the campaign was not just discussions of inflation and employment; they knew it was a great many other things as well.

One of the great things about having the debates and having so many people watching is that the candidates get away from talking out of one side of their mouth down South and out of the other side in the Northeast, and differently still in the far West. They cannot do that in nationally televised debates.

An interesting measure of a campaign is how candidates deal with regional issues, and such issues are not necessarily going to come up in national debates. I cannot recall whether Jimmy Carter was asked about deregulation of natural gas prices in one of the debates. I doubt it, but he certainly campaigned in Texas and Louisiana and Oklahoma on that issue. Perhaps if the debates were regularized and the candidates did not feel they had to be so terribly cosmic, they might get around to regional questions.

CHARLS E. WALKER, cochairman of the 1976 Debates Steering Committee: I think that the League of Women Voters very much wanted the questioners to get together—as they talk about doing before presidential press conferences—to be sure they covered the waterfront pretty well in their questions. Maybe if that had happened the *Playboy* thing would have come up; I don't know. But they refused to do so, right?

KARAYN: From the very beginning we picked people as a team, not as individuals. I left it up to each group of questioners to decide whether they would get together, and I said I would not attend. The panel for the first debate was the only panel that did not get together; the members refused. They said something which, as a journalist, I have never understood—they felt there would be collusion if they met before the debate. On the second debate I got more insistent and told them, "You are picked as a team and you had better get together." On the third one I was invited to the session, and I said I would observe. It really helped. From the time the questioners came together till the time of the debate, the three of them refined the questions and talked among themselves,. That was really great. I knew what they all said they were going to say when they first got together and what they ended up with on the next night, and it improved 100 percent.

WITCOVER: I can tell you why that first panel was concerned about collusion. Several years earlier reporters who covered the White House regularly and irregularly were very concerned that Nixon was not being pressed on issues; there was no follow-up. A group of us got together and held a breakfast to which most newspapers sent people. We decided that we would at least try to follow up questions more. There was no discussion about who would ask the questions or what the questions would be. To make sure that the White House would not be able to accuse us of collusion, we sent John Osborne to inform Ron Ziegler that this was what we were going to do. Within days, Herb Klein had written a letter to the New York *Times* accusing us of collusion.

KARAYN: On a panel like ours it worked out much better. For example, for the last debate a very good civil rights question was thought up by Bob Maynard. Jack Nelson turned to Maynard and said, "I think it would be better if I ask it because you are the black panelist." Maynard understood that perfectly. Nelson said, "I'll ask any question you want," and Maynard said, "No, ask any civil rights question you want." Nelson took Maynard's question, and it worked out far better than if they had not talked it over beforehand.

WITCOVER: In that same vein, the reporters who were asking questions in the vice-presidential debate—Walter Mears, and I have forgotten who the others were—

KARAYN: Hal Bruno from *Newsweek* and Marilyn Berger from NBC.

WITCOVER: When they saw the order of questioning, Mears wanted to give one of his questions to Marilyn and Marilyn wanted to give one of hers to Walter. To simplify matters, they just switched seats. It turned out that because of that switch, Walter Mears asked the question of Dole that elicited his response that the Democrats were responsible for all the wars in this century. If they had gone through without making that switch, Senator Dole might be vice-president today.

KARAYN: I never knew that, but I can tell you an even funnier one. The reporters wanted to change the order of questioning, and I agreed to it because it was easier for them. But I had already, unfortunately, told Dole's people the order, and Dole's people blew their stack that evening when I told them we had changed the order of questioners. They insisted we go back to the original order, and we did. If Dole got caught, he was hoist by his own petard.

JACK DENNIS, University of Wisconsin: I would like to ask a somewhat more general question, since we have representatives of the media present. As two pilot projects, the 1960 and 1976 debates were fine; but if we think about institutionalizing the debates, I wonder if we might alter the questioners somewhat by not always having media representatives.

GERMOND: I think there is every reason to use any group of questioners. No matter who is used they will not come up with questions that the candidates haven't had in one form or another and that they don't have answers for, good, bad, or indifferent. When Bob Dole said the politically "wrong" thing in the vice-presidential debate, it was not because of the question; it was because that was what Bob Dole wanted to say. He is a very good politician on his feet. There is no reason in the world why the questioners should all be journalists. They pick reporters because there is a presumption of objectivity, however far-fetched that may be, and it makes it easier on the debates' sponsors.

WALKER: I disagree very strongly with that. To give an example, in one of the preconvention debates an economic expert was selected. He was great in the warm-up and had some great questions, but he froze on the show. As a person who has done a bit of television and still gets pretty nervous when appearing on an unrehearsed think-on-your-feet show as "The Advocates," I'll take a Jim Gannon any day in the week before I'll take the president of the American Economic Association. I am strongly in favor of journalists in whatever specialization you name.

KARAYN: A couple of times the journalists asked me what kind of role they should take. I said, "I think you should be the electorate's surrogate. Ask questions you think the electorate would ask." We went through elaborate procedures in the forums in the primaries, trying to get experts and test them out. I would hold a luncheon for twenty people, partly to feel them out. When we were in Miami preparing for a forum on social transfer programs, the leading authority in this country on social security was there. He brought Elie Abel, the moderator, a fifteen-page memo on how the social security system should be changed and started talking about it. I said to Elie, "He can't be used," and Elie said, "Why not?" I said, "My God, first of all, if he asks a question I don't think anybody will understand him. Second, if a candidate could give a reasonable answer to it, I would think the candidate is suspect, because he has been spending too much time diddling around with social security and not enough running as a candidate for the Democratic nomination."

Jack Dennis has a very good point. Presidents are not elected because they are experts in economic policy or foreign policy or health care. They are elected because they are thought to be good leaders who select good advisers to help them, and because they are believed to have a grasp of the issues.

GERMOND: There is an interesting point in what is happening right now in the assessments of Jimmy Carter. People are saying that all he does is take advice from people from Georgia who talk mushmouthed. Nobody ever asked him about his coterie of close advisers, or who he would bring into the government, or any questions like that during the debates, because they weren't deemed to be "substantive."

KARAYN: No, wait; that is where you are wrong. Jack Nelson asked Carter in the last debate: "Sir, you have a problem being elected president because you have surrounded yourself with very young, inexperienced, and regional people. Where are you going to get the advice?"

WITCOVER: I think that for all the faults of the debate format, it did, to some degree, test the ability of the candidates to communicate. Only a president who can communicate is likely to build the kind of mandate for himself around the country that will enable him to take charge. One of the first things Carter did when he became president was to set himself to building a broader mandate by communicating, sometimes in person. That is very important, if a president is expected to be a leader primarily and an expert on various subjects secondarily. The performance of the candidates in debate can be pretty revealing.

STEVEN CHAFFEE, University of Wisconsin: Some people are concerned that the debates draw attention away from what you're calling "the real campaign." My questions are: One, what is the real campaign if the debates aren't part of it? And two, if there is one that can be identified, how is it available to the majority of people, who get most of their news from television and consequently know precious little about what is going on?

GERMOND: I did not make myself clear. I don't think of debates as not being part of the real campaign. They are very much a part of it. I am concerned that they might become a substitute for the entire campaign, that they will dominate the campaign. During the 1976 campaign I did a lot of door-to-door, totally unscientific reporting, just to learn what people were saying. I was struck—as anyone who did that was—by the number of people who really thought that the only obligation they had in paying attention to the campaign was to watch the debates. That, I think, is a serious problem.

CHAFFEE: What else is there to watch?

GERMOND: I think they should watch the television news and read the Madison *Capital Times*, if they are serious. I realize we are talking about an elite voter, but only about 10 percent of the people make the decision.

CHAFFEE: According to Patterson and McClure's content analysis, television news does not give any content. It tells that somebody made a speech, but it does not say what was said. The ads give a little bit, but that seems to be a pretty thin substitute. Nixon's ads in 1972 were a pretty contrived business, but that was the Nixon campaign, in the absence of debates.

GERMOND: That is true. I suppose I am talking about an elitist viewpoint, because I live in Washington, and people here read both Washington papers, and the New York *Times*, and the *Wall Street Journal*, and *Time*, and *Newsweek*, and they watch a lot of television and have access to a great deal of material. They get a lot more out of the Washington *Post* than they do out of the television networks. Nonetheless, the idea that anyone can make a judgment on the basis of three ninety-minute sessions in a television studio, no matter how good the questions and how clever the format—I think that is nonsense.

WITCOVER: Can I add to that? Both Jack Germond and I believe that the campaign can and should be an educational process for voters and also for candidates. We covered the Nixon campaign in 1968, when Nixon seldom rubbed up against a live voter. Everything that was done in the campaign was controlled and pointed toward television. Even when he was out on the stump, his speeches were given at a time—usually in the late morning, near an airport—that would give the television people fast access to New York in time to make the evening news.

We both would object to having candidates running in television studios almost entirely, whether in debates or on paid commercials. When there is a finite amount of money that can be spent in a campaign—$21.8 million in 1976—and the candidates spend more than half on television, it turns the whole process into something different from what it has always been.

It is a serious problem when candidates elect to spend so much money on paid television that grass-roots politics is diminished. As a reporter who covered the campaign last year, one of the things that surprised me most was that whenever I went to a medium-sized city or a large city, let alone small towns, there was no physical evidence of a campaign going on. In the past, when there was no limitation on money, the smallest towns would have a headquarters for the campaign. People would come into the campaign headquarters, maybe just to get a bumper sticker or a button, and then go out into the community, where there would be a ripple effect. Because of the decision to spend so much money on television, almost every city I was in had no campaign going on, unless the candidates happened to be there that day. I think that is a serious problem, and the more television is used and the more money it costs, the more something has to be done to keep grass-roots politics alive.

JOAN BERNOTT, Federal Election Commission: Mr. Witcover, I have two comments. The first is that you seem to have a bias for grass-roots politics, which I don't understand. I would like to ask you to explain why you think grass-roots politics is necessarily a better form of politicial communication than television communication. Second, how is it possible? To be realistic, Jimmy Carter can do grass-roots politics in Plains, but in any place much larger it is all media politics.

WITCOVER: Grass-roots politics is not going to work without head-quarters, without bumper stickers, without buttons, and without people going around speaking on behalf of the candidate. I am not saying that grass-roots politics should be the whole campaign. I am saying it should be part of the campaign, and something ought to be done to require the candidates to do that kind of campaigning.

The whole election process should be a learning process, not only for the voters but also for the candidates. The more the campaign is confined to a television studio, especially in paid commercials—which surveys have indicated people really believe as much as the debates—the more the campaign will be totally prone to manipulation. The illustration I gave before about Nixon showed that the more emphasis there is on television, the more manipulation is likely.

BERNOTT: Because there is less give and take between the candidate and the voters?

WITCOVER: No, because most television is controlled. The only time candidates go on television when it is not controlled is in the debate format. When candidates have control of their own television time, they lie, distort, and exaggerate. I think it is essential to have debates, if only to counteract the impact of paid commercials.

As far as grass-roots politics is concerned, I believe in the involvement of people. In 1976 there was very little involvement of people, and one of the main reasons was that there was no money to stimulate it.

GERMOND: When we talk about grass-roots politics, we do not necessarily mean that the candidate himself goes down and shakes hands on Main Street. That becomes a media event and quite often it is as phony as television.

If debates are a regular part of the campaign, they cut the value of the commercials a great deal, because people see the candidates in the debate format. The value of a debate, as opposed to a commercial, is that a debate is a real situation, as real as anything can be on television. A commercial does not have that quality. To the extent that it is not worthwhile for candidates to spend money on television commercials, maybe they will spend it on other things.

KARAYN: Let me ask one last question. We have talked a lot about the media here, and one of my criticisms of the coverage in 1976 was that it made the debates too important. The voter expected too much of

213

the debates; they were going to be everything to the voter and resolve all his hesitations.

I have always thought the debates should be just the kicking-off place, where the public and the press would go at candidates and explore the major issues in greater depth. One of my great criticisms of the press—especially television but also print journalism—is that with rare exceptions most reporters the day after a debate never picked up on half the things that were said.

On the first debate, for instance, Elizabeth Drew pointed out that Carter had been campaigning for nine months on his long list of social programs, but there was no money for them, and he could not tell on the debate where the money was coming from. There were a lot of things to throw at President Ford about how he was going to stop unemployment and still stop inflation. But not one paper went after that. They spent all of their time telling about how the candidates looked. There was even a box in the New York *Times* explaining that Ford wore a vest because he thought it looked presidential!

If the debates are overwhelmed with image, so are the media covering them. I think the debates should be only a jumping-off place. Even in four and a half hours, which is a lot of television time, it is impossible to cover every subject. And when there are only forty-two questions to cover every subject facing a president, they cannot possibly hit every one. Is that a fair criticism?

GERMOND: I think that is very valid because of the whole show-biz, sports-writer syndrome that affects political reporting. But you are talking about reeducating the whole news business, and I would say don't bet the rent money on that. It is a long process.

BIBLIOGRAPHY

Compiled by Evron M. Kirkpatrick

Adler, Richard, ed. *Television as a Social Force: New Approaches to TV Criticism.* New York: Praeger, 1976.

Agranoff, Robert. *The Management of Election Campaigns.* Boston: Holbrook Press, 1976.

————. *The New Style in Election Campaigns.* Boston: Holbrook Press, 1976.

Alexander, Herbert E. "Political Broadcasting: What Is Its Impact on Elections?" New York: Center for Information on America, 1964.

Alsop, Stewart. "Coming Attack on Lyndon Johnson." *Saturday Evening Post,* March 28, 1964, p. 15.

American Political Science Association. *Report of the Commission on Presidential Campaign Debates.* Washington, D.C., 1964.

Angle, Paul M., ed. *Created Equal? The Complete Lincoln-Douglas Debates of 1858.* Chicago: University of Chicago Press, 1958.

Apple, R. W., Jr. "The Little Debates." *Reporter,* December 6, 1962, pp. 36–38.

Arons, Leon, and Mark A. May, eds. *Television and Human Behavior.* New York: Appleton-Century-Crofts, 1963.

Ascoli, Max. "Intermezzo." *Reporter,* November 10, 1960, p. 18.

"At CBS, Blank Check for 1964 Debates." *Broadcasting,* November 25, 1963, p. 66.

"At Last, Action on Section 315." *Broadcasting,* February 24, 1964, p. 78.

Auer, John Jeffery, and Henry Lee Ewbank. *Discussion and Debate: Tools of a Democracy.* New York: Appleton-Century-Crofts, 1941.

Bagdikian, Ben J. "Television—'The President's Medium'?" *Columbia Journalism Review,* Summer 1962, pp. 34–38.

————. *The Information Machines.* New York: Harper and Row, 1971.

Barnouw, Erik. *The Image Empire.* New York: Oxford University Press, 1970.

Barrow, Lionel C. "Factors Related to Attention to the First Kennedy-Nixon Debate." *Journal of Broadcasting* 5 (Summer 1961): 229–238.

Becker, Samuel L. "Presidential Power: The Influence of Broadcasting." *Quarterly Journal of Speech* 47 (1961).

Bendiner, Robert. "How Much Has TV Changed Campaigning?" *New York Times Magazine*, November 2, 1952, p. 13.

Bennett, Ralph K. "Television and the Candidates." *National Observer*, May 20, 1968.

Berelson, Bernard, and M. Janowitz. *Reader in Public Opinion and Communication.* 2nd ed., New York: Free Press, 1959.

Berelson, Bernard R., Paul F. Lazarsfeld, and William N. McPhee. *Voting— A Study of Opinion Formation in a Presidential Campaign.* Chicago: University of Chicago Press, 1954.

Blumler, J. G., and D. McQuail. *Television in Politics: Its Uses and Influences.* Chicago: University of Chicago Press, 1969.

Bogart, Leo. *The Age of Television.* New York: Frederick Unger Publishing Co., 1958, chap. 5, "The Political Effects of Television."

Boorstin, Daniel. *The Image: A Guide to Pseudo-Events in America.* New York: Harper Colophon Books, 1964.

Boyd, Richard W. "Popular Control of Public Policy: A Normal Vote Analysis of the 1968 Election." *American Political Science Review* 66 (1972): 429–449.

Braden, Waldo W. "The Big Shows vs. the Solemn Referendum." *Vital Speeches* 28, no. 17 (1962): 542–544.

Bradley, Rulon LaMar. "The Use of the Mass Media in the 1960 Election." Ph.D. dissertation, University of Utah, 1962.

"British Parties Rule out Great Debates." *Broadcasting*, March 9, 1964, p. 91.

Bullitt, Stimson. *To Be a Politician.* Rev. ed. New Haven: Yale University Press, 1977.

Burdick, Eugene, and A. J. Brodbeck, eds. *American Voting Behavior.* Glencoe, Ill.: Free Press, 1959.

"The Campaign." *Time* 76, no. 18 (1960): 9.

Campbell, Angus. "Has Television Reshaped Politics?" *Columbia Journalism Review*, Fall 1962.

Campbell, Angus, Gerald Gurin, and Warren E. Miller. "Television and the Elections." *Scientific American* 188, no. 5 (1953): 46.

———. *The Voter Decides.* Evanston: Row, Peterson, 1954.

Campbell, Angus, Philip E. Converse, Warren E. Miller, and Donald E. Stokes. *The American Voter.* New York: John Wiley and Sons, 1960.

———. *Elections and the Political Order.* New York: John Wiley and Sons, 1966.

Cantor, Robert. *Voting Behavior and Presidential Elections.* Itasca, Ill.: Peacock Publishers, 1975.

Cater, Douglass. "Notes from Backstage." *Reporter*, November 10, 1960, pp. 19–20.

Center for the Study of Democratic Institutions. *The Great Debates.* Santa Barbara, 1962.

Chaffee, Steven H., ed. *Political Communication: Issues and Strategies for Research.* Beverly Hills, Calif.: Sage Publications, 1975. See articles by Becker, McCombs, and McLeod and by Kraus and others.

Chester, Edward W. *Radio, Television and American Politics.* New York: Sheed and Ward, 1969.

Commager, Henry Steele. "Washington Would Have Lost a TV Debate." *New York Times Magazine,* October 30, 1960, p. 13.

Converse, Philip E. "Public Opinion and Voting Behavior." In Fred I. Greenstein and Nelson W. Polsby, eds. *Handbook of Political Science.* Reading, Mass.: Addison-Wesley, 1975.

Coons, John E., ed. *Freedom and Responsibility in Broadcasting.* Boston: Northeastern University Press, 1961.

Cortney, Phillip. "Responsibility of Television to the People." *Vital Speeches* 26, no. 8 (1960): 252–254.

Cousins, Norman. "Presidents Don't Have to Be Quiz Masters." *Saturday Review,* November 5, 1960, p. 34.

Crozier, Michel J., Samuel P. Huntington, and Joji Watanuki. *The Crisis of Democracy.* New York: New York University Press, 1975.

Cunningham and Walsh, Inc. *Television and the Politicial Candidate.* New York, 1959.

Danders, Robert E. *The Great Debates.* Freedom of Information Center Publication no. 67. Columbia, Mo.: University of Missouri School of Journalism, 1961.

"Debate No. 2." *Time* 76, no. 16 (1960): 17–23.

Dennis, Lloyd B. "Lincoln Debates Easily Arranged." *New York Times,* September 26, 1960, p. 25.

Dexter, Lewis A., and David M. White, eds. *People, Society and Mass Communications.* Glencoe, Ill.: Free Press, 1964.

Dreyer, Edward C. "Political Party Use of Radio and Television in the 1960 Campaign." *Journal of Broadcasting* 8 (Summer 1964): 211–217.

———. "Media Use and Electoral Choices: Some Political Consequences of Information Exposure." *Public Opinion Quarterly* 35 (Winter 1971–1972): 544–553.

Dreyer, E. C., and W. A. Rosenbaum, eds. *Political Opinion and Electoral Behavior: Essays and Studies.* Belmont, Calif.: Wadsworth, 1966.

Edelman, Murray. "The Politics of Persuasion." In James David Barber, *Choosing the President.* Englewood Cliffs, N.J.: Prentice-Hall, 1974, pp. 149–173.

"Facing the Televoter." *Economist,* April 20, 1964, p. 222.

Fagan, Richard R. *Politics and Communication: An Analytic Study.* Boston: Little, Brown, 1966.

Farley, Lawrence T., and John S. Marks. "Campaign Events and Electoral Outcomes." Paper delivered at the American Political Science Association Annual Meeting, Chicago, Ill., August 29–September 2, 1974.

Federal Communications Commission, *Survey of Political Broadcasting.* Washington, D.C., May 1963.

Freeley, Austin J. "The Presidential Debates and the Speech Profession." *Quarterly Journal of Speech* 47, no. 1 (1961): 60–64.

Froman, Lewis A., and John K. Skipper. "Factors Related to Misperceiving Party Stands on Issues." *Public Opinion Quarterly* 26, no. 2 (1962): 265–272.

Frost, David. *The Presidential Debate, 1968*. New York: Stein and Day, 1968.

Gelman, Morris J. "TV and Politics: '62," *Television Magazine*, October 1962, pp. 64–67.

Gilbert, Robert E. *Television and Presidential Politics*. N. Quincy, Mass.: Christopher Publishing House, 1968, chap. 5, "The Kennedy-Nixon Contest of 1960."

Glaser, William A. "Television and Voting Turnout." *Public Opinion Quarterly* 29, no. 1 (1965): 71–86.

Glick, Edward M., ed. *The New Methodology: A Study of Political Strategy and Tactics*. Washington, D.C.: American Institute for Political Communication, 1967.

"Goodbye, Great Debate." *New Republic*, September 26, 1960, p. 5.

Gould, Jack. "Candidates on TV—The Ideal and Others." *New York Times Magazine*, October 28, 1962, pp. 26–27.

Graber, Doris A. *Verbal Behavior and Politics*. Urbana, Ill.: University of Illinois Press, 1976.

Graber, Doris A., and Young Yun Kim. "Media Coverage and Voter Learning During the Presidential Primary Season." Paper prepared for the Annual Meeting of the Midwest Political Science Association, Chicago, April 21–23, 1977.

"A Great T.V. Debate?" *Commonweal* 71, no. 26 (1960): 687–688.

Greenberg, Bradley S. "Voting Intentions, Election Expectations and Exposure to Campaign Information." *Journal of Communications*, September 1965, pp. 149–160.

Hagner, Paul R., and John P. McIver. "Attitude Stability and Change in the 1976 Election: A Panel Study." Paper prepared for the Second Annual Meeting of the Midwest Association for Public Opinion Research, Chicago, November 18–20, 1976.

Hagner, Paul R., and John Orman. "A Panel Study of the Impact of the First Debate: Media Events, 'Rootless Voters,' and Campaign Learning." Paper prepared for the Annual Meeting of the American Political Science Association, Washington, D.C., September 1–4, 1977.

Hagner, Paul R., and Leroy N. Rieselbach. "The Presidential Debates in the 1976 Campaign: A Panel Study." Paper prepared for the Annual Meeting of the Midwest Political Science Association, Chicago, April 21–23, 1977.

Halloran, James D., ed. *The Effects of Television*. London: Panther Books, 1970.

Hamilton, William. "The Victory Was Video's." *Christian Century* 77, no. 48 (1960): 1409–1410.

Harrington, Alan, Don W. Kleine, W. G. McLaughlin, Kenneth Boxroth, and Harvey Wheeler. "Debating the Great Debate." *Nation*, November 5, 1960, pp. 342–348.

Herring, E. Pendleton. *The Politics of Democracy*. New York: W. W. Norton, 1940.

Higbie, Charles E. "1960 Election Studies Show Broad Approach, New Methods." *Journalism Quarterly*, Spring 1961, pp. 164–170.

Hofstetter, C. Richard, and Robert H. Trice. "Television News, Foreign Policy, and Presidential Campaigns: The Case of 1972." Paper prepared for the meeting of the Midwest Political Science Association, Chicago, April 21–23, 1977.

Hovland, Carl I. "Effect of the Mass Media on Communication." In Gardner Lindzey, ed. *Handbook of Social Psychology*. Cambridge, Mass.: Addison-Wesley, 1954, vol. 2.

Hughes, Emmet John. "52,000,000 TV Sets—How Many Votes?" *New York Times Magazine*, September 25, 1960, pp. 78–80.

Johns, James T. "Television and Politics '64." *Beam*, June 1964, pp. 6–11.

Katz, Elihu. "Platforms and Windows: Broadcasting's Role in Election Campaigns." *Journalism Quarterly*, Summer 1971, pp. 304–314.

Katz, Elihu, and Paul F. Lazarsfeld. *Personal Influence: The Part Played by People in the Flow of Mass Communication*. New York: Free Press, 1955.

Kelley, Stanley, Jr. *Professional Public Relations and Political Power*. Baltimore: Johns Hopkins University Press, 1956.

———. *Political Campaigning: Problems in Creating an Informed Electorate*. Washington, D.C.: Brookings Institution, 1960.

———. "Elections and the Mass Media." *Law and Contemporary Problems*, Spring 1962, pp. 307–326.

———. "Campaign Debates: Some Facts and Issues." *Public Opinion Quarterly* 26, no. 3 (1962): 351–366.

Kessel, John. "Comment: The Issues in Issue Voting." *American Political Science Review* 66 (1972): 459–465.

Ketchum, McLeod, and Grove. *The Effects of Political Convention and Campaign Television Coverage upon Politics in the United States*. Pittsburgh, 1960.

Kingdon, John W. *Candidates for Office: Beliefs and Strategies*. New York: Random House, 1968.

Kirkpatrick, Evron M. " 'Toward a More Responsible Two-Party System': Political Science, Policy Science, or Pseudo-Science," *American Political Science Review* 65, no. 4 (1971): 965–990.

Kirkpatrick, Jeane J. *Dismantling the Parties: Reflections on Party Reform and Party Decomposition*. Washington, D.C.: American Enterprise Institute, 1978.

———. *The New Presidential Elite*. New York: Russell Sage Foundation and Twentieth Century Fund, 1976.

Klapper, Joseph T. *The Effects of Mass Communication*. Glencoe, Ill.: Free Press, 1960.

Kraus, Michael. *The United States to 1865*. Ann Arbor: University of Michigan Press, 1959.

Kraus, Sidney, ed. *The Great Debates*. Bloomington, Ind.: Indiana University Press, 1962.

Kraus, Sidney, and Dennis Davis. *The Effects of Mass Communication on Political Behavior*. University Park, Pa.: Pennsylvania State University Press, 1976.

Kraus, Sidney, ed. *The Great Debates: Carter vs. Ford, 1976*. Bloomington, Ind.: Indiana Universty Press, forthcoming.

Krock, Arthur. "The Polite Debate." *New York Times*, October 9, 1960, p. E–11.

Land, Herman. "Television and Elections." *Television Magazine*, April 1956, pp. 47–49.

Lang, Kurt, and Gladys Lang. *Politics and Television*. Chicago: Quadrangle Books, 1968.

———. "The Mass Media and Voting." In E. Burdick and A. J. Brodbeck, eds. *American Voting Behavior*. Glencoe, Ill.: Free Press, 1959, chap. 12, pp. 217–235.

———. "The Mass Media and Voting." In Bernard Berelson and Morris Janowitz, eds. *Reader in Public Opinion and Communication*. New York: Free Press, 1959.

———. "Ordeal by Debate: Viewer Reactions." *Public Opinion Quarterly* 25 (Summer 1961): 277–288.

Latham, Earl, ed. *American Government Annual, 1960–1961*. New York: Holt, Rinehart, and Winston, 1960.

Lazarsfeld, Paul F., Bernard Berelson, and Hazel Gaudet. *The People's Choice*. 2nd ed. New York: Columbia University Press, 1948.

Levin, Murray B. *Kennedy Campaigning: The System and the Style as Practiced by Senator Edward Kennedy*. Boston: Beacon Press, 1966.

Lipset, Seymour M., Paul F. Lazarsfeld, Allen H. Barton, and Juan Linz. "The Psychology of Voting: An Analysis of Political Behavior." In Gardner Lindzey, ed. *Handbook of Social Psychology*. Cambridge, Mass.: Addison-Wesley, 1954, vol. 2.

McGrory, Mary. "Ladies and Gentlemen: In This Corner . . . !" *America* 107, no. 25 (1962): 767.

MacNeil, Robert. *The People Machine: The Influence of Television on American Politics*. New York: Harper and Row, 1968.

Martin, John Bartlow. *Adlai Stevenson of Illinois: The Life of Adlai Stevenson*. New York: Doubleday, 1976.

Martin, L. John, ed. "The Role of the Mass Media in American Politics." *Annals of the American Academy of Political and Social Science* 427 (September 1976).

Mayer, Martin, *Madison Avenue, USA*. New York: Harper, 1958.

Mendelsohn, Harold. "TV and Youth: A New Style for Politics." *Nation*, June 6, 1966, pp. 669–673.

Mendelsohn, Harold, and Irving Crespi. *Polls, Television and the New Politics.* Scranton, Pa.: Chandler Publishing, 1970.

Merrill, J. R., and C. H. Proctor. *Political Persuasion by Television: Partisan and Public Affairs Broadcasts in the 1956 General Election.* East Lansing: Michigan State University, 1959.

Miami University, Department of Marketing. *The Influence of Television on the Election of 1952.* Miami, Ohio: Oxford Research Associates, December 1954.

Mickelson, Sig. *The Electric Mirror.* New York: Dodd, Mead, 1972.

———. "TV and the Candidate." *Saturday Review,* April 16, 1960, pp. 13–15.

Middleton, Russell. "National Television Debates and Presidential Voting Decisions." *Public Opinion Quarterly,* Fall 1962, pp. 426–429.

Miller, Warren E. "The Political Behavior of the Electorate." In Earl Latham, ed. *American Government Annual, 1960–1961.* New York: Holt, Rinehart, and Winston, 1960.

Miller, Warren E., and Teresa Levitin. *Leadership and Change.* Cambridge, Mass.: Winthrop, 1976.

Miller, Warren E., and Donald E. Stokes. "Constituency Influence in Congress." *American Political Science Review* 57, no. 1 (1963): 45–56.

Minow, Newton N., John Bartlow Martin, and Lee M. Mitchell. *Presidential Television.* New York: Basic Books, 1973.

Mitofsky, Warren J. "The 1976 Presidential Debate Effects: A Hit or a Myth." Paper delivered to the Annual Meeting of the American Political Science Association, Chicago, August 31–September 3, 1976.

"The Money Is Not the Object." *Broadcasting,* April 20, 1964, p. 52.

National Academy of Television Arts and Science. *TV and Politics: A Forum.* New York, 1968.

Nie, Norman H., Sidney Verba, and John R. Petrocik. *The Changing American Voter.* Cambridge, Mass.: Harvard University Press, 1976, chap. 10, "The Rise of Issue Voting."

Nimmo, Dan. *The Political Persuaders: The Techniques of Modern Election Campaigns.* Englewood Cliffs, N.J.: Prentice-Hall, 1970.

Nixon, Richard M. *Six Crises.* New York: Doubleday, 1962.

Page, Benjamin I., and Richard Brody. "Policy Voting and the Electoral Process: The Vietnam Issue." *American Political Science Review* 66 (1972): 979–995.

Paley, William E. "Television and the Presidential Campaign." Address before the Poor Richard Club of Philadelphia, January 17, 1953.

Patterson, Thomas E., and Robert D. McClure. *The Unseeing Eye: The Myth of Television Power in National Politics.* New York: G. P. Putnam's Sons, 1976.

"Political Television." *New Republic,* August 15, 1960, pp. 6–7.

Polsby, Nelson W., and Aaron Wildavsky. 4th ed. *Presidential Elections: Strategies of American Electoral Politics.* New York: Charles Scribner's Sons, 1976.

Pool, Ithiel de Sola. "TV: A New Dimension in Politics." In Burdick and Brodbeck, eds. *American Voting Behavior*. Glencoe, Ill.: Free Press, 1959.

Pool, Ithiel de Sola, Robert P. Abelson, and Samuel L. Popkin. *Candidates, Issues, and Strategies*. Cambridge, Mass.: MIT Press, 1964.

Prisuta, Robert H. "Mass Media Exposure and Political Behavior." *Educational Broadcasting Review*, June 1973, pp. 167–173.

Pulse, Inc. "How Viewers Vote: A Special Pulse Study Checks Before and After Effects of TV on Attitudes Toward Candidates." *Television Age*, April 1956, pp. 56–57.

Ranney, Austin, and Willmoore Kendall. *Democracy and the American Party System*. New York: Harcourt, Brace, 1956.

Reddick, DeWitt C., ed. *The Role of the Mass Media in a Democratic Society*. Papers and Descriptions from a Conference at the University of Texas, February 6–7, 1961. Austin: University of Texas Public Affairs, 1961.

RePass, David E. "Issue Salience and Party Choice." *American Political Science Review* 65 (1971): 389–400.

Republican National Committee. *How to Use TV in a Political Campaign*. New York, 1962.

Reston, James. "The Second Debate." *New York Times*, October 8, 1960, p. 10.

———. "The Fourth Debate." *New York Times*, October 22, 1960, p. 10.

Robinson, Michael J. "Public Affairs Television and the Growth of Political Malaise: The Case of the Selling of the Pentagon." *American Political Science Review* 70, no. 2 (1976): 409–432.

———. "American Political Legitimacy in an Era of Electronic Journalism: Reflections on the Evening News." In Richard Adler, ed., *Television as a Social Force: New Approaches to TV Criticism*. New York: Praeger, 1976.

———. "The TV Primaries." *Wilson Quarterly*, Spring 1977, pp. 80–83.

———. "Television and American Politics, 1956–1976." *Public Interest*, no. 48 (Summer 1977), pp. 3–39.

Robinson, Michael J., and Clifford Zuken. "Television and the Wallace Vote." *Journal of Communication*, Spring 1976, pp. 79–83.

Roe, Yale. *The Television Dilemma*. New York: Hastings House, 1962.

Rose, Richard. *Influencing Voters: A Study of Campaign Rationality*. New York: St. Martin's Press, 1967.

Rovere, Richard. "Letter from Chicago." *New Yorker*, October 8, 1960, pp. 167–174.

Rubin, Bernard. *Political Television*. Belmont, Calif.: Wadsworth, 1967.

Salant, Richard S. *The 1960 Campaign and Television*. Columbia, Mo.: University of Missouri Freedom of Information Center, 1961.

———. "The Television Debates: A Revolution That Deserves a Future." *Public Opinion Quarterly* 26, no. 3 (Fall 1962): 335–350.

Sarnoff, David. "Television's Role in American Democracy." New York: NBC, 1963.

———. "The Time to Plan for the 1964 Presidential Campaign Is Now." *McCalls*, September 1961, p. 16.

———. "What's Right with Television." New York: NBC, 1962.

Sears, David, and Jonathan L. Freeman. "Selective Exposure to Information: A Critical Review." *Public Opinion Quarterly* 31 (Summer 1967): 194–213.

Sears, David O., and R. E. Whitney. "Political Persuasion." In I. de Sola Pool and W. Schramm, eds. *Handbook of Communication.* Chicago: Rand McNally, 1973.

Shayon, Robert Lewis. "A 'Political Clinic' Program." *Saturday Review*, November 17, 1962, p. 38.

———. "Elections by Electronics." *Saturday Review*, March 14, 1964.

———. "Pavlov and Politics." *Saturday Review*, January 23, 1960, p. 28.

"Should a President Be Required to Debate His Election Opponent on TV?" *Senior Scholastic*, May 8, 1964, pp. 16–17.

Simon, Herbert A., and Frederick Stern. "The Effect of Television upon Voting Behavior in Iowa in the 1952 Presidential Election." *American Political Science Review*, June 1955, pp. 470–477.

"Small Screen, Super Weapon." *Newsweek*, August 19, 1963, pp. 76–77.

Sorauf, Frank J. *Party Politics in America.* 3rd ed. Boston: Little, Brown, 1976.

Spencer, Walter Troy. "The Agency Knack of Political Packaging." *Television Magazine*, August 1968, pp. 76–79.

Stanton, Frank. "Case for Political Debates on TV." *New York Times Magazine*, January 19, 1964, p. 16.

Steinberg, Charles S., ed. *Mass Media and Communication.* New York: Hastings House, 1966.

Steiner, Gary. *The People Look at Television.* New York: Knopf, 1963.

Stern, Philip M. "The Debates in Retrospect." *New Republic*, November 21, 1960, pp. 18–19.

Stevenson, Adlai. "Plan for a 'Great Debate'." *This Week Magazine*, March 6, 1960, pp. 14–15.

"Talk about Debates Tones Down, but Keeps on." *Broadcasting*, December 2, 1963, pp. 82–83.

"Television and Politics." *Television Magazine*, July 1960, pp. 46–49.

"Television Politics: All Star Cast?" *Economist*, February 8, 1964, pp. 486–487.

Thomson, Charles A. H. *Television and Presidential Politics.* Washington, D.C.: Brookings Institution, 1956.

———. *Television, Politics and Public Policy.* Reprint no. 25. Washington, D.C.: Brookings Institution, 1958.

Thomson, Charles A. H., and Frances M. Shattuck. *The 1956 Presidential Campaign.* Washington, D.C.: Brookings Institution, 1960.

Trenaman, J., and D. McQuail. *Television and the Political Image.* New York: Hillard House, 1963.

"TV Debates in '64." *New Republic*, November 7, 1960, p. 6.

"TV's $20,000,000 Gift to the Presidential Campaign." *Sponsor*, November 7, 1960, pp. 29–32.

"TV Zooms in on GOP." *Business Week*, February 22, 1964, pp. 32–34.

U.S. Congress, Senate, Committee on Commerce, Communications Subcommittee. *Final Report, Freedom of Communications*. Report no. 994, pt. 3, 87th Congress, 1st Session, 1961.

————. *Political Broadcasting*. Hearings, July 10–12, 1962. 87th Congress, 1st Session.

U.S. Department of Commerce, Bureau of the Census. *Statistical Abstract of the United States, 1977*. Washington, D.C.: Government Printing Office, 1977, p. 508, table 813.

Verba, Sidney, and Norman H. Nie. *Participation in America: Political Democracy and Social Equality*. New York: Harper and Row, 1972.

Whale, John. *The Half Shut Eye: Television and Politics in Britain and America*. London: Macmillan, 1969.

White, F. Clifton. "Presidential Debate of 1976." Paper delivered at the Annual Meeting of the American Political Science Association, Chicago, August 31–September 3, 1976.

White, Theodore H. *The Making of the President 1960*. New York: Atheneum, 1961.

————. *The Making of the President 1964*. New York: Atheneum, 1965.

————. *The Making of the President 1968*. New York: Atheneum, 1969.

————. *The Making of the President 1972*. New York: Atheneum, 1973.

Wicker, Tom, Kenneth P. O'Donnell, and Rowland Evans. "Television in the Political Campaign." *Television Quarterly*, Winter 1966, pp. 13–26.

Willis, Edgar E. "Little TV Debates in Michigan." *Quarterly Journal of Speech* 48, no. 1 (February 1962): 15–23.

Wilson, James Q. *The Amateur Democrat*. Chicago: University of Chicago Press, 1962.

Witcover, Jules. *Marathon: The Pursuit of the Presidency 1972–1976*. New York: Viking, 1977.

Wykoff, Gene. *The Image Candidates*. New York: Macmillan, 1968.

CONTRIBUTORS

STEVEN H. CHAFFEE is Vilas Research Professor in the School of Journalism and Mass Communication at the University of Wisconsin-Madison. He has published several books and articles on the role of mass communications in American society and politics.

RICHARD B. CHENEY served as White House chief of staff to President Ford from 1974 to 1976. In 1978 he was elected to the House of Representatives from Wyoming.

JACK DENNIS is professor and chairman of the Department of Political Science at the University of Wisconsin-Madison. He has published a number of books and articles on political socialization and on popular support for the institutions of democratic government.

JACK W. GERMOND and JULES WITCOVER have since 1977 written a daily syndicated column on national politics appearing in more than eighty newspapers across the country. Mr. Germond is former Washington bureau chief for the Gannett newspapers and assistant managing editor of the *Washington Star*. Mr. Witcover has written several books, of which the most recent is *Marathon: The Pursuit of the Presidency, 1972–1976*.

JAMES KARAYN was the director of the 1976 presidential debates for the League of Women Voters. He is currently president and general manager of WHYY, Inc., in Philadelphia and executive director of Campaign '78 Survey Debate Project.

EVRON M. KIRKPATRICK has been executive director of the American Political Science Association since 1954 and professorial lecturer in

225

government at Georgetown University since 1959. Prior to that he served as professor of political science at the University of Minnesota and as deputy director of the Office of Intelligence Research, United States Department of State. In 1963–1964 he was a member of the APSA's Commission on Presidential Campaign Debates.

STEPHAN LESHER is executive vice-president of Rafshoon Communications. Formerly a writer for *Newsweek* magazine, he has written two books, *A Coronary Event* and *Vested Interest*. PATRICK CADDELL is president of Cambridge Survey Research and President Jimmy Carter's chief pollster. GERALD RAFSHOON is the founder and president of Rafshoon Communications, currently on leave to serve as assistant for communications to President Carter.

NELSON W. POLSBY is professor of political science at the University of California, Berkeley. From 1970 to 1976 he served as managing editor of the *American Political Science Review*. He has written a number of works on American and British politics and is the coeditor of the seven-volume *Handbook of Political Science*.

NICHOLAS ZAPPLE served as communications counsel to the United States Senate Committee on Commerce from 1949 to 1975, in which capacity he participated in formulating all communications legislation passed in the period.